Ethical Archaeologies: The Politics of Social Justice

Series Editors:

Cristóbal Gnecco
Tracy Ireland

More information about this series at
http://www.springer.com/series/7559

Tracy Ireland • John Schofield
Editors

The Ethics of Cultural Heritage

*W*orld

*A*rchaeological

*C*ongress

Founded 1986

 Springer

Editors
Tracy Ireland
University of Canberra
Bruce, ACT
Australia

John Schofield
Department of Archaeology
University of York
York, United Kingdom

ISBN 978-1-4939-1648-1   ISBN 978-1-4939-1649-8 (eBook)
DOI 10.1007/978-1-4939-1649-8
Springer New York Heidelberg Dordrecht London

Library of Congress Control Number: 2014948465

Printed on acid-free paper

Springer is part of Springer Science+Business Media (www.springer.com)

Ethical Archaeologies: The Politics of Social Justice

Archaeology remains burdened by modern/Western values. Codified, these values harden into ethics with specific cultural and temporal foundations; indeed, ethics are contextual, shifting and negotiated entanglements of intent and practice that often conflict. Yet, archaeologists may uncritically mask these contexts unless they are adequately aware of the discipline's history and of their location in a globalised world order with its imprint of imperial, colonial and neocolonial values. A responsible and socially committed archaeologist must historicise his or her ethical principles, showing how contingent they are and what kind of needs they are serving.

By adopting a global coverage that brings together academic activism for a historicised ethics, universally created lacunae surrounding disciplinary concepts such as the archaeological record, stewardship and multivocality, as well as broader concerns of race, class and gender, can be discussed and acted upon. The four volumes comprising the *Ethical archaeologies: the politics of social justice series* discuss historically based ethics in the practice of archaeology and related fields—anthropology, museology, indigenous and heritage studies, law and education—and highlight the struggle for social justice, in which the discipline can participate.

In this series, we take that social justice is broadly about equality and the right to freedom from any kind of discrimination or abuse. It is about seeking to transform the current order of the world, in which the hegemony of the Western cosmology still reigns with its ideas of individuality, linear time, development, competition and progress. Thus, social justice is also about the positioning in our research and disciplinary practices of nonmodern values about life, time, past, place and heritage.

Hardened into reified principles, as they continue to be, ethical concerns have served to reproduce epistemic hierarchies and privileges. If archaeologists are content with what the ethical preoccupations of the last two decades have achieved, their trumpeted engagement with politics and justice is meaningless. If the ethics of archaeology continues to simply further embed disciplinary privileges, social justice is not a horizon of fulfilment. If ethics is just a disciplinary preoccupation, a way of better accommodating the discipline to changing times, social justice is an empty expression. For these reasons, this series aims to position the values of equality and freedom from all discrimination at the centre of archaeological thinking and practice. The four volumes are not toolkits or guides for standardised, universal and ethical conduct, but critically informed, self-reflective discussions of ethical problems and potentials.

Cristóbal Gnecco
Tracy Ireland

Acknowledgments

We would like to thank Aedeen Cremin for editorial assistance, Teresa Krauss at Springer for her wise guidance of this project, as well as each of the contributors to the book for their patience and positive response to reviews and critiques. We also thank Cristobal Gnecco for his strong vision for the series, rigorous editorial work and tireless project management over the years that this four volume collection took to pull together. Tracy would like to thank Nels Urwin for just about everything else.

Contents

Part II   Ethics in Practice

Contributors

Susan Barr Directorate for Cultural Heritage, Oslo, Norway

Elizabeth Bonshek Heritage, Museums and Conservation, Faculty of Arts and Design, University of Canberra, Bruce, ACT, Australia

Erika R. Ceeney International Studies, Faculty of Arts and Design, University of Canberra, Bruce, ACT, Australia

Sarah Colley School of Archaeology & Ancient History, University of Leicester, Leicester, UK

Adam B. Dickerson International Studies, Faculty of Arts and Design, University of Canberra, Bruce, ACT, Australia

John Hurd ICOMOS ISCEAH, London, UK

Tracy Ireland Faculty of Arts and Design, University of Canberra, Bruce, ACT, Australia

Richard Mackay Godden Mackay Logan Pty Ltd Heritage Consultants, Redfern, Australia

Susan McIntyre-Tamwoy James Cook University and Archaeological and Heritage Management Solutions Pty Ltd., Waterloo, NSW, Australia

Stuart Palmer St James Ethics Centre, Sydney, Australia

Andreas Pantazatos Centre for the Ethics of Cultural Heritage, Durham University, Durham, UK

Ana Luisa Sánchez Laws Media Arts and Production, Faculty of Arts and Design, University of Canberra, Bruce, ACT, Australia

John Schofield Department of Archaeology, University of York, York, UK

Emma Waterton Institute for Culture and Society, University of Western Sydney, Penrith, NSW, Australia

Steve Watson Business School, York St John University, York, UK

About the Authors

Susan Barr is founding past president and now vice president of the ICOMOS International Scientific Committee on Polar Heritage. She is the senior advisor in polar heritage at the Norwegian Directorate for Cultural Heritage and has worked solely with polar heritage and history since 1979. After her degree in historical archaeology, she became the first full-time heritage officer for the Norwegian High Arctic, later moving to the Norwegian Polar Institute and then to her current position in 1998. She has extensive field experience from much of the Arctic and parts of the Antarctic and has published books and articles relating to polar history and heritage. Email: susan.barr@ra.no

Elizabeth Bonshek is an anthropologist, researcher and lecturer in Museum Studies at the University of Canberra, Australia. Her recent publications include co-editorship of, and contributions to, *Melanesia: Art and Encounter* (2013), a scholarly companion to the British Museum collections from Melanesia. Her primary research interest focuses on the material culture and cultural heritage of the Pacific. She has carried out fieldwork in Papua New Guinea and Solomon Islands. Elizabeth is interested in all aspects of material culture studies, museums as ethnographic sites and 'contact zones'. Email: elizabeth.bonshek@canberra.edu.au

Erika R. Ceeney studied cultural heritage and sociology at the University of Canberra. At present she works for the Australian Federal Government. Her research interests include indigenous issues, the ethics and politics of cultural heritage and contemporary feminist thought.

Sarah Colley's current research examines the significance of digital communication technologies for archaeological theory and practice. She also collaborates on digital archive and video projects with colleagues from the University of Sydney, University of Leicester, Australian National University and elsewhere. Sarah has a diverse range of research, teaching and professional experience in archaeology, cultural heritage management and archaeological education, and her many scholarly publications include a book and two edited volumes. Her Ph.D. and postdoctoral research involved studying fish and mammal bones and marine shells from archaeological sites in Britain and south-east Australia to examine past environments, diets and economies. More recently, Sarah Colley was a senior academic in Archaeology at the University of Sydney where she conducted research and taught courses on Australian Aboriginal and historical archaeology, public archaeology, cultural heritage management and archaeological theory, methods and practice. Email: sc532@le.ac.uk

Adam B. Dickerson studied philosophy and history at the University of New South Wales, Australia, and has taught in both Communication and International Studies at the University of Canberra for the last 10 years. He is the author of *Kant on Representation and Objectivity* (Cambridge, 2004) and various papers in cultural history, epistemology and the philosophy of language. Email: adam.dickerson@canbera.edu.au

John Hurd is the president of the International Advisory Committee of ICOMOS and president of the International Scientific Committee on Earthen Architectural Heritage. He is the former head of conservation, Global Heritage Fund. He has worked extensively throughout Asia, particularly the arid high deserts of Central Asia where he was a senior conservation consultant to UNESCO. John is a fellow of the Society of Antiquaries of London. Email: john.hurd@icomos.org

Richard Mackay AM—B.A. (Hons.), M.B.A., M.A.A.C.I.—is a partner of Godden Mackay Logan Pty Ltd., Heritage Consultants and an adjunct professor at La Trobe University. He has more than 20 years of experience in cultural resource management and tourism. He is the current chair of the Australian World Heritage Advisory Committee and was a member of the Commonwealth State of the Environment 2011 Committee. He has served as a member of the State Heritage Council and is an expert member of the ICOMOS Scientific Committee for Cultural Tourism. He was also a member of the Australia ICOMOS Burra Charter Working Party. He is currently the team leader for the Angkor Heritage Management Framework project. In 2003 he was made a member in the General Division of the Order of Australia for services to archaeology and cultural heritage management. Email: richardm@gml.com.au

Susan McIntyre-Tamwoy is the associate director of Archaeological and Heritage Management Solutions Pty Ltd. She is also an adjunct senior research fellow in the School of Arts and Social Sciences at James Cook University. She is a past president of Australia ICOMOS and is currently the president of the International Scientific Committee on Intangible Cultural Heritage. She has worked on cultural heritage projects extensively throughout eastern and northern Australia and in the Asia Pacific region. Her research interests are wide ranging and include indigenous heritage in tropical regions, climate change and cultural heritage, world heritage and bio-cultural heritage. Email: SMcintyre-Tamwoy@ahms.com.au

Stuart Palmer is responsible for the consulting, leadership and learning services of St James Ethics Centre. Through these services, the Ethics Centre supports the integrity of individuals, leaders and organisations, helping them to align their decisions and actions with their own considered values and principles. The work of the Ethics Centre includes diagnostic research projects investigating the character, culture and alignment of organisations, regional leadership development programmes, ethical awareness and good decision-making training and a free and confidential ethical counselling line, Ethi-call. Stuart received his doctoral degree in philosophy of mind from the University of Sydney. Prior to joining the Ethics Centre, Stuart worked as a lawyer and banker. Stuart also serves as a non-executive director and volunteers as a Lifeline telephone counsellor and primary school ethics teacher. Email: stuart.palmer@ethics.org.au

Andreas Pantazatos (Ph.D.) is a co-director of the Centre for the Ethics of Cultural Heritage (CECH) at Durham University where he leads postgraduate seminars on the ethics of archaeology and cultural heritage. He also teaches ethics and applied philosophy at Durham's Philosophy Department. His main research interests are philosophy of archaeology and cultural heritage, focusing on the ethics of stewardship and trusteeship and the ethics and epistemology of museums. Email: andreas.pantazatos@durham.ac.uk

Ana Luisa Sánchez Laws is an assistant professor at the University of Canberra teaching Media Arts and Production. Her research focuses on the use of new technologies to address contested topics in museums and issues of diversity and social inclusion. She has written a book on these issues, *Panamanian Museums and Historical Memory* (Berghahn Books 2011). Her most recent research deals with the creation of digital artefacts to communicate cultural and natural heritage, with projects involving institutions such as the Panama Viejo Monumental Complex, a World Heritage Site and the Questacon Science Centre in Canberra, Australia. She is also a practising artist, with works most recently exhibited at the Museo Reina Sofia and Centre Pompidou. Email: Ana.SanchezLaws@canberra.edu.au

Emma Waterton (Ph.D.) is based at the University of Western Sydney in the Institute for Culture and Society. Her interests include unpacking the discursive constructions of 'heritage'; explorations of tourism, heritage and affect; thanatourism; visuality; and explorations of innovative methodologies. She has over 30 publications since 2005, including one authored [*Politics, Policy and the Discourses of Heritage in Britain* (Palgrave Macmillan 2010)] and one co-authored monograph (*Heritage, Communities and Archaeology* (with Laurajane Smith, Duckworth 2009), five co-edited volumes (with Routledge, Ashgate and Cambridge Scholars Press) and three guest-edited special issues. She has served on the editorial board for *Sociology* (2008–2010) and is currently part of the editorial board for the *Journal of Heritage Tourism* (2012–ongoing) and the *International Journal of Heritage Studies* (2013–ongoing). She was an assistant editor for the *International Journal of Heritage Studies* from 2009 to 2013. Email: e.waterton@uws.edu.au

Steve Watson is a professor of Cultural and Heritage Leadership at York St John University, United Kingdom. He teaches on a variety of modules concerning the cultural industries, consumer culture, tourism and heritage. His research interests are in the areas of cultural and heritage tourism and travel writing, and he has lectured on these topics around the United Kingdom and in Australia, Spain and the United States. His current focus of interest is the role of affect and emotion in the study of heritage and representations of Spain in travel literature. Recent publications include *The Cultural Moment in Tourism* with Emma Waterton and Laurajane Smith (Routledge, 2012) and *The Semiotics of Heritage Tourism* with Emma Waterton (Channel View, 2014). Email: S.Watson@yorksj.ac.uk

About the Editors

Tracy Ireland is an archaeologist and heritage practitioner who joined the University of Canberra in 2009 and is currently head of the Discipline of Humanities. She previously led the Canberra office of Godden Mackay Logan, Heritage Consultants, lectured at the University of Sydney and worked as the senior archaeologist for the NSW Heritage Council. Tracy publishes on historical and landscape archaeology, heritage conservation and the cultural politics of the past. Tracy's current work focuses on the Material Memories Project examining the conservation of archaeological remains and heritage place making in settler societies. Email: tracy.ireland@canberra.edu.au

John Schofield is the head of the Department of Archaeology at the University of York and director of studies in Cultural Heritage Management. John was previously an archaeologist with English Heritage, an organisation he joined following the completion of his Ph.D. research in 1989 and where he remained until 2010. He had numerous roles in that time, within heritage protection and policy, taking on the role of head of military programmes in 2000. During his last 10 years with English Heritage, his outreach responsibilities included regular teaching commitments in the United Kingdom and overseas, not least at the universities of Southampton and Bristol. John is a fellow of the Society of Antiquaries of London, a member of the Institute for Archaeologists and a docent in Cultural Heritage, Landscape and Contemporary Archaeology at the University of Turku (Finland). He has published extensively in the fields of cultural heritage, archaeology of the recent and contemporary pasts and the archaeology of conflict. Email: john.schofield@york.ac.uk

Chapter 1
The Ethics of Cultural Heritage

Tracy Ireland and John Schofield

Introduction

It is widely acknowledged that all archaeological research is embedded within cultural, political and economic contexts and that all archaeological research falls under the heading 'heritage'. Most archaeologists now work in museums, other cultural institutions, government agencies, nongovernment organisations and private sector companies, and this diversity ensures that debates continue to proliferate about what constitutes appropriate professional ethics within these related and relevant contexts. Cultural heritage is seen by many as an 'industry', and the ethical and social dimensions of research practices come sharply into focus because of the complexity of stakeholders and vested interests within this industry. Whether heritage work is paid, or creates revenue, for private companies or the public purse; is in compliance with laws and regulations; requires the consent of indigenous or other groups; or simply because it deals with things or concepts that people feel strongly about, it is always entangled in local to global forms of geopolitics, cultural diplomacy, investment and economics, forms that intersect in complex and sometimes surprising ways with public memory and the politics of identity and recognition. As Schofield puts it: 'It is the inevitability and universality of valued places filling our world that gives heritage strong social relevance and purpose'. For all these

T. Ireland (✉)
Faculty of Arts and Design, University of Canberra, Bruce, ACT 2601, Australia
e-mail: tracy.ireland@canberra.edu.au

J. Schofield
Department of Archaeology, University of York, King's Manor,
York YO1 7EP, UK
e-mail: john.schofield@york.ac.uk

© Springer Science+Business Media New York 2015
T. Ireland, J. Schofield (eds.), *The Ethics of Cultural Heritage*,
Ethical Archaeologies: The Politics of Social Justice 4,
DOI 10.1007/978-1-4939-1649-8_1

social reasons (not to mention those which are economically and politically driven) heritage has become central to our experience of the world' (this volume).

Debates about the ethics of cultural heritage in the twentieth century were focused on the need to establish standards of professionalism and on the development of the particular skills and expertise required for rigorously objective conservation. These developments aimed to establish the authority of heritage conservation experts and public trust in the authenticity of the outcomes of the heritage process. The ethics of cultural heritage have therefore often been conceived of in terms of three types of responsibilities: to the 'archaeological record' (or stewardship), to 'diverse publics' (or stakeholders) and to the profession and the discipline (Zimmerman et al 2003:xiff). This volume builds on recent approaches that move away from treating ethics as responsibilities to external domains and to the discipline and which seek to realign ethics with discussions of theory, practice and methods (e.g. Meskell 2010; Meskell and Pels 2005). The chapters in this collection chart a departure from the tradition of external heritage ethics, to a broader approach underpinned by the turn to human rights, issues of social justice and the political economy of heritage, conceptualising ethical responsibilities not as pertaining to the past but to a future-focused domain of social action.

Ethical Transformations

While it has been more usual to approach the ethical issues deriving from aspects of cultural heritage theory and practice or from the nature of the places and objects that constitute heritage, here we approach heritage as an *inherently ethico-political problem* because it is one of the ways in which societies actively shape the meaning of the past in the present and thus construct a particular vision of their collective future (Ricouer 1999: 9). Paul Ricouer has suggested that the 'duty to remember' allows for the possibility of an ethical *rapprochement* with the wounds of history—an imperative that is directly focused on the construction of the future. In particular he suggests that this duty to remember involves 'fighting against the erosion of traces', so that the future can inherit the archives of the past, which can then be used to 'grow' and to prevail against the 'destruction of time'. The notion of destruction that he develops in this argument is based on Aristotle's ontological category of destruction, the tendency of time to destroy what humans construct—a tendency which must be acted against if humans are to 'grow'. Finally, Ricouer sees the ethical component of memory work as its ability to act against the triumphalism of history and its focus on the victors (1999:10).

Ricouer's analysis is helpful in this discussion of the ethics of cultural heritage because his use of the Aristotelian concept of 'destruction' illuminates the deep western cultural roots of the modern heritage notion of *conservation* as inherently good and ethical, as in fact necessary for human growth. Thus, during the course of the twentieth century, the practice of heritage conservation can be seen as shifting from one defined by unspoken but ostensibly shared western aesthetic and stewardship values, towards building methods for objective, scientific forms of conservation and heritage management, through to the development of ethics, standards and codes of practice aimed at making cultural values explicit and allowing for the recognition of cultural relativities. The context and foundation for this history of transformation are key ruptures in international geopolitics and intellectual thought. Following on from the events of the Second World War and the holocaust, these have included the rise of postmodernism and collapse of positivism, the impact of the postcolonial critique and the global human rights movements, including indigenous rights and feminism. However, while 'universal' heritage concepts such as authenticity have been problematised as socially and culturally contingent in past decades, contemporary conservation ethics continue to embody aspects of all this historical accumulation—so that conservation still tends to be seen as aiming for objective scientific accuracy rather than as an argument for, or form of rhetoric on behalf of, particular interpretations and cultural values (e.g. Matero 2000; Otero-Pailos et al 2010). Also relevant here is Derrida's concept of 'archive fever' that the self-conscious creation of the archive, the act of preservation, only occurs at the point of the 'structural breakdown' of the memory—the archive will never be as spontaneous and alive as the original experience or even the memory of that experience (Derrida 1995:11). Thus, heritage has also been recognised as a process which changes the nature of what has been categorised as heritage by reifying and commodifying places and practices in ways that may have negative effects for those whose culture is thus appropriated (e.g. Handler and Gable 1997).

The history of cultural heritage, as a distinctive subset of memory work, can be seen as an ethical tug-of-war between its use by powerful formations such as nation states to instantiate national histories and identities and its use by less powerful groups to fight against forms of forgetting. Much has been written about the dominance of nation states in these activities, and the ethical and social justice concerns that the nations' tendency towards exclusivity creates. More recently scholarly focus has turned to the impacts of economic and cultural globalisation and the ethical quandaries that emerge from local-global tensions and how global discourses of heritage intersect with local politics and economics (e.g. papers in Labadi and Long 2010). In this context, considerable attention has been paid to the UNESCO World Heritage Convention as an agent of globalisation in its promulgation of western notions of heritage as authentic and material and to cultural tourism as a neocolonial form of exploitation, responsible for either the suppression of unpalatable memories or perhaps the even more ethically suspect business of thanatourism (e.g. Stone and Sharpley 2008). The 2003 UNESCO *Convention for the Safeguarding of Intangible Cultural Heritage* was seen as a much needed corrective to the Eurocentrism of the World Heritage List in its intention to recognise cultural diversity. However, it has also been found to reflect the cultural hierarchies of the West, confusing intangibility with endangered evanescence and obscuring how intangible heritage is embodied and intertwined with the material and social world (Kirshenblatt-Gimblett 2004; Smith and Akagawa 2009).

Ricoeur's optimistic view of the ethical potential for memory work has perhaps been less influential in critiques of heritage than have concerns about its unethical use. However, despite the predominance of these top-down critiques, heritage is clearly a complex field of power relations between the privileged and the underprivileged, the empowered and the dispossessed, and the history of modern heritage shows a robust jostling amongst groups to ensure that the field does not simply 'celebrate the victors' but is also a place where the politics of social justice are negotiated. Cornerstones of the new museology and of transforming heritage management practices include ethical engagements with issues such as social inclusion, radical transparency and the potential for shared guardianship of heritage (Marstine 2011 and see Sánchez Laws this volume). The twentieth century focused on the rights of indigenous people to control their cultural heritage and on demands for the repatriation of human remains and cultural materials collected by imperial institutions and continues to be an ongoing concern for twenty-first century heritage management and museums, and decolonisation is clearly an unfinished project (see papers by Ireland and Dickerson this volume). Similarly the problem of looting of archaeological sites and the illicit trade in antiquities has only intensified in recent decades in the context of continuing threats to communities and their heritage posed by war and other forms of violence and by political and religious forms of iconoclasm (e.g. Stone 2011). In the twenty-first century, debates over climate change, ecological risk and sustainability, digital technologies and forms of communication, as well as the growing global inequalities caused by these factors combined with economic globalisation, will provide triggers for continued momentous shifts in ethical thinking and practice in this field.

Ethical Domains

The chapters in the first section of this collection survey key 'domains' within which distinctive ethical challenges for cultural heritage are encountered and which we believe will be of growing importance in the future. The first four chapters review fields that represent areas of intensifying challenges for cultural heritage theory and practice: digital heritage (Colley), tourism (Watson), community engagement (Waterton) and climate change (MacIntyre, Barr and Hurd). Colley's comprehensive review of ethics and digital heritage considers the ethical and sociopolitical questions raised by digital technologies in the field of cultural heritage. She points out that current ethical issues with the use of new digital technologies mirror earlier concerns voiced by indigenous communities about research-driven archaeology and its external agenda that returned no obvious benefits back to communities and in some cases also transgressed sensitive cultural protocols. Thus, she notes, in pre-emptive moves designed NOT to mirror the history of indigenous communities and archaeology, indigenous critics are now urging indigenous people to undertake experimentation with digital technologies and their heritage themselves, before allowing others access. As in many of the chapters in this collection, she also considers questions of authenticity—here in relation to the creation of digital heritage, the interpretations it produces and the rhetorical methods it employs. Another common theme in this collection is the ethic of conservation or stewardship. As Colley explores, the digital realm challenges conventional notions of how culture should be conserved and archived. Questions of access—how ethically appropriate access can be maintained and who has the responsibility to maintain it—recur throughout her detailed narrative that stretches from social media use to sophisticated data visualisations. She concludes that an ethical challenge for all cultural heritage professionals is the need to engage with the digital realm, suggesting that 'digital citizenship' will be a key aspect of future professionalism—opting out is simply not an option.

Watson's chapter undertakes the significant challenge of overviewing the huge domain of ethics and heritage tourism. While obviously not an emerging area for cultural heritage analyses, like the field of digital heritage (and of course now closely interlinked with the dynamism of the digital realm), tourism is likely to be a continued location where both old and new ethical debates will interweave and proliferate. Watson approaches ethics as a lens through which heritage tourism might be evaluated and first asks how, methodologically speaking, we might attempt to 'find the good' (in Aristotelian terms) in tourism and in how heritage interpolates with this local/global political and economic formation. The 'good' he suggests is usually found in economic benefits and the 'bad' in the unequal power relations of the participants, the commodification of culture, the inauthentic and inaccurate interpretations and the adverse impacts on the materiality of heritage—all of these themes are well rehearsed in the heritage tourism debate. However, Watson suggests that none of these are *necessary conditions* that must continue to determine the nature of these heritage and tourism engagements. Authenticity, for instance, he suggests, 'need not be sought in the heritage object itself, but in subjective responses to it'. Finally he opens a potential space for ethical engagement and, in an approach that aligns with Schofield's case studies in the second part of this collection, suggests that the concept of 'place' may partly provide this, particularly where it can incorporate some sense of locality and the interests of host communities, in all their diversity.

Waterton's chapter picks up the concepts of heritage and community, already a central theme of the previous two chapters, underlining how they are intertwined and in some ways mutually constituted subjects. She sets out to historicise the use of the concept of community in the social sciences and public policy and in heritage research more specifically. Because of the sensitivity and methodological challenges of working with groups of peoples, she suggests that there has been a lack of critical debate about community engagement in heritage studies—about what it means, how we can measure the success of methods and outcomes and the extent to which they achieve our ethical aspirations. She makes the further important point that the issues that we often deal with as being ethical problems for heritage, such as the impacts of tourism or the looting of archaeological sites, are in reality only partial views of far broader societal problems. The fact that heritage studies continues to replicate such limited views reflects the tendency to be concerned only with disciplinary interests and the way in which the discipline's objects of study must be protected—a failure to practice ethical self-reflexivity and transform practices with the insights thus generated.

MacIntyre-Tamwoy, Barr and Hurd focus on heritage and the question of climate change—asking what is the moral imperative for affluent nations to take responsibility for projected negative consequences and how can they support less affluent nations, which may have already suffered the impacts of colonialism, war and other activities associated with long histories of exploitation. In particular they focus on the need for knowledge sharing and collaborative approaches, not just to heritage management but to research and policy making, and on the major need for transparency in all these processes, ensuring that communities, as well as governments and experts, have access to all possible evidence and analysis relevant to local conditions.

The following three chapters in this section focus on domains that have already seen significant critique and analysis in the revision of the main professional codes of ethics for heritage over the past decades. Dickerson and Ceeney, Ireland and Pantazatos all drill down to explore heritage's codified ethic of stewardship in very different contexts. Philosophers Dickerson and Ceeney approach the questions surrounding the ethics of the repatriation of human remains from the perspective of publicly acceptable, normative ethics. Their chapter provides an example of how public institutions might conduct a morally reasoned argument in search of an acceptable ethics of repatriation, noting that such arguments are constrained by what may be found to be acceptable by different groups in different circumstances rather than what might be right or true according to any external codes or standards.

Ireland's chapter looks at how heritage stewardship has worked to perpetuate forms of 'imperial debris' in a range of settler society locations (Stoler 2008). The practices of historical archaeology and conservation in situ provide a visible materiality that can be used in a range of memory-making activities, enhanced by the affective, sensory qualities of archaeological ruins that evoke the 'old world' of Europe and its deeply layered urban histories. Here in situ conservation is shown to be not only a technique whereby archaeological remains are made visible but also the means by which they visibly testify to their authenticity, a rhetorical argument for progressive historicism and the legitimacy of the settler nation. Archaeology, in this case, provides the condition of possibility for the perpetuation of strategies of control but also significantly for strategies of resistance. Finally in this section, Pantazatos provides an in-depth analysis of stewardship—the notion that archaeologists, by virtue of their special training, are the rightful custodians of the traces of the past. In a constructive analysis of the history of this idea, Pantazatos suggests recasting stewardship as an ethics of care and respect that foregrounds not the care of the material so much as the relationships between people and communities that coalesce around these material things.

Ethics in Practice

The papers in the second section of this collection consider ethics in practice, through case studies and real-world situations where the full range of conflicts, competing interests and values come in to play. These case studies situate ethics at the core of their practices rather than as exterior to their research aims or in the realm of professional codes or university ethics committees. Anthropologist Bonshek provides a 'thick description' of how she set about responding to the aims of the 'new museology' in a traditional field work setting, practising as an anthropologist living amongst, and reliant upon, her host community in Wanigela, Collingwood Bay in Papua New Guinea. She carefully steps us through the anthropological and museological genealogy of the collecting mission that she had been charged with, providing deep context for the process of ethnographic collecting, how it has changed through the decolonising of anthropology and museology and how these changes have impacted on the research and collecting concerns of anthropological museums. In particular Bonshek describes her own process of reconciling her research and professional mission with her personal need to respond ethically to the obligations of appropriate reciprocity. While she had a professional responsibility to comply, and to be seen to comply, with the ethical codes of her employing institution, hers is a good illustration of how heritage work is rarely, if ever, a case of simply applying a code, but in working towards a personal understanding of what she believed to be ethical and what was seen by the people she was working with to be right.

In a contrast to Bonshek's personalised case study, Mackay and Palmer set out a framework for ethical decision-making developed in response to the need to provide the visibility and transparency that is demanded in the complex field of international cultural and political obligations at the World Heritage site of Angkor in Cambodia. Mackay and Palmer's array of stakeholders is vast: Angkor is Cambodia's premier heritage site, of key economic importance to the nation, and perhaps *the* iconic 'lost ruin' that lingers as a colonial ghost in the cultural imaginary of the west. This case is particularly instructive in showing how a detailed framework for practical ethics was developed that could be used by consultants, funding agencies, UNESCO and other stakeholders to demonstrate the basis for decision-making—so that the outcomes of their professional tasks not only satisfied their own personal ethics but more particularly allowed for, and indeed invited, scrutiny of the decisions made and actions undertaken. Mackay and Palmer refer to the concepts underlying the framework for heritage practice provided by the Burra Charter (Australia ICOMOS 1999), which is widely used as the benchmark for heritage practice in Australia and has a growing following internationally. They show that while the Burra Charter was not in fact developed as a code of ethics, because it is a values-based management approach, it embeds a commitment to the concept of culturally different values and the possibility that contested and competing values may be irreconcilable and need to be accepted as thus. They provide a strong supporting argument for an ongoing ethical role for the heritage expert who can contribute to bringing benefits back to less powerful communities or individuals and to building frameworks for sustainable development and empowerment, in the context of the highly complex political and economic realities of the field that today constitutes World Heritage.

Unlike Mackay and Palmer and Bonshek's preoccupations as outsiders working in the 'field', Sánchez Laws explores how trust might be rebuilt between a community and its heritage institutions following a period of dictatorship, upheaval and violence in Panama. Sánchez Laws not only develops an argument for what she sees as the moral obligation of the heritage sector in Panama to deal with a difficult heritage of conflict and to actively collect, curate and preserve the material evidence of this period but also is concerned with exploring what kinds of institutional structures are needed to rebuild trust and re-establish the social compacts upon which democracy might be enacted. She works through very specific strategies including providing transparency for how the museum is governed as well as a suggestion that trust may be enhanced if the museum is seen more in the traditional role of collector, custodian and conserver and as less embroiled in the contentious politics of representation and interpretation. Sánchez Laws' close attention to the details of how the museum is embedded in, and might actively build, 'thick' and 'thin' social relationships of trust reminds us of what is taken for granted in more complacent liberal democracies and thus the power relations and 'imperial debris' that continue to persist unacknowledged in so-called first-world locations (Stoler 2008).

Finally Schofield considers the implications of the implementation of the 2005 European Framework Convention on the Value of Heritage (the Faro Convention) and suggests that perhaps the most ethical response is to do away with the concept of 'heritage' (as traditionally defined) altogether—considering the way in which heritage has focused on special significance to particular groups, excluding groups which express their feelings of belonging and comfort in places and locations that defy the very category of heritage. Schofield discusses the ethical implications of heritage regimes that reify categories of value, such as age and rarity, and the special language of 'heritage', suggesting that such regimes devalue the attachment that some social groups feel to contemporary aspects of place, particularly minority or alternative groups. This discussion reinforces how the aesthetics of heritage remain defined by the patina of age and classical notions of beauty, rather than by the sense of belonging or attachment that people feel, and the ethical challenges this sets up for those who believe that heritage should be more about people than things. The structures of heritage management and legislation are in fact deliberately constructed so that not everyone's heritage matters and so that heritage that reflects the grand narratives of the nation is prioritised as more significant. Here lies perhaps the greatest ethical challenge for heritage practitioners who, as Meskell has put it, 'hope that their interventions might intercalate with the broader aims of social justice, restitution and improving the lives of those we work with' (2010: 854). However, we are also keenly aware of how difficult heritage work can be when values, ownership and access are contested and how subtly it can happen that powerful social groups appropriate the language and methods of heritage that were in fact developed to work against their dominance.

Conclusions

This volume does not set forth a consistent argument on what the key ethical issues in cultural heritage are or how they should best be approached. There are inconsistencies and some significant differences in the approaches of the authors of the following chapters; however, there are also some key similarities. All the authors in this collection approach the ethics of cultural heritage very broadly and as inherently entangled with politics and economics. Ethics are not approached as specifically defined categories that are referred to at key points in designing, undertaking and evaluating heritage work but as a constant questioning of the potential impacts, benefits and implications of heritage work and as embedded in all levels of theory and practice as well as in personal allegiances and belief systems. All, in different ways, approach heritage as an inherently ethico-political problem—some focus on the continued task of embedding normative, publicly useful and acceptable ethics in the work of institutions, such as museums and the management of World Heritage; others are more concerned to deconstruct heritage's foundational concepts including communities, conservation, stewardship and authenticity and to understand the ethical implications of the often 'blackboxed' nature of these ideas. Some also seek to reconcile professionalism and disciplinary identity and the future of the 'expert' (see Schofield 2014), with enabling and positive ethical approaches. Although the authors in this collection have different approaches to, or are more or less concerned with, how ethics have embedded disciplinary or expert privilege in the past, each is committed to developing a better understanding of the ethico-political implications of their work and how it may contribute to a political, social justice agenda. As Watson concludes, ethical approaches help us to form our critique of current practices and shape debates; however, only political action will contribute to social change (this volume).

References

Australia ICOMOS. (1999). *The Burra charter: The Australia ICOMOS charter for places of cultural significance*. Available via DIALOG: http://australia.icomos.org/publications/charters/. Accessed April 2, 2013.

Derrida, J. (1995). *Archive fever (translated by Eric Prenowitz)*. Chicago: University of Chicago Press.

Handler, R., & Gable, E. (1997). *The new history in an old museum: Creating the past at colonial Williamsburg*. Durham: Duke University Press.

Kirshenblatt-Gimblett, B. (2004). Intangible heritage as metacultural production. *Museum International, 56*(1–2), 52–65.

Labadi, S., & Long, C. (Eds.). (2010). *Heritage and globalisation*. Oxford: Routledge.

Marstine, J. (2011). The contingent nature of the new museum ethics. In J. Marstine (Ed.), *The Routledge companion to museum ethics: Redefining ethics for the twenty-first-century museum* (pp. 3–26). Oxford: Routledge.

Matero, F. (2000). Ethics and policy in conservation. *Getty Conservation Institute Newsletter* 15 (1): 5–9.

Meskell, L. (2010). Human rights and heritage ethics. *Anthropological Quarterly, 83*(4), 839–860.

Meskell, L., & Pels, P. (2005). *Embedding ethics*. Oxford: Berg.

Otero-Pailos, J., Gaiger, J., & West, S. (2010). Heritage values. In S. West (Ed.), *Understanding heritage in practice* (pp. 47–87). Manchester: Manchester University Press.

Ricouer, P. (1999). Memory and Forgetting. In R. Keaney & M. Dooley (Eds.), *Questioning ethics: Contemporary debates in philosophy* (pp. 5–11). Oxford: Routledge.

Schofield, J. (Ed.). (2014). *Who needs experts? Counter-mapping cultural heritage*. Farnham: Ashgate.

Smith, L., & Akagawa, N. (Eds.). (2009). *Intangible heritage*. Oxford: Routledge.

Stoler, A. L. (2008). Imperial debris: Reflections on ruins and ruination. *Cultural Anthropology, 23*(2), 191–219.

Stone, P. (Ed.). (2011). *Cultural heritage, ethics and the military.* Woodbridge: Boydell and Brewer.

Stone, P., & Sharpley, R. (2008). Consuming dark tourism: A thanatological perspective. *Annals of Tourism Research, 35*(2), 574–595.

Zimmerman, L., Vitelli, K. D., & Hollowell-Zimmer, J. (Eds.). (2003). *Ethical issues in archaeology.* Walnut Creek: Altamira Press.

Part I
Ethical Domains

Chapter 2
Ethics and Digital Heritage

Sarah Colley

Introduction

This paper discusses ethical and sociopolitical questions raised for cultural heritage by digital technologies and presents two archaeological case studies from Australia. The paper was first drafted in May 2012 for a scholarly edited book produced in hard copy by the Springer publishing company with the usual processes of review and production. Had I published my work via a blog it would have become public immediately. Readers may have posted comments and started online communication. Our experiences, perceptions and roles as authors, consumers, producers or users of formats, genres and platforms and the actual and perceived qualities of the 'product' would be different. How would peer review apply? What about referencing? Who owns the intellectual property of discussion content? Would the blog be archived? Despite innovations in scholarly e-publication (Richards 2006; Kansa 2007; Shanks 2009:554-555; Kansa *et al.* 2010), most Australian universities only recognise peer-reviewed books and research papers (older media formats) as 'research outputs' to comply with government funding rules, making digital products of lower value. These are just some examples of the transformative nature of digital technologies.

Digital mapping and surveying technologies have long been used to study archaeological sites and cultural places (e.g. Coller 2009), and libraries were the first heritage institutions to engage significantly with digital technologies (e.g. networked information systems) in the 1980s (Evans 2006:549-555). There has since

S. Colley (✉)
School of Archaeology & Ancient History, University of Leicester, LE1 7RH, UK
e-mail: sc532@le.ac.uk

© Springer Science+Business Media New York 2015   13
T. Ireland, J. Schofield (eds.), *The Ethics of Cultural Heritage*,
Ethical Archaeologies: The Politics of Social Justice 4,
DOI 10.1007/978-1-4939-1649-8_2

been development and wide use in heritage of online databases, search engines, imaging and multimedia applications, interactive communication technologies and social networking platforms. Current trends include data portals and cloud services for online research collaboration (e.g. Shanks 2007; AHAD 2012; Ross 2012). Archaeology has a long history of both using and discussing use of digital technologies (e.g. Hodder 1999; Lock 2003; Zubrow 2006; Evans and Daly 2006; Shanks 2007, 2009; Webmoor 2008; Ryzewski 2009), and since the 1990s the UK Archaeology Data Service (ADS) has promoted international standards of best practice for archaeological and heritage data management and online publication (Richards 2008). Libraries, archives, museums, art galleries and other memory institutions are also significant developers and users of digital technologies (Cameron and Kenderdine 2007; Parry 2007; Silberman 2010).

Digital technologies involve dematerialisation, compression, high-speed access, non-linear access, manipulability and qualitative changes in the production, form, reception and use of 'media' (Lister *et al.* 2009:9-48; Shanks 2009:550). Their history and significance is best understood through interdisciplinary perspectives from media and cultural studies, political economics, histories of technology and society and the history and philosophy of science, biology, psychology, cybernetics, computer science and anthropology (Lister *et al.* 2009; Harrison 2009:76; Harrison and Schofield 2009:197-198). Ideas about technologies and society discussed by Marx and extended by social theorists and philosophers of the Frankfurt School (e.g. Adorno, Horkheimer, Marcuse, Habermas) are relevant to understanding sociopolitical dimensions of digital technologies (Lister *et al.* 2009:395). In developing a post-phenomenological perspective on ethics of technology and technology design, Verbeek (2011) builds on work of Ihde (philosophy of technology), Foucault (power and ethics) and Latour (Actor Network Theory) and foregrounds the hybrid character of humans and technologies. Discussions of representation, virtual reality and hyperreality in digital cultural heritage and archaeology frequently draw on theories of, e.g. Benjamin, Baudrillard and Bourdieu (Cameron 2007; Harrison and Schofield 2009:197) and many other thinkers and artists (Cochrane and Russell 2007:3). Scholars of the history of technology and society discuss dystopic and utopic 'technological imaginaries' where fears and hopes for society and the future are projected onto or imagined through technologies and influence the way new technologies are produced, marketed, received and adopted (Brittain and Clack 2007:58; Lister *et al.* 2009:68-73; Morgan 2009:470). New technologies remediate (extend, remedy, refashion or reframe) older forms, processes and practices (e.g. McLuhan, Levinson, Bolter and Grussin cited in Russo and Watkins (2007:154)). Reviewing ethical questions (Who owns the past? What is authentic heritage? What defines professional archaeology?) through the 'lens' of digital technology provides new insight into existing and emerging heritage practices.

Cultural heritage is something valuable for past, present and future generations that people want to keep. It may be *tangible*, e.g. material artefacts, buildings and places or *intangible*, e.g. values and ideas associated with or symbolised by tangible cultural heritage and cultural practices, representations and skills with enduring cultural significance for future generations. The UNESCO (2003) *Charter on the*

Preservation of Digital Heritage defines digital heritage as 'unique resources of human knowledge and expression' that include 'cultural, educational, scientific and administrative resources' and 'technical, legal, medical and other kinds of information created digitally, or converted into digital form from existing analogue resources'. For 'born digital' resources there is 'no other format but the digital object'. Digital heritage includes texts, databases, still and moving images, audio, graphics, software and web pages and other formats. According to UNESCO these merit preservation so they remain 'accessible to the public' apart from sensitive and personal information. De Lusenet (2007) argues that UNESCO concepts of digital heritage as static objects are inadequate. Digital heritage includes items that are, or represent, dynamic processes and patterns of use which share more common features with intangible heritage. In discussing intellectual property, cultural rights and copyright legislation in Vanuatu, Geismar (2005:32) likens conceptualisations and practices of women's woven materials to those that apply to open-source software.

Archaeological Ethics

Archaeologists have debated ethics since at least the 1930s (Wildesen 1984:3). Ethics are about values and what is right and wrong. Professional standards govern quality, appropriate actions and behaviours. Professional archaeologists have ethical responsibilities to maintain standards. Numerous charters, codes and guidelines about ethics and professional standards are published and updated online by archaeological organisations, museums associations and heritage groups worldwide. Key international organisations for heritage include UNECSO, ICOM and ICOMOS. Archaeological associations include WAC, EAA (transnational); AAA, ACCAI, AIMA (Australia); and RPA (formerly SOPA), AIA, SAA, SHA (USA) and IfA (UK). Some codes are highly detailed and prescriptive while others state broad intent. They emphasise different aspects of practice and espouse values that may be openly stated or only implied through wording and emphasis.

Most codes state that professional archaeologists have special rights to, e.g. access, excavate, record, study and interpret material remains that are significant to 'the public' for scientific, historical, cultural or social reasons. Archaeology is promoted as a public benefit enterprise. Actions and attitudes of archaeologists are assumed to have real-world consequences for the profession, other people and society. Archaeologists must help conserve finite material remains of the past ('the conservation ethic') and keep materials and information produced by archaeology for current and future generations through 'stewardship'. Archaeologists have responsibilities towards others including the profession (colleagues, trainees, students), traditional owners and descendants with special cultural rights, legal owners, businesses and clients who pay for archaeology, 'the public' and governments. Archaeologists must act legally. Professional guidelines define minimum standards for archaeological work and discuss intellectual property, confidentiality, publication, sharing archaeological data, public outreach and education.

Archaeologists work within national legal and policy frameworks that, e.g. provide protection for archaeological sites and heritage places or mandate community consultation. They work with other professions (anthropologists, historians, scientists, journalists, teachers, museum professionals, archivists, librarians) who have their own professional standards. Whether archaeologists always act ethically is obscure and joining professional associations is rarely obligatory, but archaeology is also regulated by legislation, policy and 'public' opinion including social and cultural mores. Governments and heritage agencies may only grant access to field areas or issue excavation permits to people who meet certain criteria. Professional organisations can sanction members who transgress ethical codes by cancelling membership or public disassociation. There may be informal consequences of acting unethically. However, an archaeologist who 'does the wrong thing' cannot be deregistered. They can still call themselves an archaeologist. Many people without formal training or qualifications participate in archaeology and interpret material remains of the past. Boundaries between 'professional' and other types of archaeologists are permeable.

Encoding ethical principles in charters and formal statements does not resolve the reality of contested and conflicting heritage values (Smith et al 2010). Codes of ethics are frameworks to help professionals and other stakeholders make decisions and judgements. Ethics are always historically contingent, highly dependent on context and linked to politics of power (Meskell and Pels 2005; Hamilakis and Duke 2007). Archaeology and other heritage practices are influenced by sociopolitical factors and formations such as capitalism, colonialism, nationalism and identity politics. Who sets ethical agendas? Who benefits from ethical, and unethical, practice? Who can most and least afford to act ethically?

Political Economy and Digital Heritage

Digital technologies can be expensive. Once new technologies become standard, heritage practitioners and communities in wealthier countries can usually afford to use them. Even cheaper technologies may be less accessible, or not accessible, to people with low incomes or who live in places where some technologies are unavailable for economic or political reasons. Physical abilities, digital literacy levels, language and cultural attitudes effect technology use (Joyce and Tringham 2007; Mason 2007:232; Lister *et al.* 2009:185-187).

Developing innovative technologies usually requires large capital investment. Neo-liberal capitalism, governments and businesses have vested interests in promoting and marketing particular kinds of digital technologies to consumers. In 2000 the European Council of Ministers wanted the European Union to become 'the most competitive and dynamic knowledge-based economy in the world, capable of sustainable economic growth with more and better jobs and greater social cohesion' (Evans 2006:553). Hemsley *et al.* (2005a) and Ioannides *et al.* (2010) showcase some of hundreds of national and transnational European Commission funded projects that apply technologies to cultural heritage. The European heritage sector has often been a 'technology driver' for scientific and research and development organisations and businesses (Hemsley *et al.* 2005a, b). Funding programmes of the 1990s and early 2000s aimed to produce major global engagement between the cultural sector and digital technology industries. Hemsley *et al.* describe such projects as progressive and good for economic development but note 'false dawns and dashed hopes' (2005c:296-297), a lack of 'successful business models' and that digitisation of 'cultural assets' did not generate expected money for the cultural sector or businesses trying to capitalise on them. Take-up and application of technological developments potentially of interest to users was judged 'well below early expectations' due to organisational barriers, copyright and economics. Fragmented national European cultural technology industries could not compete with large US and Japanese companies while 'major pan-European commercial activities' proved unsuccessful due to, e.g. language barriers. Despite some interesting projects and success in enabling access to people with disabilities (papers by Weisen, Bowen, Bornemann-Jeske and Scherer in Hemsley *et al.* 2005a), Hemsley *et al.* (2005b) regard efforts by international professional cultural heritage organisations ICOM (International Council of Museums) and CIDOC (International Committee for Documentation) as being more effective in, e.g. setting digital information standards. Governments can spend significant public funds developing and applying technologies to cultural heritage that are unsuccessful. Whether the money should be spent on things of greater public benefit is a political question. Framing cultural assets, including digital ones, as marketable commodities concerns ethics.

Ethics and Technology Design

Theorists discuss the affordance offered by technologies, i.e. their potential to function or be used in particular ways. Different technologies may support, encourage or determine ethical, or unethical, behaviours depending on their design (Verbeek 2011:50-58). Ethical technologies could be, for example, web pages that allow users to view but not download, copy, alter or redistribute digital assets or which restrict access to online information deemed culturally sensitive by Aboriginal people. In this case it is ethical to restrict access to information. In other cases providing open access to information is ethical. Unethical technologies could be those that support online sale of illegally acquired antiquities or force practitioners, through inflexible data entry interfaces on compulsory government websites, to record data in ways that create unnecessary work or support contentious research agendas. Many commentators regard community participation in heritage afforded by Web 2.0 platforms as 'democratic' and therefore a good thing (Webmoor 2008:190; Evans 2006; Broderick *et al.* 2009). Joyce and Tringham (2007) advocate using digital technologies for feminist communication and political action. Backhouse (2006) asks whether adoption of technology is good or bad for UK contract archaeology units faced with mountains of digital data and limited resources.

Designing and applying innovative digital technologies to cultural heritage can be complex. When professionals initiate projects, negotiating informed consent from stakeholders for actions that impact on cultural heritage is an ethical prerogative. This may be difficult when technologies change rapidly, or it is not obvious how best to use them. Community stakeholders and clients often lack technological knowledge to make informed decisions. Ethical codes state that heritage professionals should not undertake work for which they are not qualified, should update their skills through professional training and development and should seek to provide advice that supports the best interests of stakeholders and cultural heritage resources by seeking advice and working in an interdisciplinary way.

Shanks (2007) proposes that technologies for archaeology and heritage need conscious design and implementation to be ethical. He favours principles of agile design where technical and project managers work closely with clients, users and other stakeholders in an iterative manner so that consultation, testing and feedback are automatically incorporated into the design and development process. This mirrors some aspects of community-based archaeologies initially developed in response to objections raised by Australian and other indigenous communities about the ethics of archaeology driven by external research agendas of non-Aboriginal people that brought no obvious community benefits and in some cases transgressed cultural protocols (Colley 2002:102-105). Agile design methodologies and community-based archaeologies diverge in their aims and context but raise similar issues about governance, negotiation, participation and learning.

Cultural Information Standards

Cultural heritage professionals must abide by 'the conservation ethic' and work to ensure that cultural heritage does not get lost or destroyed. Vast quantities of digital information and heritage are currently at risk due to economics of technology production, organisational constraints, digital illiteracy, lack of political will and costs of compliance with digital archiving standards (Richards 2008; Billenness 2011). This challenges the basic tenet of most ethical codes of heritage practice.

Archives and libraries have led development of cultural information standards (policies, guidelines and methods) for collection, preservation and access to digital information about cultural heritage (Mason 2007). The UK ADS has developed information standards for archaeological and heritage data, software and complex digital objects and media (Richards 2008). Museums, art galleries and other memory institutions also deal with a broad range of digital information and items (Parry 2007). Digital data and objects need active curation (Richards 2008:174) and prior planning for collecting, preservation, access and publication (McCarthy 2007:255-256). Also essential is design and production of administrative, descriptive and technical metadata (data about data) that needs to be standardised at some level (Mason 2007:225; Kansa et al. 2010). For digital archives to remain understandable in future, metadata and content also needs to include information about the broader context of their production (McCarthy 2007:257; Witmore 2009:517; Sanders 2011).

Archaeologists are ethically obliged to make their research data publicly accessible, but the metadata standardisation needed to achieve this online can act to promote particular types of archaeological research design over others with implications for theory and practice (Hodder 1999; Cochrane and Russell 2007:14; Witmore 2009). Similar issues apply to museums (Cameron and Robinson 2007; Parry 2007). Mason (2007:228-230) observes that development of shared information standards for digital cultural heritage requires trust and cooperation between stakeholders and willingness to share both information and costs. Principles of federation work best and are more ethical as they embed negotiation and openly acknowledge sociopolitical realities such as digital divides, diversity of practice and cultural and other sensitivities.

Individuals and organisations can store material items and hard-copy documents in the reasonable expectation they will remain stable and accessible. Digital media and technologies are unstable and quickly become redundant or obsolete for commercial and organisational reasons (McCarthy 2007:246; Richards 2008). Preserving digital heritage requires active intervention, technical expertise, infrastructure and funding beyond the reach of most private individuals and organisations (BRTF 2008). Digital items are stored on networked servers which are shared places and raise questions of privacy, security, access, control and costs. Techniques for conserving digital heritage (Carroll 2008:247) include technology preservation (maintaining obsolete hardware and software), emulation (creating new programmes to replicate the look and functionality of older software) and migration (transferring data, information and content from older to newer media formats). Migration is the most widespread method favoured by libraries and archives and requires digital information be stored in formats that can be accessed by open source software and with metadata that conforms to international standards, e.g. Dublin Core (Mason 2007; Richards 2008). Digital preservation also requires institutions to maintain computer systems into the future and sign international agreements on sustainability (BRTF 2008).

Digital heritage preservation services are offered through some government libraries, archives and museums and for archaeology by, e.g. the UK-based ADS http://archaeologydataservice.ac.uk, the USA-based Digital Archaeological Record (tDAR) http://www.tdar.org and some European institutions aligned to the ARENA project (Richards 2008:176). Despite these efforts, much digital heritage remains at risk because only some practitioners have access to necessary services. Even in the UK where digital preservation of archaeological information is mandated by government and which has better resources than many other countries, some digital heritage still remains at risk.

Commonly used software and file formats are commercial products developed by businesses that restrict public access to their coding to protect intellectual property. Whether such proprietary software and file formats remain usable into the future depends on market forces. Heritage conservation ethics are predicated on principles of public ownership, open access to information and the 'public right to know' tempered only by consideration of privacy, confidentiality of commercial information and cultural rights of traditional owners and descendants (McCarthy 2007:253). Sustainable digital archiving and preservation assumes open-access file formats and protocols (Kansa *et al.* 2010). It could be regarded as unethical for heritage practitioners to use proprietary software to make unique and irreproducible records of important heritage information unless future public access can be assured. This is clearly impractical and undesirable given the enthusiasm with which professionals and communities embrace commercially produced digital technologies and apply them to cultural heritage. Using such technologies delivers significant public benefit which must be balanced against the constraints of conservation. A pragmatic approach is for heritage practitioners to develop greater awareness and understanding of ethical and other consequences of using these technologies in different ways (i.e. digital literacy). Some technologies are used as tools to record and help conserve tangible and intangible heritage. Others are research tools, are communication devices or have research and heritage value in their own right (Evans 2006:569). Technologies may combine several functions simultaneously and defy easy categorisation.

A recent European Commission funded initiative recognised digital preservation as an urgent and serious matter demanding action from government and businesses at international level with the growing rate of digital data creation 'rapidly outstripping the rate of growth in data storage technologies' (Billenness 2011:3). With insufficient market demand for private industry to develop digital preservation products, governments were urged to provide funding incentives for industry and introduce regulation, including modifying copyright laws and ensuring digital preservation featured on university computer science curricula. Ideal and ethical future technology design (e.g. self-preserving objects) should make digital preservation seamless, simple and automatic (Billenness 2011:4; Evans 2006:564; Witmore 2009). Yet it could also be unethical for technologies to automatically keep information for posterity without also making users aware and offering choices. Collecting and storing digital information raises questions about security, ownership and privacy which are currently regulated by legislation and, e.g. university research ethics protocols. Digital Rights Management becomes more complicated when information is made accessible online and is commonly described as 'a problem' in the heritage literature. What kind of problem depends on context and whose rights are being protected or advanced by withholding, restricting or making information freely and openly accessible or by imposing copyright charges, royalty fees and restricted terms of use. There are particular concerns about online access to culturally sensitive information and digital heritage belonging to indigenous people (Hollowell and Nicholas 2008; Bowrey and Anderson 2009; Brown 2007). Ethical codes governing ownership, permissions and appropriate use of indigenous cultural heritage have been developed and are updated through ongoing discussion between representatives of indigenous communities, museums, archaeologists and other heritage professionals in Australia, New Zealand, North America and elsewhere (e.g. WAC, AIATSIS). Guidelines for ethical and culturally appropriate practice embedded into government heritage policy and research ethics protocols in Australia extend to digital heritage (e.g. recognising cultural rights of Aboriginal and Torres Strait Islander peoples, negotiating informed consent from appropriate traditional owners prior to fieldwork and publication, access to and ownership of cultural materials and information). Guidelines and policies that seek to empower traditional owners in decisions about cultural heritage do not erase colonial history and legacies of inequality. This concerns politics rather than being specifically about digital rights management.

Professional archaeologists have responsibilities to publish findings and share data with colleagues and the public (Fagan 1995; Kansa 2007; Beaudry 2009). Codes allow professionals to retain exclusive access to their own research data, provided they own the rights, until they finish analysis and publish their work. Publication also establishes their intellectual property rights in their research products. Digital technologies offer new and exciting options for publication that can be interactive and afford deep access to heritage data and information in ways impossible in hard copy. However, current government research funding policies that undervalue innovative publication formats are blocking progress. New business models, including pay walls and sponsorship, are also needed to cover the costs involved in scholarly digital publication (Richards 2006, 2008).

Collecting and preserving digital heritage but not making it public (e.g. creating 'dark' archives) is ethical when restricting access to sensitive information. Harvesting and data mining from the Internet potentially allows archivists and others to collect everything publicly accessible online and store it automatically. For digital cultural heritage de Lusenet (2007:173) asks 'Are we going to keep everything because it is possible? What has happened to the idea that heritage has some value attached to it?' She queries the legality and ethics of archivists capturing and keeping conversations on social networking sites without permission, yet this is the basis for successful Google and Facebook business models. Interoperability of technologies supports access, information sharing and digital preservation. McCarthy (2007:248) regards silos of unconnected knowledge banks as undesirable for cultural heritage. Facebook, now commonly used in heritage practice, is a 'walled garden' designed so Google and other sites cannot index most of its content (Arthur 2012). Objects created inside the Second Life (SL) virtual world cannot generally be exported, so archaeologists and heritage practitioners using SL for research face data loss unless they continue to pay SL use fees (Morgan 2009:483). Digital preservation, whether provided by a private company or public organisation, does cost money. However it could be considered unethical for private companies earning money from donated public data not to also provide means for users to export their own content should they wish. When the Yahoo! product GeoCities closed down in 2009, the Archive Team worked to export, store and make content publicly accessible before it was lost (The Wayback Machine 2012). What are the ethics of this?

Case Study: New South Wales Archaeology Online

New South Wales Archaeology Online (NSW AOL) http://nswaol.library.usyd.edu.au is a website with full text search and display functionality and a sustainable digital archive of previously unpublished and hard to access heritage consultancy reports about the historical archaeology and colonial history of the state of NSW in southeastern Australia (Gibbs and Colley 2012). Stages 1 and 2 are part grant funded by the NSW agency responsible for managing post AD 1788 archaeology and by significant in-kind support from content donors, academic staff and research affiliates at the University of Sydney, local consulting archaeology companies and the University of Sydney Library. This is the first project of its kind in Australia. Neither the federal nor any state or territory government mandates or routinely helps fund preservation of digital information about Australian historical archaeology. There is limited and extremely patchy provision for similar services for Aboriginal and maritime archaeology. There is also no mandated NSW repository for physical collections of artefacts recovered by archaeological excavation of historical sites. Hard-copy reports of fieldwork, some with digital content on CD-ROM, are lodged with relevant agencies for planning consent. Many documents can only be read by visiting physical storage locations in different parts of Sydney and elsewhere in NSW (which has a land area of over 800,000 km^2) or by requesting loan of private copies. Some digital content is now being made accessible online by private websites of consultancy businesses but not in any consistent or sustainable way. The reports and archives are important for research about Sydney and NSW archaeology (e.g. Clarke et al 2012) for which no other resources are available. Many items are missing from public collections, including work produced by academics, students and consultants between the 1970s and 1990s in hard-copy formats which helped establish the subdiscipline of historical archaeology in NSW and Australia. NSW AOL has borrowed 'at risk' hard-copy reports from private donors for professional scanning and digital preservation through the library.

For Stage 2 (May 2011 to May 2013) we started auditing born-digital (images, databases, GIS files, websites, etc.) and hard-copy items (reports, recording sheets, drawing and maps, photographs, slides, film, etc.) produced since the mid-1990s and held by private consultancy companies and numerous government agencies involved in NSW heritage. There is so much material that even a complete audit is beyond the scope of our current grant. This material only describes terrestrial historical archaeology in NSW. Maritime and Aboriginal heritage and archaeology are managed under separate legislation and are not yet part of NSW AOL. Other Australian states and territories manage their own Aboriginal, historical and maritime archaeology and heritage independently and under different legislation. Codes of ethics for Australian archaeology include statements about professional responsibilities to conserve heritage, archive information and make data publicly accessible. In practice this is neither working nor workable.

We started NSW AOL to support our research and university teaching with technical support from experts in sustainable digital archiving at the University of Sydney Library. The library will curate Stages 1 and 2 content as a university research collection. We were awarded grant funding from a NSW government heritage infrastructure scheme that specifically excludes 'research' and expires mid-2013. A small group of mainly Sydney-based consultancy companies and research affiliates donated time and content out of interest and from their professional responsibility to conserve information and make data publicly available. NSW AOL is also useful for consultants' own work and promotes their businesses which operate in a competitive market. The NSW AOL website resides on university servers and must comply with the University of Sydney branding guidelines and website policies.

There are limits to goodwill contributions. The global financial crisis has reduced funding for universities and government services. Currently the library cannot undertake additional technical development work until further notice for organisational reasons. NSW AOL has been well received and successful, but we have only recently been able to start work on publishing hard-copy peer-reviewed publications about the project due to significant funding-related time constraints in university workplaces. Developing NSW AOL is time consuming even with grant funding. The university cannot credit our digital product as a research output even when we add proposed new research and scholarly content. Academic staff are not paid as service providers for the heritage industry or the public. We recently met with a university lawyer to tighten our permissions policy following a complaint about plagiarism in a report previously made publicly accessible by NSW AOL. Paid to act in the university's best interests by offering advice designed to minimise costs and risks, the lawyer asked us why university resources were being used to make information freely available to people outside the university at all. Such policy decisions are not yet made by university lawyers, although we do comply with legislation and university regulations.

Deciding 'What happens next?' has driven frequent changes in project scope and methodology and meetings with stakeholders, potential collaborators and technical experts offering advice or soliciting paid work. The challenge is to manage relationships between people, organisations, regional archaeological practice, technology and economics. Some people who are willing to share their older information online will not release more recent or current information due to business competition. Others may not wish to draw public attention to 'substandard' work produced under the commercial pressures of development-driven archaeology. Fear of 'airing dirty linen in public' inhibits information sharing in archaeology elsewhere and in other disciplines (Ford 2010; Pisani 2011). Most of us want to showcase our better work. A donor was disappointed that online PDF versions of their documents were inaccurate copies of the originals. Poor image reproduction in the PDF versions misrepresented the real quality of mapping and photography they created for clients and reflected badly on their consultancy business. This is understandable, but current Internet bandwidths only support making compressed and smaller PDF versions of reports available online.

Some archaeologists offered scanned PDF copies of reports, including about Aboriginal and maritime archaeology, planning to discard the hard copies to save space. Currently we are unable to accept such content. Metadata entry is relatively expensive. We pay project staff to complete this to a high standard, and our grant is already committed. Enabling donors to enter their own metadata is not an option on the current website. University policy forbids external users uploading publicly accessible content. Even if permission was granted which seems unlikely, digital rights compliance costs are prohibitive, especially for any Aboriginal information. The University of Sydney Library cannot currently accept files in PDF format for digital preservation as part of NSW AOL because PDF does not match their digital preservation criteria. The NSW AOL website delivers PDF versions of sustainably archived TIFF files that remain invisible to users. The XTF-based full-text search and display functionality of the website helps users find information and access document content. NSW AOL is currently configured both as a research tool and a sustainable digital archive. Future plans include uploading selected 'at risk' images, adding commentary to better contextualise collections and producing online publications linked to the archive reporting scholarly research on regional archaeology.

Visualisation and Virtual Realities

Visualisation and interactive and immersive multimedia technologies have been widely and enthusiastically adopted in cultural heritage practice. Their significance both *to* and *as* research and practice is theorised as remediation of illustration, mapping, photography and cinematography and by discussing representation, simulation and virtual reality (Earl 2005, 2006; Gillings 2005; Cochrane and Russell 2007; Barceló 2007; Perry 2009). Such technologies raise questions about essential qualities of 'real' and 'virtual' material objects and places (e.g. Pujol and Champion 2012) and discuss notions of authenticity and truth. Trust, truthfulness and transparency are professional and ethical values. An opinion survey showed that local people trusted North American museums to be accurate and authentic (Hazan 2007:135). Ethical codes for archaeology, museums and archival practice stress professional obligations to retain and value authenticity and uphold intellectual integrity by separating factual evidence from interpretation and unfounded opinion. The problematic concept of authenticity is central to heritage theory (Smith *et al*. 2010). Truth, 'actuality' (c.f. Harrison 2009:85) transparency and realism are slightly different concepts. Anxieties have been provoked for museums by the reproducibility and 'immaterial' nature of digital objects based on fears that real (material) objects and artworks are threatened by mechanical reproduction and simulation (Cameron and Kenderine 2007:4; Parry 2007:61-66). Trade in faked antiquities is a potential concern given developments in 3D printing technologies that could in future materialise 'untruthful' digital objects in realistic looking ways.

How realistic or truthful must a digital visualisation be to be useful, less useful, ethical or unethical? This depends, as always, on context. Realistic visualisation was not that important to Morgan's research on the functional design of prehistoric features at a reconstruction of the Çatalhöyük archaeological site in the Second Life (SL) virtual world (2009:478), but she notes that archaeologists working with other SL virtual reconstructions of Çatalhöyük found them 'too real' or 'too sterile' (2009:481-2). Convincing 3D audiovisual simulations that look or seem 'real' due to advances in computer imaging technologies, but blend fact and fiction, are regarded as unethical and unprofessional by some researchers and heritage practitioners unless production is contextualised and made transparent by including paradata documenting interpretative processes that make the degree of reliability of the visualisation clear (Sanders 2011; Bentkowska-Kafel *et al*. 2012). The *London Charter for the Computer-Based Visualisation of Cultural Heritage* (2009) sets out principles for rigorous, scholarly digital visualisation based on intellectual integrity and reliability, documentation, sustainability and access. It is aimed at computer visualisation in research and professional practice and 'those aspects of the entertainment industry involving reconstruction or evocation of cultural heritage' but not for visualisation in 'contemporary art, fashion or design'. Given challenges of separating facts from interpretation, this would be difficult to implement for archaeology except when discerning the facts is possible or socially important (e.g. in some kinds of archaeological science or for legal and forensic cases concerning rights claims or criminality).

Visualisation technologies have been embraced by some archaeologists to actively challenge boundaries between science and arts, truth and fiction, and because such technologies can enhance engaged, experiential and creative practices as part of archaeology (Cochrane and Russell 2007; Joyce and Tringham 2007; Webmoor 2008; Ryzewski 2009; Shanks 2009; Witmore 2009). Where 'contemporary art, fashion or design' or 'entertainment' stop and professional archaeology and heritage management start is not clear as discussed by Holtorf (2007, 2009, 2010) for archaeology, popular culture and 'the experience society'. Holtorf accepts and celebrates fictionalised popular representations of archaeology while Pyburn (2008) regards this as professionally dishonest.

Indigenous critiques of digital technologies and cultural heritage by Brown (2007) and Bowrey and Anderson (2009) employ visualisations by indigenous artists using digital and other media to communicate ideas about cultural appropriation. Brown (2007) urges indigenous people to apply digital technologies to their own cultures before others do so on their behalf. Spiritual and cultural qualities customarily transferred into reproductions and representations of material Maori *taonga* (treasures) extend to digital simulation. Digital technologies can be valuable for cultural repatriation provided their use is governed by communities in culturally appropriate ways (Brown 2007:85).

Context, genres, modes of delivery and audience understandings and expectations are crucial to such debates. Digital media representations of archaeology and cultural heritage are viewed, consumed, experienced, appreciated, ignore or disliked in actual places using differently formatted, sized, shaped and placed screens and audio equipment in public or private social contexts (Shanks 2009:551-552; Graves-Brown 2009:210). Without denying the power of professional media advertising (Holtorf 2009), presumably most mature and media literate audiences appreciate differences between 'reality' and fictional reconstruction in heritage visualisation. The 'wow' factor of the technology (Lister *et al.* 2009:141-5) may be part of the appeal, even for heritage and archaeology, although as computer-generated visualisation becomes increasingly common in heritage interpretation it can become mundane, boring or annoying to some (Silberman 2010).

Questions of the 'real' are pivotal to archaeology's ambiguous relationship with professional print and broadcast media and film producers (Brittain and Clack 2007:46). Archaeologists criticise 'the' media for inaccurate reporting, misrepresenting archaeology as trivial entertainment and undermining professional authority (Taylor 2007:190-194). 'New' digital media technologies (e.g. blogs and online platforms like Flickr, YouTube and Facebook) and cheaper audiovisual equipment and software allow audiences to produce and distribute their own media content online using different formats. Archaeologists and others can represent themselves and tell their own 'media' stories to potentially wide public audiences. This has significantly transformed established business models and practices of traditional media who now also produce 'new' media themselves (Lister *et al.* 2009:262). This throws interesting light on archaeologists' existing concerns with media 'professionals' about unethical practice. If archaeologists become media producers themselves, they can tell their own stories in their own ways, and they need to act professionally and reflect on media ethics. As Brittain and Clack (2007:41) discuss for professional media, visual and audio multimedia present 'more complicated' issues than print media when representing people involved in archaeological and heritage projects, especially in cross-cultural contexts. When professional archaeologists perform 'engaged' fieldwork and heritage practice (as discussed by, e.g. Ryzewski 2009) using technologies to closely document people's behaviours, reactions and opinions, and not just archaeological information, they have professional obligations to seek informed participant consent and to think about privacy and surveillance, particularly if content will be made public online. This depends on circumstances and who is involved. Some people like being on camera and performing to public audiences. Others may not want to share their opinions and attitudes with a wider audience or have their actions and appearance documented for public broadcast. Technology may impact on outcomes, for example, when being recorded for public podcast changes how people act or what they say. Who controls the editing and the story? Can people easily opt out with no social or other costs? Is there a 'take-down' policy if participants object to web content? Coercion is possible when participants are students, employees or in less powerful positions. University research ethics codes now govern such practices.

The ethics of archaeologists using traditional media coverage for self-promotion or to foster public support for particular types of archaeology are discussed by Brittain and Clack (2007:36). Even posting information on a basic website immediately and unavoidably raises questions of representation, branding and online identity. Are ethics and professional issues raised by the self-representation, branding and advertising implied by 'broadcasting yourself' on YouTube, for example, any different to traditional media?

Given highly flexible design options (Morgan 2009:479-481; Harrison 2009:83), what should or could the avatar of a professional archaeologist look like in a virtual world when they are there conducting research? Should they be 'obviously' identifiable as a professional archaeologist (whatever that implies) when interacting with other residents? Should they remain anonymous? To what extent are other residents in virtual worlds 'community stakeholders' as discussed in archaeological codes of ethics governing actual worlds?

Case Study: Archaeological Communication and Digital Technologies

Similar questions apply when archaeologists use other social networking platforms and interactive communication technologies for their work. A 2011 interview survey of professional archaeologists and heritage practitioners based in Australia aims to investigate relationships between professional communication in archaeology, heritage practice and impacts of digital technologies (Colley 2014). Thirty participants provided information about the organisational context of their work, their work-related communication and use of digital technologies. Preliminary analysis shows that respondents used a wide range of hardware and software for work and they were generally more positive than negative about them. Technologies saved time, made work quicker and easier, were effective and allowed people to store, access and share more information. People liked the instant communication, quick online publication and being able to communicate better with colleagues and the public. Others liked using technologies for improved visual presentations, data analysis and visualising spatial information. Problems included limited bandwidth, 'crashing', outdated hardware and software and inadequate technical support. People disliked software that was hard to use, or remember how to use, and technologies that were not interoperable. Expense was an issue for self-employed consultants and in workplaces where employers did not cover technology costs. Some people disliked steep and continual learning curves, having to constantly reskill or having to work with others with different levels of digital literacy. One person complained of 'dazzling' technology that was not needed or useful. Technologies could be misleading, distracting and create unreasonable expectations of instant replies (e.g. student emails to university-teaching staff). Technologies were considered barriers to some kinds of work-related communication. Some people preferred tangible and hard copy to digital media and were worried about digital preservation, costs of metadata compliance and imposed data standardisation.

Attitudes to social media and interactive communication platforms (e.g. Facebook, Twitter, LinkedIn, blogs, wikis, etc.) were polarised. Some heritage professionals in Australia cannot access social media and similar web technologies from work as they are blocked by government employers. Stated benefits of using such media included being able to share research more easily and reach interdisciplinary research communities, making professional contacts with a very wide range of people, work-related advertising and connecting with students, younger people and the wider public. Some university-teaching staff thought social networking sites engaged students better than mandated university online learning platforms like WebCT and Blackboard Learn. One university researcher liked the freedom of being able to 'fly under the university media and marketing people's radars and circumvent university branding guidelines'.

Others expressed concern about privacy and misuse of personal data by private companies or thought that using social media presented an unprofessional image, was pointless or was 'ephemeral'. It is ethical for university-teaching staff to maintain professional distance from students. Inappropriate personal content and communication on, e.g. Facebook presents the danger of transgressing such boundaries. Some professional archaeologists said they disliked social media or considered themselves too old to use them. Others were not interested or did not have phones that supported access. Other online tools failed to match expectations when, e.g. few people contributed and sites attracted limited visitors. Online communication tools (emails lists, forums, blogs, wikis) presented challenges of dealing with negative and derogatory comments, e.g. 'people feel they can hide behind anonymity and say things they would not dare say to your face'.

Digital technologies present convergent issues for heritage practice regardless of institutional or disciplinary context. These also apply to others who produce and manage digital content and wish to archive or make it publicly accessible online, including media professionals, journalists, creative practitioners, businesses and communities and private individuals. The 'public sphere' online raises questions about public and private spaces (c.f. Graves-Brown 2009) the nature of 'online communities' and appropriate professional and private behaviours in digital spaces. Themes of 'digital citizenship' about access, commerce, communication, literacy, etiquette, law, rights and responsibilities, health and well-being, security and self-protection (Ribble 2012) are not specifically about heritage, but digital communication technologies blur boundaries between public and private and workplace and home and impact on heritage practitioners as private citizens and consumers.

What Happens Next?

Making provision for digital preservation to prevent loss of archaeological and heritage information is the major ethical and professional challenge facing our profession. Principles enshrined in existing ethical and professional codes are extensible to digital technologies in most cases, even though only some codes discuss technology. Research for this paper suggests it is useful, necessary and ethical for archaeologists and other heritage practitioners to extend their digital literacy to help them make better decisions about the use and application of technologies in their work.

New technologies in general have acted to fragmented professional media production and audiences and participants increasingly prefer to engage with familiar content that expresses values they already hold (Lister et al. 2009:202-4). To some extent this mirrors fragmentation in current archaeological theory and practice. In discussing archaeological theory, with admittedly less focus on practice, Johnson (2010:183-184, Figs. 12.1 and 12.2) presents two cartoons illustrating changing interactions and communication between archetypes of archaeologists of different theoretical persuasions, e.g. processualists, post-processualists of different kinds, feminists and, in my opinion, a highly 'unrealistic' Classical Archaeologist. In Fig. 12.1 (by Simon James) illustrating 1988, the public is an 'irritating distraction', the Classical Archaeologist prefers to read books on his own, while the others argue passionately with each other about who is right or wrong. In Fig. 12.2 (by Matthew Johnson) showing 1998, the public have wandered off to do something else, the Classical Archaeologist still reads his books on his own, and the other groups have long stopped talking to each other and only engage with people who share their perspectives. If we updated the image to 2012, presumably even the Classical Archaeologist would be downloading e-journals from the web, and archaeologists in all groups would be checking e-mails or using their mobiles to text people not even in the picture. A digital cloud would be gathering overhead beckoning everyone to start standardising at least some of their metadata for online collaboration and to aid digital preservation. Some archaeologists would be observing the scene, taking pictures on their hand-held mobile devices and producing video blogs. The 'the public' and everyone would be online somewhere if not actually in the same physical location at the same time. I have visualised this picture in words rather than copying and extending the original images, as this is quicker and cheaper, if probably less effective, than obtaining necessary reproduction rights. It is legal and ethical to describe other people's work if I include a bibliographic reference. Digital technologies raise many practical, ethical and sociopolitical challenges, and they are a transformative and interesting part of archaeology and heritage practice.

Acknowledgements I thank Martin Gibbs, Anne Bickford, Kenneth Aitchison and Robin Torrence for feedback on earlier drafts. NSW AOL is part funded by a grant from the NSW Office of Environment and Heritage and NSW Heritage Council. The *Archaeological Communication and Digital Technologies* project was seed funded by a 2009 University of Sydney Faculty of Arts Research Support Scheme Grant.

References

AHAD (Australian Historical Archaeology Database). http://www.latrobe.edu.au/humanities/research/australian-historical-archaeology-database-ahad. Accessed May 19, 2012.

Arthur, C. (2012, April 28–29). Too quiet in the walled garden (Sydney Morning Herald Weekend Edition, News Review: 22). *Guardian News & Media*.

Backhouse, P. (2006). Drowning in data? Digital data in a British contracting unit. In T. L. Evans & P. Daly (Eds.), *Digital archaeology: Bridging method and theory* (pp. 50–58). London: Routledge.

Barceló, J. A. (2007). Automatic archaeology: Bridging the gap between virtual reality, artificial intelligence and archaeology. In F. Cameron & S. Kenderine (Eds.), *Theorizing digital cultural heritage: A critical discourse* (pp. 437–455). Cambridge: MIT Press.

Beaudry, M. C. (2009). Ethical issues in historical archaeology. In T. Majewski & D. Gaimster (Eds.), *International handbook of historical archaeology* (pp. 17–29). London: Springer.

Bentkowska-Kafel, A., Denard, H., & Baker, D. (Eds.). (2012). *Paradata and transparency in virtual heritage*. London: Ashgate.

Billenness, C. S. G. (Ed.), (2011, May 4–5). *The future of the past: Shaping new visions for EU-research in digital preservation*. Report on the Proceedings of the Workshop, Cultural Heritage and Technology Enhanced Learning, European Commission Information Society and Media Directorate-General, Luxembourg, 4–5 May 2011.

Bowrey, K., & Anderson, J. (2009). The politics of global information sharing: Whose cultural agendas are being advanced? *Social & Legal Studies, 18*(4), 479–504.

Brittain, M., & Clack, T. (2007). Introduction: Archaeology and the media. In T. Clack & M. Brittain (Eds.), *Archaeology and the media* (pp. 11–65). Walnut Creek: Left Coast Press.

Broderick, M., Cypher, M., & Macbeth, J. (2009). Critical masses: Augmented virtual experiences and the xenoplastic at Australia's Cold War and nuclear heritage sites. *Archaeologies, 5*(2), 323–343.

Brown, D. (2007). Te Ahu Hiko: Digital cultural heritage and indigenous objects, people and environments. In F. Cameron & S. Kenderine (Eds.), *Theorizing digital cultural heritage. A critical discourse* (pp. 77–92). Cambridge: MIT Press.

BRTF (Blue Ribbon Task Force on Sustainable Digital Preservation and Access). (2008). http://brtf.sdsc.edu/about.html. Accessed May 13, 2012.

Cameron, F. (2007). Beyond the cult of the replicant. Museums and historical digital objects: Traditional concerns, new discourses. In F. Cameron & S. Kenderine (Eds.), *Theorizing digital cultural heritage: A critical discourse* (pp. 49–76). Cambridge: MIT Press.

Cameron, F., & Kenderdine, S. (Eds.). (2007). *Theorizing digital cultural heritage: A critical discourse*. Cambridge: MIT Press.

Cameron, F., & Robinson, H. (2007). Digital knowledgescapes: Cultural, theoretical, practical, and usage issues facing museum collection databases in a digital epoch. In F. Cameron & S. Kenderdine (Eds.), *Theorizing digital cultural heritage: A critical discourse* (pp. 165–192). Cambridge: MIT Press.

Carroll, M. S. (2008). From data to knowledge: Creating and managing archaeological data for the future. In F. P. McManamon, A. Stout, & J. A. Barnes (Eds.), *Managing archaeological resources: Global context, national programmes, local actions* (pp. 241–256). Walnut Creek: Left Coast Press.

Clarke, A., Colley, S., & Gibbs, M., (Eds.), (2012). *Landscapes and materiality: Historical and contemporary archaeology in the Sydney basin*. Special Issue of *Archaeology in Oceania*, 47 (2).

Cochrane, A., & Russell, I. (2007). Visualizing archaeologies: A manifesto. *Cambridge Archaeological Journal, 17*(1), 3–19.

Coller, M. (2009). SahulTime: Rethinking archaeological representation in the digital age. *Archaeologies, 5*(1), 110–123.

Colley, S. (2002). *Uncovering Australia: Archaeology, indigenous people and the public*. Sydney: Allen and Unwin.

Colley, S. (2014). Social media and archaeological communication: An Australian survey. *Archäologische Informationen,* Early View. http://www.dguf.de/index.php?id=9. Accessed April 29, 2014.

De Lusenet, Y. (2007). Tending the garden or harvesting the fields: Digital preservation and the UNESCO Charter on the Preservation of Digital Heritage. *Library Trends, 56*(1), 164–182

Earl, G. P. (2005). Video killed engaging VR? Computer visualizations on the TV screen. In S. Smiles & S. Moser (Eds.), *Envisioning the past: Archaeology and the image* (pp. 204–223). Oxford: Blackwell.

Earl, G. P. (2006). At the edges of the lens: Photography, graphical constructions and cinematography. In T. L. Evans & P. Daly (Eds.), *Digital archaeology: Bridging method and theory* (pp. 191–209). London: Routledge.

Evans, T. (2006). Research policy and directions. In L. MacDonald (Ed.), *Digital heritage: Applying digital imaging to cultural heritage* (pp. 549–574). Oxford: Elsevier.

Evans, T. L., & Daly, P. (Eds.). (2006). *Digital archaeology: Bridging method and theory*. New York: Routledge.

Fagan, B. (1995). Archaeology's dirty secret. *Archaeology, 48*(8), 14–17.

Ford, M. (2010). Archaeology: Hidden treasures. *Nature, 464*(, 826–827.

Geismar, H. (2005). Reproduction, creativity, restriction: Material culture and copyright in Vanuatu. *Journal of Social Archaeology, 5*(1), 25–51.

Gibbs, M., & Colley, S. (2012). Digital preservation, online access and historical archaeology 'grey literature' from New South Wales, Australia. *Australian Archaeology, 75*, 95–103.

Gillings, M. (2005). The real, the virtually real, and the hyperreal: The role of VR in archaeology. In S. Smiles & S. Moser (Eds.), *Envisioning the past. Archaeology and the image* (pp. 223–239). Oxford: Blackwell.

Graves-Brown, P. (2009). The privatisation of experience and the archaeology of the future. In H. Cornelius & P. Angela (Eds.), *Contemporary archaeologies: Excavating now* (pp. 201–213). Frankfurt am Main: Peter Lang.

Hamilakis, Y., & Duke, P. (Eds.). (2007). *Archaeology and capitalism: From ethics to politics*. Walnut Creek: Left Coast Press.

Harrison, R. (2009). Excavating second life: Cyber-archaeologies, heritage and virtual communities. *Journal of Material Culture, 14*(1), 75–106.

Harrison, R., & Schofield, J. (2009). Archaeo-ethnography, auto-archaeology: Introducing archaeologies of the contemporary past. *Archaeologies, 5*(2), 185–209.

Hazan, S. (2007). A crisis of authority: New lamps for old. In F. Cameron & S. Kenderdine (Eds.), *Theorizing digital cultural heritage: A critical discourse* (pp. 133–148). Cambridge: MIT Press.

Hemsley, J., Cappellini, V., & Stanke, G. (Eds.). (2005a). *Digital applications for cultural and heritage institutions*. London: Ashgate.

Hemsley, J., Cappellini, V., & Stanke, G. (2005b). Introduction and international overview. In J. Hemsley, V. Cappellini, & G. Stanke (Eds.), *Digital applications for cultural and heritage institutions* (pp. 1–13). London: Ashgate.

Hemsley, J., Cappellini, V., & Stanke, G. (2005c). Conclusions and future trends. In J. Hemsley, V. Cappellini, & G. Stanke (Eds.), *Digital applications for cultural and heritage institutions* (pp. 295–300). London: Ashgate.

Hodder, I. (1999). *The archaeological process*. Oxford: Blackwell.

Hollowell, J., & Nicholas, G. (2008). Intellectual property issues in archaeological publication: Some questions to consider. *Archaeologies, 4*(2), 208–217.

Holtorf, C. (2007). *Archaeology is a brand! The meaning of archaeology in contemporary popular culture*. Walnut Creek: Left Coast Press.

Holtorf, C. (2009). Imagine this: Archaeology in the experience society. In H. Cornelius & P. Angela (Eds.), *Contemporary archaeologies: Excavating now* (pp. 47–64). Frankfurt am Main: Peter Lang.

Holtorf, C. (2010). Heritage values in contemporary popular culture. In G. S. Smith, P. M. Messenger & H. A. Soderland (Eds.), *Heritage values in contemporary society* (pp. 43–54). Walnut Creek: Left Coast Press.

Ioannides, M., Fellner, D., Georgopoulos, A., & Hadjimitsis, D. (Eds.), (2010). *Digital heritage. Third International Conference, EuroMed 2010*, Lemesos, Cyprus, November 8–13 2010, Proceedings (SpringerLINK Lecture Notes in Computer Science, Vol 6336).

Johnson, M. (2010). *Archaeological theory: An introduction* (2nd ed.). Oxford: Wiley-Blackwell.

Joyce, R., & Tringham, R. (2007). Feminist adventures in hypertext. *Journal of Archaeological Method and Theory, 14*, 328–358.

Kansa, E. (2007). Publishing primary data on the World Wide Web: Opencontext.org and an open future for the past. *Technical Briefs in Historical Archaeology, 2*, 1–11.

Kansa, E. C., Kansa, S. W., Burton, M. M., & Stankowski, C. (2010). Googling the grey: Open data, web services, and semantics. *Archaeologies, 6*(2), 301–326.

Lister, M., Dovey, J., Giddings, S., Grant, I., & Kelly, K. (2009). *New media: A critical introduction* (2nd ed.). London: Routledge.

Lock, G. (2003). *Using computers in archaeology: Towards virtual pasts*. London: Routledge.

London Charter for the Computer-Based Visualisation of Cultural Heritage. (2009). http://www.londoncharter.org/. Accessed May 4, 2012.

Mason, I. (2007). Cultural information standards: Political territory and rich rewards. In F. Cameron & S. Kenderdine (Eds.), *Theorizing digital cultural heritage: A critical discourse* (pp. 223–243). Cambridge, MA: MIT Press.

McCarthy, G. (2007). Finding a future for digital cultural heritage resources using contextual information frameworks. In F. Cameron & S. Kenderdine (Eds.), *Theorizing digital cultural heritage: A critical discourse* (pp. 245–260). Cambridge, MA: MIT Press.

Meskell, L., & Pels, P. (Eds.). (2005). *Embedding ethics: Shifting boundaries of the anthropological profession*. Oxford and New York: Berg.

Morgan, C. (2009). (Re)Building Çatalhöyük: Changing virtual reality in archaeology. *Archaeologies, 5*(3), 468–487.

Parry, R. (2007). *Recoding the museum: Digital heritage and the technologies of change*. London: Routledge.

Perry, S. (2009). Fractured media: Challenging the dimensions of archaeology's typical visual modes of engagement. *Archaeologies, 5*(3), 389–415.

Pisani, E. (2011, January 15). All will be welcome at harvest of health research. Opinion. *Sydney Morning Herald*. http://www.smh.com.au/opinion/society-and-culture/all-will-be-welcome-at-harvest-of-health-research-20110114-19r78.html. Accessed May 19, 2012.

Pujol, L., & Champion, E. (2012). Evaluating presence in cultural heritage projects. *International Journal of Heritage Studies, 18*(1), 83–102.

Pyburn, K. A. (2008). Public archaeology, Indiana Jones and honesty. *Archaeologies, 4*(2), 201–204.

Ribble, M. (2012). Digital citizenship: Using technology appropriately. http://www.digitalcitizenship. net. Accessed May 15, 2012.

Richards, J. (2006). Archaeology, e-publication and the semantic web. *Antiquity, 80*(310), 970–979.

Richards, J. (2008). Managing digital preservation and access: The archaeology data service. In F. P. McManamon, A. Stout, & J. A. Barnes (Eds.), *Managing archaeological resource: Global context, national programmes, local actions* (pp. 173–194). Walnut Creek: Left Coast Press.

Ross, S.A. (2012). *NeCTAR research tools project. Federated archaeological information management systems: A heterogeneous, modular, and federated approach to archaeological information management.* Presentation at the Digital Humanities Australasia 2012: Building, mapping, connecting [Conference]—aaDH12. Canberra, Australia: ANU. http://hdl.handle.net/1885/9004

Russo, A., & Watkins, J. (2007). Digital cultural communication: Audience and remediation. In F. Cameron & S. Kenderdine (Eds.), *Theorizing digital cultural heritage: A critical discourse* (pp. 149–164). Cambridge: MIT Press.

Ryzewski, K. (2009). Seven interventions with the Flatlands: Archaeology and its mode of engagement. Contributions from the WAC-6 Session, 'Experience, Modes of Engagement, Archaeology'. *Archaeologies, 5*(3), 361–388.

Sanders, D. H. (2011). Virtual reconstruction of maritime sites and artifacts. In A. Catsambis, B. Ford, & D. L. Hamilton (Eds.), *The Oxford handbook of maritime archaeology* (pp. 305–326). Oxford: Oxford University Press.

Shanks, M. (2007). Digital media, agile design, and the politics of archaeological authorship. In T. Clack & M. Brittain (Eds.), *Archaeology and the media* (pp. 273–289). Walnut Creek: Left Coast Press.

Shanks, M. (2009). Engagement: Archaeological design and engineering. *Archaeologies, 5*(3), 546–556.

Silberman, N. A. (2010). Technology, heritage values, and interpretation. In G. S. Smith, P. M. Messenger & H. A. Soderland (Eds.), *Heritage values in contemporary society* (pp. 63–73). Walnut Creek: Left Coast Press.

Smith, G. S., Messenger, P. M., & Soderland, H. A. (Eds.). (2010). *Heritage values in contemporary society.* Walnut Creek, CA: Left Coast Press.

Taylor, T. (2007). Screening biases: Archaeology, television, and the banal. In T. Clack & M. Brittain (Eds.), *Archaeology and the media* (pp. 187–195). Walnut Creek: Left Coast Press.

The Wayback Machine. (2012). http://archive.org/web/web.php. Accessed May 18, 2012.

UNESCO. (2003). *Charter on the preservation of digital heritage.* http://portal.unesco.org/en/ ev.php-url_id=17721&url_do=do_topic&url_section=201.html. Accessed May 19, 2012.

Verbeek, P.-P. (2011). *Moralizing technology: Understanding and designing the morality of things.* Chicago: University of Chicago Press.

Webmoor, T. (2008). From silicon valley to the valley of Teotihuacan: The 'Yahoo!s' of new media and digital heritage. *Visual Anthropology Review, 24*(2), 183–200.

Wildesen, L. (1984). The search for an ethic in archaeology: An historical perspective. In E. L. Green (Ed.), *Ethics and values in archaeology* (pp. 3–12). New York: Free Press.

Witmore, C. (2009). Prolegomena to open pasts: on archaeological memory practices. *Archaeologies, 5*(3), 511–545.

Zubrow, E. B. (2006). Digital archaeology: A historical context. In T. L. Evans & P. Daly (Eds.), *Digital archaeology: Bridging method and theory* (pp. 10–32). London: Routledge.

Chapter 3
Ethics and Heritage Tourism

Steve Watson

Introduction

The purpose of this chapter is to assess the ethical implications of heritage tourism as it is presently constituted and practised. The questions this implies seem fairly clear at first sight: What constitutes heritage tourism and what are its effects? What ethical problems have been posed and how has heritage tourism been challenged on ethical grounds? How do ethics engage with heritage tourism practices and what are the results and implications of such an engagement? Yet any such clarity is immediately confounded by the complexities surrounding each of these questions and a tendency to limit debate to the well-rehearsed issues of tourism impacts (environmental and cultural) and how these might be mitigated through effective management and the talismanic qualities of the word 'sustainability'.

My intention is to explore the complex relationships between ethics and heritage tourism in a way that avoids 'managerial' solutions whilst leaving some space for thinking about an ethical framework within which heritage tourism might be examined. I do not offer an ethics *of* heritage tourism, in the way that MacCannell (2011) offers an *Ethics of Sightseeing*. I think this is a slightly different task, and in any case, MacCannell needed a book rather than a chapter to work through his penetrating and insightful analysis. Nor do I offer an ethics *in* heritage tourism as this would presuppose that there are some or at least some worth looking for. What I do propose is to look at ethics *and* heritage tourism, to put the two things side by side and see what connections and judgements can be made. In doing so, I will attempt to examine heritage tourism through an ethical lens and evaluate it in terms of what it is and what it does when seen in this way.

S. Watson (✉)
Business School, York St John University,
Lord Mayor's Walk, York YO31 7EX, UK
e-mail: S.Watson@yorksj.ac.uk

© Springer Science+Business Media New York 2015
T. Ireland, J. Schofield (eds.), *The Ethics of Cultural Heritage*,
Ethical Archaeologies: The Politics of Social Justice 4,
DOI 10.1007/978-1-4939-1649-8_3

The core of my argument, to provide some orientation and momentum, is that an ethical case is needed for heritage tourism as it is most frequently practised. Furthermore, I contend that ethics should be made an explicit part of the way heritage tourism is critically examined, if we accept that ethics are implicated in debates about what it is and how it operates. I am thinking here particularly about politics, power relations, commodification and other issues that have come to be discussed in advancing the so-called heritage debate. The value of engaging with ethics in this way is that it provides an analytical sidelight that reveals things about the way that heritage tourism works and what ensues as a result. It is important, however, not to create too much abstraction: the ethics should be politically grounded and the politics should be ethically informed. The remaining question that I will attempt to address in this essay is whether it is possible to sustain a concept and practice of heritage tourism that stands up to ethical scrutiny and a rendering of it that responds to ethical and political critiques.

Ethics and Method

For ethics, however, to provide a lens through which heritage tourism might be evaluated, it has to begin with a question that is philosophically grounded and not just political, namely, what 'good' does it do, if any? Conventional normative and applied ethics would suggest the need for an evaluation that makes judgements about what is the right course of action in particular situations and circumstances and, when certain conditions obtain, how an agency or an individual ought, therefore, to act. It would be difficult to improve on MacCannell's (2011:50–51) penetrating sense of this in applying Aristotelian ethics to tourism:

> According to Aristotle [...] it is necessary to know 'the good' to determine whether any given action is ethical. Those who emphasised fun and pleasure as the central organizing feature of the tourism field can no longer be allowed to dodge the question: what is the good of tourism and sightseeing and how does it connect to the pleasure of the tourist? Minimally, this involves searching for the good in the relationship of fantasy, symbolism, and reality as provoked at an attraction. Is it the good of visiting Auschwitz the way it symbolizes the dignity of its victims in the face of unspeakable cruelty, or is it in the way it symbolizes the evil of their Nazi oppressors? Is it in the fantasy identification it solicits from tourists? And what about the fantasy identification with the Nazis? Or is it in the banal orderliness and cold efficiency of the actual layout of buildings, streets, Crematoria? What is the good of Disneyland? No tourist should walk away from their experience without ethical concerns.

For MacCannell, the emphasis is on looking at an individual's response to the potential that every attraction has to provoke ethical questions and doubt. My concern is to look at the practice of heritage tourism, the way it is done and its effects and, if it does any good, how this is mapped across its means and its ends. This Kantian-utilitarian polarity, however it resolves itself, is actually very useful in studies of tourism, because an evaluation of *the good* often turns on whether ends justify means. In tourism, these are most often expressed in terms of assumed economic benefits, but with heritage included, they also connect, if rather vaguely, with other values such as education, cultural enrichment, sharing common values, celebrating human achievement and the need to protect and conserve heritage in ways that have been enshrined in the UNESCO World Heritage Conventions.

Heritage thus endows tourism with a kind of moral ballast that it might not otherwise possess, especially if it presents an alternative to what is sometimes framed as hedonistic tourism, the tourism of beaches, commercial resorts, extravagant nightlife, sexual adventure and the way that all this is represented and marketed (Shields 1991; Game 1991; Diken and Laustsen 2004; Brunt and Davis 2006; Pritchard and Morgan 2010). The immorality, or amorality, of hedonistic tourism undoubtedly casts heritage tourism in a contrastingly positive light. But even without this 'good thing by comparison' prop, heritage is also favourably compared with the present 'against what's dreadful and dreaded today', as Lowenthal (1998: xiii) put it, and in a reflection of popular sentiment about the 'good old days', so that the idea that 'heritage must be a general good is now a general faith' (1998: 67). It is a good thing because it is connected with a myriad of virtues: it displays the achievements of humanity and the splendours of art and architecture, and it provides reference points for national identity and local customs. Its objects accrue value not only in having survived the many tests of time but in showing it and in representing an authenticity that is virtuously contrapuntal to the artifice of modernity.

Heritage thus rendered is for everyone and available for the price of an admission ticket to a museum, a stately home or an ancient monument. It is the leveller of past privileges; a key that has opened the door for the masses to consume in an afternoon what the bounteously endowed elite spent their whole lives enjoying. It socialises private luxury by representing it as a public benefit, and in the process, it also socialises the costs of stewardship and preservation. Heritage is educational. It teaches us about past transgressions and how to avoid them in the future. It demonstrates both human wickedness and great triumphs for our edification. It underpins our identity and justifies our place in the world. Its truths are empirically manifest in stone and other materials and in traditions and beliefs. That heritage is a *good thing* is more than amply demonstrated in the monumental tangibility (or financial value) of its objects and in the practices and beliefs connected with them.

Yet the aesthetics of heritage and the experts who underwrite its value provide guarantees not only of provenance but, by extension, of a particular version of the past. This is the secret work of heritage objects (Watson and Waterton 2010) and the *heritage debate* of the last 25 years has, in its deconstructive fervour, done much to destabilise and challenge many of the consensual assumptions about the good that heritage is and does. Heritage, thus examined, has rather withered, at least in the academy, where there is an uneasy truce between those who would defend the values it harbours and those who, from a critical constructivist perspective, would point to the discourses that such value underpins and the ends they serve. Smith (2006) has provided what amounts to a culmination in this thinking with the idea of the Authorised Heritage Discourse (AHD), an ideologically modulated narrative of the past largely represented through its materiality, selection and display. Heritage is thus a process rather than a collection of objects, one that endows powerful class and nationalistic interests with qualities of consensus and commonsense at the expense of other oppositional and subaltern renderings of the past. There is no such *thing* as heritage. Rather, it is constructed in the social and discursive arrangements that support powerful interests.

An ethical position, therefore, would be one that made judgements about such discourses and the ends they serve. It might furthermore abjure an interest in objects and a belief in their inherent value and redirect attention to the heritage discourses that are active in a particular place at a particular time. So whilst, for example, it is difficult to disavow the merits of economic well-being and shared understanding, there is a serious debate not only about what is gained and lost along the way but also about what principles and interests are served in the process as a whole. The heritage debate has thus ordered and constituted a field of critical deconstructive analysis within which, I argue, ethics has an important role. An important concomitant of this is that ultimately, the philosophical debate about ethics is grounded in politics, with ethics informing practice that has social, economic and political implications. Is there anything that heritage tourism ought to do or be like in order to address its detractors and do some good in the world?

Finding 'The Good' in Heritage Tourism

I have suggested that heritage tourism can be ethically evaluated in terms of the extent to which it does good and how this is mapped against its means and its ends. But by what standards can it thus be evaluated and what might the issues be that demand such attention? MacCannell's (2011:ix) concept of 'good' appears to reflect broad enlightenment principles: 'It is only by rigorous and consistent application of ethics to action that human beings can become more courageous, temperate, liberal, generous, magnanimous, self-respecting, gentle and just'.

Whilst this list seems difficult to gainsay, it might also suggest the need for emphasis, amendment or elaboration. For example, in referring to what is 'just', we might be inclined to suggest that this encompasses, in an explicit way, social justice, equity, the redress of grievances and the righting of wrongs. Such an embellishment would not seem outside the spirit of an enlightened perspective; after all, the Constitution of the United States no less makes provision for such redress, and Rawls (1993: 346) cites it as a basis for political action in the face of an unjust and oppressive government. So, to advance a little, we might accept a *broad* notion of 'good' informed, *broadly*, by *broad* enlightenment principles such as those expressed by MacCannell, with some embellishments—if this helps. Good intentions might thus be discerned, which leads us to Kant, and the idea that we can judge the good in actions not by anything inherent in them, which is always subject to qualification based on circumstantial and contextual effects, but on the will to be good, which cannot easily be reduced to anything less (Kant 2012).

But is it reasonable to look for the good in heritage tourism when there is already a significant body of knowledge and practice dedicated to finding and rectifying its negative effects? A whole literature, for example, has grown up around the environmental, social and cultural impacts of tourism and how these can be ameliorated by the application of principles of sustainability that contain a suitably sensitive awareness of the problems and pitfalls and at least some measures to deal with them. Tourism has many consequences, each of which demands ethical scrutiny. Consequentialism suggests that even the best intentioned acts and practices may bring unintended results that could be negative. This becomes even more complicated when agencies and individuals are either unaware or uninterested in such consequences, sometimes naively perhaps, sometimes blinkered or knowingly diverted by partisanship, politics or profit. It could be argued, for example, that there is, at best, a naive consequentialism about heritage tourism if its good intentions mask a material gain for some at the expense of others, either through exploitatively commercial activity that pays low wages and does not, therefore, produce balanced shares of benefit, or through the commodification of culture that diminishes its meaning (see, e.g. Cohen 1988, although this has since become a well-trampled path, especially when linked with ideas about authenticity).

It is clear, therefore, that in order to evaluate the ethics of heritage tourism, we must use a framework that weighs the good it achieves, in its broadest sense, against the negative consequences that are charged against it, and we should, perhaps, make a distinction between those of benign intent who may be unaware or naive about those consequences and those who exploit heritage tourism for gains that are not fairly distributed or which diminish in some way any original or indigenous meaning.

No universal law is offered here, or palliative or answers at an operational level. The best that can be achieved is to invoke a moral sense in the way that we view heritage tourism and hope that such an awareness might be called upon, perhaps as a matter of obligation when heritage tourism is both produced and consumed. What is offered here can only be a selection of those issues since a more comprehensive examination would require a book, as Dean MacCannell has demonstrated in relation to sightseeing. I examine, therefore, some of the key issues, claims and counterclaims of heritage tourism, in the knowledge that others might wish to add or subtract from this selection or find it wanting in some way.

Economic Ends

In order to address the question of whether economic benefits justify the means in heritage tourism, we would need to know not only the value of heritage tourism in economic terms but also the way in which that value was distributed. A narrow distribution, or an exploitative one, would in itself raise ethical questions about who really benefits. It would also raise questions about whether the past should be sequestered for such purposes, especially if the gain was privatised.

Heritage as a category of cultural production has been closely associated with tourism for a long time, because it provides resources and itineraries for sightseeing. In historical terms, this is perhaps best exemplified by the cultural significance of the Grand Tour (Adler 1989) and afterwards in the expansion of leisure travel in the nineteenth century (Lowenthal 1985, 1998). Tourism in its latter day industrial manifestation has also become heavily dependent on the material of heritage as a source of attraction *assets*. This, in turn, is part of what has become a relentless process of touristic representation and the re-representation of places and spaces that were formerly associated with other types of capital accumulation, such as mining, agriculture and heavy industry (Dicks 2000: 33–37). Heritage tourism is sometimes seen, therefore, as an economic lifeline in locations deprived of the primary or heavy industries that once sustained them, a form of development that has also extended to industrial cities (Zukin 1991). Indeed, it is in heritage that the tourism industry finds much of its significance in social and economic terms, especially since the fragmentation of the traditional, 'Fordist', mass market tourism that predominated in the nineteenth and twentieth centuries (Urry 2002).

The fundamental question, however, is how any negative consequences might be identified and weighed against the obvious benefits of economic well-being or regeneration. We might also conjecture that any such equation for evaluating these effects might vary considerably between different regions and countries. As for the value of heritage tourism in financial terms, this in itself would seem a hard enough question and could easily confound further speculation. In the United Kingdom, however, the Heritage Lottery Fund (HLF) has recently commissioned a report on precisely this question—Investing in Success, subtitled Heritage and the UK Tourism Economy (Heritage Lottery Fund/Visit Britain 2010). The evidence offered, in an array of staggering facts and figures, is impressive. For example, in the words of Dame Jenny Abramsky (2010:1), Chair of the HLF, 'the size of the heritage-tourism sector is in excess of £12.4billion a year and supports an estimated 195,000 full-time jobs—this makes the sector bigger than the advertising, car or film industries'. But there was some politics even here, for this triumph would surely persuade the government that such a lucrative 'industry' should be invested in, especially where cuts and other priorities might weigh in. This report would provide the data, the 'missing numbers', that would demonstrate once and for all the size and scale of the contribution made by heritage to the national economic well-being:

> As this document demonstrates, heritage is not a luxury or a pleasant recreational pastime, but an integral part of our future. Heritage – and particularly heritage-based tourism – has never been more important to the UK's economy. We need to say so (Abramsky 2010:3).

When the oft-quoted 'multiplier effect' is factored into the equation, however, the value of tourism rises to over £20bn, with the best part of half a million people employed. Faced with this, how could anyone doubt that heritage tourism is a good thing? It sounds like the only industry in rude health after the financial crisis, and with figures like these, might it not lead us triumphantly from the depths of the recession? The past, paradoxically, is giving us a future, the true legacy of all those buildings, all that archaeology, colourful pageantry and timeless tradition.

Even accepting that it is not possible to generalise from the UK experience, it does seem peevish, if not economically reckless to foster a moral debate in the face of such unmitigated good. Would we want our ethical critique to put people out of work, to destroy an industry when there are so few others to provide income in hard-pressed communities? The motives of the HLF and others also seem pure; they are not reckless capitalists or wicked bankers and the various bywords of worthiness crop up through the report: communities, authenticity, sustainability, place-making and identity. Indeed, to question such motives and such achievements would in itself seem unethical. And yet, questions remain that should be addressed and that need at least to be aired from an ethical position. How honest, for example, is the rendering of heritage in this economic sphere? Is it just nostalgic rhetoric or populism? What does it mean? What does it do? Surely, it would be unethical to leave unexamined things that are worthy of serious enquiry, especially if the result was a morally better basis from which to derive economic benefits.

Ethics and the Heritage Debate

The heritage debate of the last 30 years has furnished many such questions, and they are worth rehearsing. MacCannell (2011) has expressed much of it with precision and economy. In what seems at first an unlikely comparison between the artist Piranesi and the symbolic strategies of Disney, MacCannell provides some compelling insights about the way that heritage tourism works, by creating its own moments of fiction that occlude all other understandings, negotiations or alternative discourses. Origins are thus replaced with unequivocal but fictional narratives that appear to mark a progression that points the way to the present, to us, now:

> Within the Piranesi/Disney frame, heritage-in-use cannot be encountered as heritage until it has been killed and cooked for consumption by tourists. There is no historical dialectic in this frame. The only thing proffered to the tourist is the self-congratulation of bland conservative ideology. Any memory of different versions of the past grappling with different desires for the future is doubly suppressed, first at the unveiling of the monument or the opening of the park and second by the elevation of objects and events that pretend to stand outside of their own history (MacCannell 2011:150–151).

This passage seems to touch so much on the heritage debate that it is almost a summary. But it also prompts a return to ethics as a valid basis for critical reflection. What right do official or commercial versions of heritage have to 'stand in' for all others, variants, oppositions, dissonances and activism?

Whilst, therefore, it is hard to refute the economic arguments in favour of heritage tourism, despite its fragile transferability to other jurisdictions and concerns about equity in the distribution of income, it does still have a broader ethical case to answer, touching on the way it frames, symbolises, imagines, essentialises and narrativises the past and in this way constitutes dominant discourses that affect and limit the way we understand it. We are entitled to ask some searching questions about the nature of heritage display and its translation into tourism: what kind of new cultural movements are responsible for this display, and what does the display seek to reveal (or obfuscate)? How do such transformations take place and why? What are these new forms of cultural consumption and what do they mean?

For Kirshenblatt-Gimblett (1998:149–151), heritage is a new form of cultural production that 'produces something new' by adding values of 'pastness', exhibition and difference that convert locations into destinations which in turn become 'museums of themselves' that can be marketed as tourist resources. The past then, as Wright (1985:75) has put it, is recoverable through the talismanic qualities of its 'bits and pieces'; it therefore has substance and reality, and moreover, it can be visited by tourists. But which bits and pieces, and who decides? For heritage tourism to claim a principled ethical position, it would have to justify an operational orientation that is focussed on those aspects that are easily marketed and consumed: the visual and the spectacular, momentous events, leading personalities and, especially, violence and warfare. If it could be demonstrated that every ruined castle or museum concerned with the engines of war had earned its place in heritage as a test of the morality of armed conflict, then it might justly claim such an ethical position; but I am not sure that it is easy to make that case. Whilst it is easy to be moved by the experience of suffering and violence, these things gain a kind of patina over time and are narrativised in ways that often emphasise technical aspects and a rarified interest in objects, material detail and entertainment. Of course there is nothing new about glamorising war, but add to this the selective/exclusionary nature of what passes for heritage (Waterton 2009, 2010) and we are left with an image of the past that is both limited and distorted. In the United Kingdom, for example, heritage tourism seems bound up with a set of discursive and representational practices that work to diminish its breadth of meaning and act to protect dominant and essentially conservative views of the national past. The extent of this reductionism and depletion of meaning is readily apparent in the English tourism 'product', which despite attempts to jazz it up in recent years is still mired in the 'rural-historic' as an authorised heritage discourse (Watson 2012). How can tourism based on this view of heritage ever find an ethical voice even accepting its economic significance?

Anti-heritage Animus

Lowenthal (1998:100) coined the term 'anti-heritage animus' to summarise and express the corpus of theoretical opposition to the concept of heritage and its uses that has characterised much of the debate on heritage since the 1980s. 'Heritage', Lowenthal states, 'is vilified as selfish and chauvinistic, nostalgic and escapist, trivial and sterile, ignorant and anachronistic. Intricacy is simplified, the diverse made uniform, the exotic turned insipid' (Lowenthal 1998:88). He goes on to identify six basic elements wherein heritage is variously assailed as chauvinistic and contested, elitist, incoherent eclectic, commercially debased and 'bad' historically. This critique still weighs heavily on heritage and raises the question of whether any serious attempt to develop an ethical, subaltern and politically oppositional view of heritage represents, in itself, a worthwhile project. If the concept of heritage is so problematic as a basis for explaining behaviour or understanding the various practices that constitute it, then further development of the concept would seem fruitless.

The question of agency is central: who controls heritage and to what end; what means are used to create heritage within touristic space and why? Clearly, the production and supply of heritage and heritage tourism is highly organised within a framework of institutions, destinations and operators. Other theorists have taken these ideas into a new realm of representational analysis, including Shields (1991), Rojek (1993), Kirshenblatt-Gimblett (1998), Urry (2002) and, more recently, Waterton and Watson (2010). The production of heritage is always in jeopardy of producing 'partial stories', and for Zolberg, the museum in particular has become a focus for disputes about the meaning of heritage objects and the accounts they represent (1998, 69). On a broader scale, Tunbridge and Ashworth (2000; see also Graham et al. 2000) argue that dissonance is an integral aspect of heritage.

Objects of heritage tourism thus become defined as such by agencies concerned with the representation of touristic space. Thus, what is considered of touristic merit is authorised and organised according to the mediating process of commodification and its powerful agents. Cheong and Miller (2000) have focused on the dynamics of touristic representation and its potential as a site for contestation, employing the Foucauldian concept of power to elucidate a tripartite system of tourists, locals and 'brokers' (operators and tourism officials). Power is thus exercised through another socially constructed 'gaze' through which each of these parties perceives the others. The potential for contestation occurs when one of these groups assumes dominance and either welcomes or rejects tourists and the meanings the latter impose on their location. The potential for conflict in such contexts has also been explored by Hale in the representation of heritage in Cornwall (2001), and Mordue (2005, 2010), who has analysed heritage tourism in York (United Kingdom) as it is 'performed', evaluated and contested in terms of Cheong and Miller's tripartite framework.

According to Mordue (2005:180–181, 2010), York's historical core now plays host to a range of 'performative signifiers', from souvenir shops to street musicians, that are expressions of a coupling of commercial activity with heritage. The process also represents a gradual dislocation of the city and its history from local meanings as it becomes re-represented for the global tourism industry. York, therefore, is a site of contestation or dissonance between a heritage understood and expressed by locals and another which is conceived and represented by local officialdom and performed by businesses and entertainers. In this way, and in celebrating its uniqueness, it is effectively and paradoxically dedifferentiated from everywhere else in the world that is attempting something similar for the purposes of global consumption (Mordue 2005; Watson 2007).

An additional risk is that the officially represented version, the *authorised* version, eventually suppresses and replaces local meanings and becomes the only reality available. An ethical position here would examine disparities in the power to define heritage and what should be displayed through the medium of heritage tourism. It should also address the effect that such selection has on local meanings of place and the practices associated with it. The classic case study of this effect is Greenwood's (1977) account of the Alarde Festival in Fuenterrabia in northeastern Spain, where the community celebrated through re-enactment its victory and survival of a siege by the French in 1638. The cramped conditions in which the festivities took place, however, prevented outsiders and tourists from viewing it effectively and tourism officials, thinking it might be of interest to visitors, redefined it as a spectacle and instructed the locals to 'perform' an abbreviated version of the event and to repeat it so that more visitors could see it. Local meaning was thus drained from the occasion and what remained had little significance for the host community. This kind of appropriation is not uncommon in heritage tourism and would seem to be unethical, although a more utilitarian perspective would make a claim for the greater good in economic terms. On the other hand, a heritage tourism which, through its representational practices and modalities of interpretation, encompassed and explored dissonance, rather than ignored or downplayed it, would seem essential in the construction of an ethical framework. It begins with an acknowledgement of the plurality of perspectives and an imbalance of power in the act of representation.

Waitt (2000: 857) proposes such a solution for the Sydney Cove development, where a 'multiplicity of viewpoints and interpretations' should be incorporated into the narrative formed by officials and operators. Whether they would do so or not within the context of the hegemonic and commercial pressures that operate on, and within, their domain is arguable, as Dicks found at the Rhondda Heritage Park in Wales (2000), but a space for other readings can at least be imagined, even where dissonance of various sorts exists. How that space is filled is part of another debate, but instigating that debate would be essential to an ethical framework and would challenge situations where a single or authorised discourse crowded out all others.

For the present purposes, then, rather than being diminished by dissonance and contestation, heritage, it could be argued, forms a potentially valuable context for open and enlightened debate about the received past and the uses to which it is put in a wide range of contexts. It may thus facilitate an ethically positioned, critical and reflective approach to the past for both the providers of heritage tourism and its recipients as both tourists and hosts and provide a counterpoint to the unexamined, hegemonic and uncritical narratives that fuelled the heritage debate. The balance of power, however, would be crucial in determining the extent to which alternative versions might be heard, and ethics, therefore, dissolves into politics.

Heritage Tourism Is Inauthentic

Tourism, of course, brings on charges of commercial debasement and 'inauthenticity', a negative consequence of the 'real' being sacrificed for the spectacular and the arresting imagery of contemporary display methods as well as a good story. Anything else risks rejection from the privileged narrative:

> Selling history or heritage is contingent on the commodity being free from any association that could hinder capital accumulation; there is little possibility of selling the local history of Calvinist Presbyterianism for instance … Selling heritage and place is therefore a highly selective business, which writes out or visually excludes anything it cannot assimilate (MacDonald 2002:64).

A compelling criticism applied, therefore, to the commercial aspects of heritage tourism is that such versions of the past are heavily dependent on, and potentially distorted by, an emphasis on the visual or spectacular, something which is held to further compromise authenticity. Thus, they tend, inevitably, towards the marginalisation and trivialisation of social experience in which complexities and contradictions are elided, and important historical, social and political significances are oversimplified (Urry 1995:161; Crouch and Lübbren 2003; Waterton 2009; Watson and Waterton 2010).

Authenticity, however, is famously represented in the work of MacCannell (1973, 1999) as the ultimate goal of touristic activity. Tourists attempt to escape from everyday life in a quest for something more fundamental. As modernity becomes replete with artifice, tourism comes to express an urgent need to find an original in some other place or time. Authenticity has another strand in the field of heritage tourism, however, as an important value in the organisation of cultural heritage by the agencies involved. For example, The UNESCO-ICOMOS document on authenticity, the 'Nara Document' (ICOMOS 2005), makes plain the importance of authenticity in every aspect of heritage presentation:

> The understanding of authenticity plays a fundamental role in all scientific studies of the cultural heritage, in conservation and restoration planning, as well as within the inscription procedures used for the World Heritage Convention and other cultural heritage inventories (ICOMOS 2005).

If authenticity is a 'good thing', it follows that any version of heritage tourism that limits or confounds it or which produces something judged to be inauthentic must be considered to have produced a negative consequence. Authenticity, furthermore, has a fugitive quality. Whenever tourists arrive in a destination, the authentic at once retreats and a contrived version is duplicitously staged for their benefit (MacCannell 1973: 593–98, 1999). What is more, such *staged authenticity* can be damaging to the original meanings attached to cultural objects and practices, changing them in order to fit with the touristic imperatives of the spectacular and the visual as was seen in Greenwood's (1977) famous case study quoted above. The *best bits* are thus selected for representation and the rest paradoxically neglected (given their authenticity) (Cohen 1988:372). The representations are, in turn, presented as 'unmediated encounters' creating 'the effect of authenticity, or realness' (Kirshenblatt-Gimblett 1998: 55).

The problem is compounded when the industry itself, perhaps in a perfect demonstration of staged authenticity, uses it as a source of attraction value. Authenticity becomes performative, and joins the lexicon of marketing-speak appropriate for historical attractions, whatever their real merit or value (Waitt 2000:836). Rendered thus meaningless, it is difficult to see how any useful definition of the term can be applied in a discourse focused on heritage tourism. Who defines what is 'authentic' and why? Is an encounter with staged authenticity any less authentic to the actors involved than an experience outside this sphere? The problem, however, is that authenticity, in whatever guise it is presented, is still an object of the tourist.

Selwyn (1996:21) is helpful here in determining a concept of authenticity that is contingent on the particular place meanings, destination and tourism development processes that are relevant to particular places at particular times and noting that authenticity has more to do with the discovery of an authentic 'self' through the act of experiencing *otherness* in different places and cultures. More experiential approaches to authenticity followed (Wang 1999), and this is a theme developed by Bagnall (2003: 88) in exploring the way that if authenticity is a significant value it exists in the performative response of the subject to the experience, for example, of a museum display.

The authenticity debate has rumbled on over the last decade with little sign of common ground emerging between the various contributions (Cohen and Cohen 2012). These range from philosophical disquisitions on experiential engagements (Steiner and Reisinger 2006) to those which emphasise the role of objects and places in framing those experiences (Belhassen and Caton 2006; Belhassen et al. 2008). Latterly, others have sought to make connections between authenticity and an emerging literature on emotional engagement (Knudsen and Waade 2010). All we can say at this stage is that authenticity remains a concept that is open to negotiated meanings formed and framed in the praxis of the operational environment, and the experience of heritage tourism in situ, especially where this provides a context for understanding the performativity around which contemporary tourism theory is currently developing. From an ethical standpoint, it is perhaps safest to suggest that authenticity can be problematic in connection with objects and places where it has become staged, but that heritage tourism can still offer authentic experiences regardless of the authenticity of the object: thus, one can authentically experience an inauthentic object, the question here being who evaluates and defines the latter. There is also a Eurocentrism about the concept that betrays its roots in Western philosophy, and Winter (2012: 181) has cast doubt on its relevance in other heritage discourses, for example, in Japan.

Heritage Tourism Is Bad History

Heritage tourism in the service of identity, ideology or commerce and heritage tourism as a colourful chaos of shallow meanings and stereotypical images all tend to the view that it produces 'bad' history, or a deliberate travesty of it. For example, Hewison (1987: 144), reaching his polemical climax, asserts that 'Heritage, for all its seductive delights, is bogus history', a theme taken up by many writers since. Wright (1985:69) sees heritage as an extraction and abstraction of history. History becomes 'the historical,' a gloss, an 'impression of pastness' redeployed as a new kind of cultural product. In fact, he rarely uses the word heritage, preferring 'historicity' to denote the process he describes. Walsh (1992:68) makes a similar point but emphasises the damage that heritage does to history in replacing it: 'instead of history we have heritage'. These historicist criticisms of heritage have led Lowenthal (1998:102) to observe that 'The crux of most aspersions against heritage is that it undermines 'real' history, defiling the pristine record that is our rightful legacy'.

MacDonald (2002: 60) suggests that the 'over signification of the commodity spectacle' has a 'naturalising effect on social relations' where issues of social justice are effectively overwritten by a surplus of touristic meanings. If heritage tourism produces bad history, then it must be seen as problematic ethically, assuming that history relies on transparent methods of enquiry and objectivity in the creation of knowledge.

Lowenthal (1998) attempts to resolve the issue with what is clearly meant to be a revelatory conclusion that history and heritage are separate categories with different purposes. Heritage tourism is no usurper of the past after all, but simply another use of it, neither plausible nor testable, but a declaration of faith, not susceptible to the validations of the historical method (Lowenthal 1998:121). Lowenthal might have saved history from heritage, but his argument does not save heritage from its critics. Lowenthal simply *owns up* for heritage. It does not matter that it has no historical veracity or method; it does not matter that it is biased, for in a sense, it is meant to be. Let history keep its method and its 'truth'. And yet, even this is dangerous ground.

One of the problems with the concept of heritage as 'bad' or debased history is the epistemological status of history itself. To place history on a pedestal and claim it is the right and proper form of engagement with the past is to invest it with a mythic and rarefied quality that historians themselves have questioned (Carr 1987; Marwick 1989). Nowadays, it seems almost too obvious to say that history is what historians write about rather than what took place in any absolute sense. Historians may own their histories, but nobody owns the past.

For Samuel, history is a 'house of many mansions' with narratives that change over time and always subject to prevailing influences (Samuel (1998):204). It seems unreasonable, therefore, to criticise heritage tourism for the damage it does to history when history itself tells partial stories, but it also seems unreasonable to align poor interpretation with well-researched history. An ethical position might therefore seek to instil a quality in heritage tourism that reflects integrity and honesty on the part of its producers and a duty, perhaps, to indicate sources and methods (where this does not already occur).

Towards an Ethical Framework

The ethical critique of heritage tourism outlined above is problematic in that so much of it is based on a critique of heritage in its broadest sense rather than its touristic manifestation. This is inevitable, however, if we are to avoid the kind of reductionism associated with environmental and social impacts and managerial responses to these. Hence the concern with the ethical status of heritage tourism and the key aspects of what Lowenthal termed the 'anti-heritage animus', the purpose being to provide an ethical critique of heritage tourism and to assess the ways in which this critique might be addressed. The first question is whether any of the 'problems' with heritage outlined above is a *necessary condition* of it, or whether alternative, oppositional renderings are possible. It might be proposed, for example, that the engagement between tourists and heritage could be isolated from commercial and other imperatives and represent a subaltern perspective free of dominant discourses. MacCannell (1999:156) provides a prospect that some theoretical space might be created in this avenue of thought: 'Commercialisation is pressing in on sightseeing from all sides. Still, at the heart of the act, the final contract between the tourist and a true attraction, such as the White House or the Grand Canyon, can be pure.'

Engagement might thus become more direct, less mediated, shorn of its commercial logic, messier and less selective. McCabe and Stokoe (2004:17) found something of this in the way that visitors to an English national park constructed their performance as tourists from the particularities of their engagement with the place rather than the place itself:

> Their accounts were designed to avoid or resist the implication that they visit certain places because they are popular, because other people go there, or because they are tourism places. Speakers emphasized the 'naturalness' of their engagement with places as something they have always done, and the 'ordinariness' of their trips to these places as something they 'just' do. Therefore respondents worked to maintain individuality in the face of actually 'doing being a tourist' as they were interviewed.

There may be also something of this 'authenticity in engagement' in Kirshenblatt-Gimblett's discussion of the response to the avant-garde in festival performances. For her, 'the most authentic moment occurs when the audience confronts what it does not understand' and 'requiring that [avant-garde performances] be explained, interferes with the purity of the aesthetic experience, because from an avant-garde perspective, explanation mediates what should be a direct encounter' (Kirshenblatt-Gimblett 1998:239–40). Audiences should be prepared thus to confront what they see and be allowed to make up their own minds about it. This could be a basis for developing MacCannell's (1999:157) suggestion that attractions could be re-socialised outside the commercial sphere. Ringgaard (2010:108–109) offers the opportunity to address this through a recasting of the concept of authenticity that is relational and subjective and in opposition to experiences and representations that are easily reproduced for touristic consumption:

> An almost unending number of places have already been chosen by the guide books: they are sights, places to be seen, and part of a global circulation of tourism. They are sights because they - for some reason – are considered worth seeing. The traveller encounters the unique under common conditions. The challenge, for some, is to make the place talk, to come to terms with it. The task is to rediscover or even recover the place.

There is an emerging view in heritage, however, that this tends to happen anyway in the encounters and engagements that take place between tourists and heritage objects. Of importance here, for example, is the work of Bagnall (2003) to which reference was made earlier, which challenges the view that visitors to heritage sites are passive and uncritical and that, rather, they are involved in a complex and discursive engagement that involves the mapping of their own memories, reminiscences, emotions and feelings of nostalgia onto heritage representations in museums. Key to this process was a sense in which they were performers of their own consumption, meeting and mediating the messages contained in the representative practices employed by sites and admitting or rejecting them according to how well they could be mapped against their own experience and emotional engagement (Bagnall 2003: 96).

Since then, the precepts of non-representational theory as developed originally by Thrift (2007) and developed extensively in Cultural Geography (Anderson and Harrison 2010) have found their way into contemporary heritage thinking. In particular, it raises issues about nonvisual and non-textual encounters with heritage and interrogates emotional and affective responses in ways that emphasise the emergence of meaning in engagement. Whilst there is not the space here to examine these issues in detail, it is important, nonetheless, to reflect on their significance for an ethical position in heritage tourism, especially in releasing from the commercial representational nexus and re-privileging the subjective and the social.

There is a sense, therefore, that there is something good in heritage quite apart from its economic value. Some of this is undoubtedly the standard rhetoric of heritage, the way it contrasts with contemporary realities and the virtues of 'authenticity'. Its objects are in jeopardy of being 'lost forever', to use a well-worn phrase, unless they are preserved and conserved 'for future generations', to use another. Heritage also contains within it, however, something of the uniqueness of the place and the quintessence of locality that makes it all the more desirable and its loss that much more difficult to bear (Nadel-Klein 2003:173–174). Sense of place in this context garners its own social significance (Schofield and Szymanski 2011). But there have always been voices in support of heritage, voices that challenged the emerging critique. Notable, for example, was Wright's (1985:80) assertion that the sheer popularity of heritage tourism attractions and activities cannot be ignored: 'we should instead be considering whether all those millions can be so entirely mistaken in their enthusiasms'. Samuel (1998:130) is the champion of such history 'from the bottom up' expressed in a myriad of local conservation societies and restoration projects, the significance of which has led him to describe the critics, famously, as 'heritage baiters'.

It is possible then that a useful basis for an ethical position in heritage tourism is the concept of place, particularly where this can be some sense of locality and the interests of host communities, accepting, of course, that there never is a single host community. The question of whose version of place identity is clearly problematic, however, and related to the contestability of place to which reference is made above. Jeong and Santos (2004:654) have investigated the ways in which dominant groups gain and sustain their status through the organisation of a community festival and yet how others in the same community contest this version of the event through their own 'meanings of place'. Walsh (1992) pointed to the need for a reconnection between people and their places through the establishment of lines of continuity that were effectively emplaced. 'The heritage on display', Goodey (1998:201) asserts, 'has not been fully reviewed by its communities'. Other research has provided a new orientation to this issue, in the ways that local people might interpret their place for tourists (MacDonald 1997:2005).

MacCannell (1998:352) tells of a lesson long learnt that 'heritage is not what the dead did and thought; it is more their manner of speaking to the living'. He goes on to make a distinction between the global industry and its presentation of 'dreamworks' and the local presentation of minor places. Thus, the stewards of minor places should be local people, who 'should be crawling all over the place with the tourists, speaking about the significance of history and heritage for them and making the tourists aware of contested heritage' (MacCannell 1998:360). The minor place should also be presented in a way that goes beyond the visual and indeed the other senses and engages 'vision, integrity, honesty and sympathetic understanding', and in which mere sightseeing is placed in the service of something more profound (MacCannell 1998:360–361). Schofield and Szymanski (2011:2–3) make a similar point about local significance, not just the tangible aspects of it but other sources of local distinctiveness such as music and culinary traditions, all of which contribute to a sense of place. Place can also provide the literal and physical context for an encounter with the past that is both subjective and intersubjective rather than formal or official and which is therefore constitutive of heritage in a different and more personal way. For Byrne (2012:27), this opens up new possibilities for engagements between tourists and heritage that express a more human dimension in past events than conventional tourism allows: 'I am interested in the potential of heritage tourism to put people in situations of critical proximity to past events and perhaps precipitate them into moments of empathy with past others'.

There may be room, therefore, in theorising ethical approaches to heritage tourism, for a more developed synthesis between ideas about place, the past and subjective responses to it. Notions of representation, institutionalised and individuated, authorised and oppositional, and of performance and consumption in situ could well provide the basis for such a theoretical movement. This might provide the beginning of a discourse between the subject and the past that is separate from purely institutionalised and authorised versions. The means might even be sought for an ethically informed approach to destination marketing based on an inclusive sense of place (Hopley and Mahony 2011). What is revealed here is a more ethically positive picture of heritage than its critics have hitherto allowed, one that is open to critical analysis through the transparency brought to it by the various deconstructions of commodification, ideology, authenticity and everything else that constitutes the practice of heritage tourism. It may even be that the very dissonance and contestation to which many authors have drawn attention could be the means of revealing a multiplicity of meanings and a transparency of debate that purely authorised accounts have failed to achieve hitherto. The fundamental question that lies at the heart of whether heritage tourism is worth understanding beyond its commercial logic is whether there is a genuine sense of something that is evoked when people meet and interact with the things of the past. If that were the case, might it provide an ethical basis for heritage tourism so that other more commercial or ideological versions would, for the first time, have to justify their existence?

Conclusion

Emerging ideas and responses to the heritage debate as it has developed since the 1980s have provided opportunities to review the ethics of heritage tourism as a cultural practice. They have also stimulated a debate that goes beyond the conventional approaches of ameliorating negative social and environmental impacts through management. The effects of the *anti-heritage animus* highlighted by Lowenthal have been explored, and the validity of some of the individual elements within that critique has been examined.

The critique of heritage tourism is a compelling one. It elucidates the social and cultural influences and issues that underpin the production and consumption of heritage tourism in contemporary contexts. Here might be found heritage at its *most criticised*, as an instrument of commerce that has also encoded power relations and authorised accounts of history, an *authorised heritage discourse,* as Smith (2006) has framed it. It is apparent, however, that the value of the heritage debate lies in the way it prompts both an ethical and political impulse drawn from a range of sources rather than a single ethical stance. A consequence of this is that whilst the critique of heritage is valid in each of the areas discussed above, none of them are *necessary conditions* of its existence as a means of engagement with the past. Authenticity for example, need not be sought in the heritage object itself, but in subjective responses to it, and dissonance may become a source of transparency and a locus of debate rather than the negative outcome of attempts to produce exclusive and dominant accounts.

An ethical position is implied, therefore, that permits the production and consumption of heritage outside the authorised versions represented by the industry and its institutional sponsors in government, quasi-government and the independent sector. Ideally, this would facilitate representation and representational practices that reconnect people with places and pasts within a transparent discourse that creates its own authenticity in the construction of subjective experience. An ethical context can revivify the heritage debate, but only political contexts can provide the means to achieve 'the good' in heritage tourism.

References

Abramsky, D. J. (2010). *Investing in success: Heritage and the UK tourism economy.* Britain: HLF/Visit.

Adler, J. (1989). Origins of sightseeing. *Annals of Tourism Research, 16,* 7–29.

Anderson, B., & Harrison, P. (2010). *Taking place: Non-representational theories and geography.* Farnham: Ashgate.

Bagnall, G. (2003). Performance and performativity at heritage sites. *Museum and Society, 1*(2), 87–103.

Belhassen, Y., & Caton, K. (2006). Authenticity matters. *Annals of Tourism Research, 33*(3), 853–856.

Belhassen, Y., Caton, K., & Stewart, W. P. (2008). The search for authenticity in the pilgrim experience. *Annals of Tourism Research, 35*(3), 668–689.

Brunt, P., & Davis, C. (2006). The nature of British media reporting of hedonistic tourism. *Crime Prevention and Community Safety: An International Journal, 8*(1), 30–49.

Byrne, D. (2012). Gateway and garden: A kind of tourism in Bali. In R. Staiff, R. Bushell, & S. Watson (Eds.), *Heritage tourism: Place, encounter, engagement* (pp. 26–44). London: Routledge.

Carr, E. H. (1987). *What is history.* London: Penguin.

Cheong, S.-M., & Miller, M. L. (2000). Power and tourism: a Foucauldian observation. *Annals of Tourism Research, 27*(2), 371–390.

Cohen, E. (1988). Authenticity and commoditization in tourism. *Annals of Tourism Research, 15,* 371–386.

Cohen, E., & Cohen, S. A. (2012). Authentication: Hot and cool. *Annals of Tourism Research, 39*(3), 1295–1314.

Crouch, D., & Lübbren, N. (Eds.). (2003). *Visual culture and tourism*. Oxford: Berg.

Dicks, B. (2000). *Heritage, place and community*. Cardiff: University of Wales Press.

Diken, B., & Laustsen, C. B. (2004). Sea, sun, sex and the discontents of pleasure. *Tourist Studies, 4*(2), 99–114.

Game, A. (1991). *Undoing the social: Towards a deconstructive sociology*. Milton Keynes: Open University Press.

Goodey, B. (1998). New Britain, new heritage: The consumption of heritage culture. *International Journal of Heritage Studies, 4*(3–4), 197–205.

Graham, B., Ashworth, G. J., & Tunbridge, J. E. (2000). *A geography of heritage, power, culture and economy*. London: Arnold.

Greenwood, D. J. (1977). Culture by the pound: an anthropological perspective on tourism as cultural commoditization. In V. L. Smith (Ed.), *Hosts and guests: The anthropology of tourism* (pp. 129–138). Philadelphia, PA: University of Pennsylvania Press.

Hale, A. (2001). Representing the Cornish: Contesting heritage interpretation in Cornwall. *Tourist Studies, 1*(2), 185–196.

Hewison, R. (1987). *The heritage industry: Britain in a climate of decline*. London: Methuen.

Hopley, C., & Mahony, P. (2011). Marketing sense of place in the Forest of Bowland. In J. Schofield & R. Szymanski (Eds.), *Local heritage, global context: Cultural perspectives on sense of place* (pp. 33–52). Farnham: Ashgate.

ICOMOS. (2005). *The Nara document on authenticity*. http://www.international.icomos.org/charters/nara_e.htm. (Accessed March 12, 2012).

Jeong, S., & Santos, C. A. (2004). Cultural politics and contested place identity. Annals of Tourism Research, 31(3), 640–656.

Kant, I. (2012). *Groundwork for the metaphysics of morals*. Cambridge: Cambridge University Press [1785].

Kirshenblatt-Gimblett, B. (1998). *Destination culture: Tourism, museums and heritage*. Berkeley: University of California Press.

Knudsen, B. T., & Waade, A. M. (Eds.). (2010). *Re-investing authenticity: Tourism, places and emotions*. Bristol: Channel View Publications.

Lowenthal, D. (1985). *The past is a foreign country*. Cambridge: Cambridge University Press.

Lowenthal, D. (1998). *The heritage crusade and the spoils of history*. Cambridge: Cambridge University Press.

MacCannell, D. (1973). Staged authenticity: Arrangements of social space in social settings. *American Journal of Sociology, 79*(3), 589–603.

MacCannell, D. (1998). Making minor places: Dilemmas in modern tourism. In J. Magnus Fladmark (Ed.), *In search of heritage as pilgrim or tourist?* (pp. 351–362). Shaftesbury: Donhead.

MacCannell, D. (1999). *The tourist: A new theory of the leisure class*. Berkeley: University of California Press.

MacCannell, D. (2011). *The ethics of sightseeing*. Berkeley: University of California Press.

MacDonald, S. (1997). A people's story: Heritage, identity and authenticity. In C. Rojek & J. Urry (Eds.), *Touring cultures: Transformations of travel and theory* (pp. 155–175). London: Routledge.

MacDonald, F. (2002). The Scottish highlands as spectacle. In S. Coleman & M. Crang (Eds.), Tourism, between place and performance. Oxford: Berghahn Books.

Marwick, A. (1989). *The nature of history* (3rd ed.). Basingstoke: Macmillan.

McCabe, S., & Stokoe, E. H. (2004). Place and identity in tourists' accounts. *Annals of Tourism Research, 31*(3), 601–622.

Mordue, T. (2005). Tourism, performance and social exclusion in 'Olde York'. *Annals of Tourism Research, 32*(1), 179–198.

Mordue, T. (2010). Time machines and space craft: Navigating the spaces of heritage tourism performance. In E. Waterton & S. Watson (Eds.), *Culture, heritage, and representation: Perspectives on visuality and the past* (pp. 173–194). Farnham: Ashgate.

Nadel-Klein, J. (2003). Fishing for heritage, modernity and loss along the Scottish coast. Oxford: Berg.

Pritchard, A., & Morgan, N. (2010). 'Wild On' the beach: Discourses of desire, sexuality and liminality. In E. Waterton & S. Watson (Eds.), *Culture, heritage, and representation: Perspectives on visuality and the past* (pp. 127–143). Farnham: Ashgate.

Rawls, J. (1993). *Political liberalism*. New York: Columbia University Press.

Ringgaard, D. (2010). Travel and testimony: the rhetoric of authenticity. In B. T. Knudsen & A. M. Waade (eds.), *Re-investing authenticity: Tourism, place and emotions* (pp. 108–120). Bristol: Channel View.

Rojek, C. (1993). *Ways of escape: Modern transformations in leisure and travel.* Basingstoke: Macmillan.

Samuel, R. (1998). Island stories, unravelling Britain, theatres of memory (Vol. 2). London: Verso.

Schofield, J., & Szymanski, R. (Eds.). (2011). *Local heritage, global context: Cultural perspectives on sense of place.* Farnham: Ashgate.

Selwyn, T. (Ed.). (1996). The tourist image: Myths and myth-making in tourism. Chichester: Wiley.

Shields, R. (1991). *Places on the margin: Alternative geographies of modernity.* London: Routledge.

Smith, L. (2006). *Uses of heritage.* London: Routledge.

Steiner, C. J., & Reisinger, Y. (2006). Understanding existential authenticity. *Annals of Tourism Research, 33*(2), 299–318.

Thrift, N. (2007). *Non-representational theory: Space, politics, affect.* London: Routledge.

Tunbridge, J. E., & Ashworth, G. J. (2000). *Dissonant heritage: The management of the past as a resource in conflict.* Chichester: Wiley.

Urry, J. (1995). *Consuming places.* London: Routledge.

Urry, J. (2002). *The tourist gaze* (2nd ed.). London: Sage.

Waitt, G. (2000). Consuming heritage: Perceived historical authenticity. *Annals of Tourism Research, 27*(4), 835–862.

Walsh, K. (1992). The representation of the past, museums and heritage in the post-modern word. London: Routledge.

Wang, N. (1999). Rethinking authenticity in tourism experience. *Annals of Tourism Research, 26*(2), 349–370.

Waterton, E. (2009). Sights of sites: picturing heritage, power and exclusion. *Journal of Heritage Tourism, 4*(1), 37–56.

Waterton, E. (2010). *Policy, politics and the discourses of heritage in Britain.* London: Palgrave Macmillan.

Watson, S. (2007). Trading places: Europe for sale. In U. E. Beitter (Ed.), *Reflections on Europe in transition* (pp. 157–175). New York: Peter Lang.

Watson, S. (2012). Country matters: the rural historic as an authorised heritage discourse in England. In R. Staiff, R. Bushell, & S. Watson (Eds.), *Heritage and tourism: Place, encounter, engagement* (pp. 107–126). London: Routledge.

Watson, S., & Waterton, E. (2010). Reading the visual: Representation and narrative in construction of heritage. *Material Culture Review, 71*, 84–97.

Winter, T. (2012). Cultures of interpretation. In R. Staiff, R. Bushell, & S. Watson (Eds.), *Heritage and tourism: Place, encounter, engagement* (pp. 172–186). London: Routledge.

Wright, P. (1985). *On living in an old country: The national past in contemporary Britain.* London: Verso.

Zolberg, V. L. (1998). Museums as contested sites of remembrance: the Enola Gay affair. In S. Macdonald & G. Fyfe (Eds.), *Theorising museums* (pp. 69–82). Oxford: Blackwell and the Sociological Review.

Zukin, S. (1991). *Landscapes of power: From Detroit to Disney world.* Berkeley: University of California Press.

Chapter 4
Heritage and Community Engagement

Emma Waterton

Introduction

For many years now, a number of scholars have been assessing the role of communities within the field of heritage studies. This is an area that is also gathering strong political backing, evidenced by the foregrounding of the term in recent international policy, such as the independent review prepared for the IUCN World Heritage Programme, titled *IUCN, World Heritage and Evaluation Processes Related to Communities and Rights* (Larsen 2012), as well as that developing at the national level, such as the *Australian Heritage Strategy* consultation. It is a term that is equally visible within broader public policy, too, taking perhaps its most obvious form in recent community cohesion debates occurring in the United Kingdom, which revolve around issues of citizenship and national values. The relationship between heritage and community is, therefore, one that has significant currency at many different levels: conceptually, in terms of heritage management practices, and, more broadly, as something that is implicitly referenced in debates about identity and cultural difference. The latter in this list may at first appear to push the chapter beyond the scope of traditional heritage management. Yet, I will argue, it is a focus of interest that nonetheless has important consequences for any consideration of ethics, especially those that take up a social justice approach. To better understand this, the chapter will reflect upon the work of Nancy Fraser and her 'politics of recognition', which will be drawn upon as a framing device for illustrating that if

E. Waterton (✉)
Institute for Culture and Society, University of Western Sydney,
Locked Bag 1797, Penrith, NSW 2751, Australia
e-mail: e.waterton@uws.edu.au

© Springer Science+Business Media New York 2015
T. Ireland, J. Schofield (eds.), *The Ethics of Cultural Heritage*,
Ethical Archaeologies: The Politics of Social Justice 4,
DOI 10.1007/978-1-4939-1649-8_4

dominant patterns of cultural value (both institutional and societal) prevent some communities from participating on a par, as peers, with others in social life, we can speak of misrecognition. Holding this in mind thus necessitates structuring the chapter around three key agendas: (1) establishing workable definitions of 'community', (2) examining ethically sound practices and methods of community engagement within the field of heritage studies, and (3) exploring the politics bound up with the uses 'heritage' and 'community' are put to in wider social life, particularly in terms of marginalisation. Across the back of all three, then, will be a broader consideration of the operationalisation of the term 'community'.

Community Defined

Like heritage, the concept of community is one that has been with us for some time. And just as heritage has a tendency to settle into the role of something that is great, good, objectified and reified (Crouch 2010), so too does community tend to speak of something convivial, gentle and idealised (see Williams 1976; Bauman 2001). For both terms, these tendencies are a product of their history. Importantly, these have been pervasive histories, ones that have aided the import of caricatures of both terms into the public policy process and popular currency, where there also exists an implied and positive relationship between the two. This echoes an observation made by Elizabeth Crooke (2010), who points out that definitions of one frequently refer implicitly to the other, so much so that while the two terms are often only loosely or vaguely defined as individual concepts (we *know* what they mean, or so the assumption goes), they seemingly draw conceptual strength from each other and together they seem untouchable. Indeed, as Crooke (2010: 17) goes on to argue, a community 'is defined and justified because of its heritage and that heritage is fostered and sustained by the creation of community'. Their relationship, it would seem, is both recursive and self-fulfilling.

While readers will undoubtedly be familiar with the historical emergence of the term 'heritage', they may be less so with that of 'community', which is a concept that began life somewhere other than in the field of heritage studies. For this broader history, we can trace the term back to sociological literature emerging at the turn of the last century which specifically explored rural towns and villages (see Warren 1956; Fox 1968). This rurality was characteristic of much of the work developing at the time, which also took community to mean a self-contained collection of people living within a specific geographic area or particular place, sharing in common ways of life. Nestled here were notions of tradition or that of a 'golden age', with appeals made to an idealisation of place (see Dicks 2000: 51). While these more traditional approaches to the term have since received sustained criticism in academic literature, they continue to linger in a policy sense where notions of community as convivial, undifferentiated and homogenous, inevitably romanticised, existing 'back in time' or within the strict parameters of social hierarchy, remain a stubborn assumption (Smith and Waterton 2009). This reification, as Pyburn (2011: 33) points out, brings with it an accompanying definition of the roles and terms those communities must adopt 'in order to have a voice in the management of heritage'. But pushing aside this policy emphasis for the time being, it should come as no surprise that the term—like 'identity' and 'culture'—exists as one of perennial interest, coming into dialogue with many scholars in all manner of disciplines. Indeed, by the midpoint of the twentieth century, it was widely acknowledged to be 'one of the most ambiguous words in sociological literature' (Smith 1940; see also Williams 1976). For some it had become a 'fantasy' (Clarke 2005, cited in Neal and Walters 2008: 280), a 'weasel word' (MacGregor 2001: 188), something tied up with so many different ways of thinking that it had come to mean virtually nothing at all (Aas et al. 2005: 30; Kumar 2005). Despite this discomfort, it remained a central interest, triggering the emergence of several key texts, many of which will be familiar to scholars working within the fields of archaeology and heritage studies. These include Colin Bell and Howard Newby's (1971) *Community Studies*; Benedict Anderson's (1983) *Imagined Communities: Reflections on the Origin and Spread of Nationalism*; Anthony Cohen's (1985) *The Symbolic Construction of Community*; Graham Crow and Graham Allen's (1994) *Community Life: An Introduction to Local Social Relations*; Paul Hoggett's (1997) *Contested Communities: Experiences, Struggles, Policies*; Robert Putnam's (2000) *Bowling Alone: The Collapse and Revival of American Community*; and Zygmunt Bauman's (2001) *Community: Seeking Safety in an Insecure World*.

As the literature continued to develop, thinner social relationships were acknowledged and the concept broadened beyond something confined to geography or social groupings to those that might exist as subgroups (Watson and Waterton 2011). Such studies focused on particular cultural groups that were seen to share certain sets of values or identities, like the business community, the LGBT community, the golf community, the deaf community and so forth. As before, these were essentialised groups, simplified and defined around apparently cohesive and power-neutral gatherings of people, but, at least, they broke beyond the traditional coupling of community with rural geographies. As this web of communities continued to emerge, so too did more critical accounts, particularly those associated with a range of marginalised and disenfranchised groups agitating for the right to also define and use the term. Theirs was an agenda primarily developing out of counter-colonial, post-conflict and non-Western contexts, in which marginalised groups sought to actively and politically respond to a range of injustices. Most commonly associated with this challenge were Indigenous projects for self-determination and control emerging within Australia, New Zealand, Canada and America (see Greer et al. 2002; Ronayne 2008). These, to borrow from Crooke (2010), were 'communities of action' dissatisfied with prevailing and denigrating conceptualisations, built in the image of a cosy and nostalgic social group. In response, scholars were forced to reject past definitions of 'community', and the concept itself came to be reworked as contested, nuanced and, ultimately, replete with the workings of power. This new level of complexity required us to think as much about difference as we do unity, likewise 'conflict *and* harmony, selfishness *and* mutuality, separateness *and* wholeness, discomfort *and* comfort', to borrow from Burkett (2001: 242).

More recently still, an additional layer of complexity has been added to the mix which draws in the elective communities developing online. All around us now, traditional areas of social life are being amended with the prefix 'e', such that we now have access to e-mail, e-commerce, e-learning, e-culture and, importantly, e-communities. Each year the statistics go up, so much so that by December 2011 32.7 % of the world's population had access to—and knowledgeable capabilities with—the Internet.[1] In geographical terms, the numbers become more impressive, with five regions—North America (with 78.6 % of the population able to access and use the Internet), Oceania/Australasia (67.5 %), Europe (61.3 %), Latin America (39.5 %) and the Middle East (35.6 %)—enjoying above average Internet usage.[2] Indeed, with each year that passes, the Internet is pulled more and more into play with a fuller range of user groups and interests. Perhaps the most cited example of literature that conceptualises life online as a form of community formation comes from Howard Rheingold's (1993) somewhat outdated concept of the *virtual community*. Rheingold's evocative exploration provided an enduring image of an unregulated, open and widely available social space in which anything goes. This democratic utopia, where there are few impediments and many opportunities, was seen as free from the state-sanctioned narratives and agendas animating real life. Here, a generic and simplified understanding of 'community' came to dominate, which offered, as Willson (1997: 145) has argued, 'the answer to the theorist's search for a less exclusionary and repressive experience of community'. This tendency towards life online took up a distinctly romantic feel, where cyberspace became something almost mythical, providing significant leverage for any form of political, social or cultural action. It was, in many ways, imagined as the quintessential 'level playing field' (Markham 1998: 155).

Like those concepts of community that went before it, however, Rheingold's virtual community has since come under scrutiny. Indeed, a number of scholars have responded with a reminder of the importance of acknowledging that narratives of inequality are carried forwards into cyberspace, which has a user group dominated not only by Western countries but a demography characterised by white, male and middle-class people (Nakamura 2000: 713). Indeed, those scholars go on to point out that cyberspace reflects the divisions and asymmetries of the 'real' world in terms of gender, sex, religion, age, class and ethnicity (Nakamura 2000; Bell 2001; Dicks 2003; McIver 2004; Brown 2007). Because of this, some scholars have characterised the Internet in decidedly negative terms, in which its endless freedom is reimagined as an inauthentic and totalising alternate reality. For these scholars, it is greeted with suspicion and distrust, and the malleability of life online becomes decidedly *undemocratic*. The same qualities that Rheingold took to be so positive conjure up a qualitatively different human experience, in which the endless possibilities for identities and narratives constructed online provide a potentially deceitful experience (Quan-Haase et al. 2002). Panic around these possibilities was later

---

[1] http://www.internetworldstats.com/stats.htm, page consulted 11 August 2012.

[2] http://www.internetworldstats.com/stats.htm, page consulted 11 August 2012.

harnessed to wider concerns that the Internet had become an unregulated place for pornography, cyber-violence, fraud and cybersex (Benwell and Stokoe 2006: 244).

What we are left with today, then, is an understanding of community that may be place based, face-to-face based or non-face-to-face based, yet all may engender attentive and active senses of engagement. The nomenclature for these types of engagement will, of course, differ along the way. What will unite them, however, is their ability to allow individuals to engage not only with strangers but also cement and develop relationships with people who may already be a part of the same extended social network. Moreover, individuals can now be acknowledged as participating in a community even if they live and work in different places and time zones. No matter how it happens—whether online or in 'real' life—communities, to rehearse Neal and Walters (2008: 280), will be 'highly contested and heterogeneous site[s] containing a range of socio-economic tensions, needs, socio-cultural exclusions and contradictions'. They will be fashioned by social and cultural experiences and political aspirations and will draw together a range of people. This is a conceptualisation that is inherently fragile and dissonant, both necessary characteristics because of their ability to draw attention to the fact that communities are continually re/constructed both consensually and contentiously. Moreover, they are saturated with complex relations of power, not all of which are distributed uniformly within any given group. As a concept, then, it is constituted and negotiated *by* and *within*, which means, as Thrift (2005: 139) points out, that not everything can be rosy all of the time, nor, as he goes on to argue, does it have to mean 'the same thing as liking others'. The point here is that while 'community' *may* be warm and friendly, it is also something we stumble into as a means of avoiding loneliness and inactivity, or resisting marginalisation, and is thus vulnerable, contingent, changing and contested (Neal and Walters 2008: 291; see also Bauman 2001; Smith and Waterton 2009).

However it is defined, 'community' is a concept no longer managed at the nexus of face-to-face encounters and has become a 'more than place' notion existing symbolically or imaginatively beyond the parameters of geography or proximity (Neal and Walters 2008: 282; see also Anderson 1983). The grander gestures of human togetherness bounded by locality have thus been replaced by routine performances of conviviality, shared interests, constructions of otherness, structures of feeling and/or everyday labours and mundane experiences. This is an observation that we, as heritage scholars, need to come to grips with, as the alternative is to equate the term with less than satisfactory conceptualisations of tradition, timelessness and nostalgia, all of which bring with them an enduring pattern of exclusion (see Matthews 2009).

Research as a Form of Engagement

What, then, does all this mean for heritage studies? To answer this question, I want to quickly revert back to the point around which this chapter pivots, which is the idea that the intersection of heritage practice and community engagements ought to be ethical. This is a theme I have written about elsewhere with Laurajane Smith (see Smith and Waterton 2009; Waterton and Smith 2010), where we have sought to place our thoughts amongst provocative moves within the academy aimed at rethinking archaeological and heritage management practices. It seems to me that such moves spring from a general discomfort with what I see as a lack of critical debate around 'community engagement', which in turn bleeds into a longer standing dissatisfaction with the way communities are conceived of within the sector. With this in mind, I have used the above (albeit brief) foray into the historical constructions of community as a means to highlight that the ways in which we think about the term have not always been useful or conducive to participation in, and empowerment *through*, research. More importantly, the more nuanced position that has been developing steadily within the scholarly literature does not seem to play out as clearly within associated policy and practice, where one-dimensional constructions of 'community' continue to dominate. This is a point reinforced by Pyburn (2011: 29), who likewise remarks upon the lacklustre theorisation of community we are often asked to work with:

> Here, I problematise the concept of community on three fronts: (1) any individual belongs to multiple communities; (2) community archaeology frequently reifies imaginary communities, which have been created by the archaeologists; and (3) community archaeology needs to consider not only descendent and local communities, but also those communities with political and economic power.

While Pyburn is talking specifically about archaeological practice, the broader point remains that drawing upon anything less than a critical understanding of community will lead to exploitative practice. This, I would argue, is the case whether we are thinking about the more obviously political engagements invoked by Indigenous community groups in their struggles over control and ownership, where our work is admittedly more nuanced and politically minded, or the more mundane engagements led by those seeking to have a stake in the understanding and interpretation of a local heritage (see Smith and Waterton 2009).

There are, to my mind, two ways to tackle this problem: target examples that illustrate a frustratingly exploitative engagement with community groups or attend to those spaces where a more ethically sound practice can be found. In this chapter, I have opted to go with the latter and the thoughts I have put together below draw from a number of influential sources. To begin, I want to acknowledge the influential voice of Linda Tuhiwai Smith and her volume, *Decolonizing Methodologies: Research and Indigenous Peoples* (1999), which was undoubtedly at the forefront of literature dealing with intersections between ethics and research methods (see also Nicholls 2009). I have also situated the chapter alongside a handful of community engagement projects that have emerged as positive examples within the field of archaeology and heritage management. Here, I am referring to long-standing projects like the Community Archaeology Project Quseir, Egypt (CAPQ), work by Shelley Greer (2010) and Annie Clarke (2002; see also Clarke and Faulkner 2005), both in areas of Northern Australia, and more recent projects such as those commenced by K. Anne Pyburn in Central Asia (2007; but see also the work by Gemma Tully 2007). The lessons emerging from these projects have been bolstered here with more general commentary offered by Yvonne Marshall (2002) and Carol McDavid's (2003, 2004) work, for example, to which I have also added those thoughts emerging from disciplines outside of archaeology and heritage, such as Ruth Nicholls' reflections on critical reflexive method. The specifics of each project will not be covered here; rather, I offer a general impression of how these projects have unfolded through the lenses of recognition, particularly their attempts to dislodge the interpretive authority of disciplinary voices in favour of granting alternative voices greater parity in the process (Rountree 2007: 14).

A key lesson that emerges out of the literature listed above is that community engagement practices need to be participatory, be non-extractive and 'give back' (Askins 2009; see also Koster et al. 2012: 200). Implicitly invoked here is the instruction to think seriously about the risks of becoming exploitative; in other words, as Koster et al. (2012: 200) argue, we can no longer afford to see communities as passive data sources that can be mined 'to serve the researcher's information needs'. A shift is needed, then, from thinking about conducting research *for* or *about* communities towards conducting research *with* and *from* communities. This means first asking people if they feel they belong to the community in question: how they fit, avoid or otherwise participate in its workings and how they understand its parameters (Pyburn 2011: 34). It also means simultaneously thinking beyond a singular 'community' and taking into account a fuller range of groupings that exist within the broader network or assemblage. These, as Pyburn (2011) points out, could include government departments, schools, the military, collectors, tourism bodies, descendent communities, religious groups, academic interests and so forth, all of which are layered with their own relations of power and structures of feeling. Questions then need to be asked about the *sorts* of research that ought to be undertaken and with which goals in mind. Indeed, a significant source of friction in community engagement practices occurs when these initial questions are ignored, as it is here that heritage professionals find themselves proposing projects that are 'designed to solve problems that do not make sense to the people they affect with strategies that depend on outside investment and pressure' (Pyburn 2011: 39). All too often, as Pyburn (2011: 39) goes on to point out, in these circumstances, we find ourselves trying to 'help' a community (often one that is not really a community at all) by inviting them to participate in something that they are not particularly interested in or do not understand. The important shift that sits at the heart of these illustrations, then, is one that moves the field away from thinking about communities (and their lives, knowledge, issues, interests, etc.) as 'subjects' towards one that is foregrounded in thinking about accountability, building trust and, ultimately, striving for relevancy (see Ronayne 2007). Pushed a little further, as Ronayne (2007, 2008) argues, this means allowing our skills and resources to be put to use in ways that we may not always anticipate. Here, an emancipatory current can be detected, one that allows for a sense of empowerment and *active* engagement. This, however, will only be achievable if our handle on control is ceded away from researchers and handed over to participants, a move that needs to take place as part of a process that does not allow the former to trump the latter by default, as is often the case today (see Meskell 2007: 443). For Koster et al. (2012), this means broadening the project of decolonisation such that we seek also to decolonise the way communities are seen and understood, as well as decolonising how expertise, itself, is portrayed and privileged.

What I am arguing for here is a research process that contests and pushes against those tidy ascriptions of 'community' found in policy and popular parlance, replete with traditions, beliefs and shared identities, so as to reveal, to borrow from Alexander et al. (2007: 788):

> ...the messier contours and intersections of individuals and groups at the level of everyday life. Rather than being an abstract category, 'community' is lived through embedded networks of individual, family and group histories, trajectories and experiences that belie dominant representations and discourses.

Ruth Nicholls, in her 2009 article in the *International Journal of Social Research Methodology*, outlines perhaps most explicitly what she sees as emancipatory and critical research practice, which she hinges around concepts of empowerment, relationality and reflexivity. Hers is a practice inspired by feminist, post-structuralist and Indigenous methodologies, through which she seeks to foreground a more nuanced conceptualisation of 'community', along with all the complexities that such a collective entails. Key here are notions of conduct and trust, both of which are achieved only when the researcher risks moving out of a position of knowledge and control into what Nicholls terms 'a liminal, in-between space' (2009: 121). In these spaces, the fragile relationship between 'the researcher' and 'the researched' is teased apart and grafted together again in new ways, guided by a multilayered reflexivity (Nicholls 2009). First in Nicholls' approach is a process of self-reflexivity, during which the researcher seeks to explicitly identify and name any hidden assumptions nestled not only within the project's methodology and conceptualisation but in the wider research framework that constitutes their employment. Nicholls then compels researchers to reflect upon their ability to identify themselves and collaborate with others: this means considering not only the interrelations between people but so too those relationships between 'institutional, geopolitical and material aspects of their positionality' (Nicholls 2009: 122). Finally, Nicholls (2009:123) suggests that those involved in community engagement projects ought also to think hard about collective reflexivity, by which she means thinking about:

> ...how the collaboration determine[s] the frames of inquiry. It also asks what were the terms of participation, who participated or did not...and what effects did this have on the outcome of social change and practical knowing for the community participants.

Evident here are similar leanings towards broader social engagements intimated by Pyburn, cited earlier, and the work by Yannis Hamilakis (2007:15), who argues that 'the ethical and socio-political arenas should not be treated as separate'. The pivot point, it seems to me, is attaining that level of reflexivity that allows a project of engagement to move beyond participation and become one that entails an openness towards learning about difference, creating new spaces for understanding and negotiating mutually accountable ways of thinking about the past in the present. Such an approach will take the discipline of archaeology and field of heritage studies far beyond the sorts of ethical arrangements cited in various codes of ethics and standards associated with their practice. This is not to suggest, as Ronayne (2008) makes clear, that such codes require abandonment—that, too, would lead to potentially exploitative relationships. Rather, the point is that these broader instruments of ethical practice need also to reference the personal, and here I mean acknowledge what people—those that exist in attachment to our notions of 'community'—think, feel, want and need.

Politicising Community Engagement

Drawing from a position similar to that advocated above, Christopher Matthews' (2009:82) provocation in a review article published in the *Public Historian* in 2009 made the following observation:

> Truly surprising is that issues of divergent values over the marketing of artifacts or the proper uses of the past constitute the very subject of this book [*Archaeological Ethics*]. The fact that these issues are constructed such that they may be considered as solely archaeological problems, rather than issues in larger social, cultural, and ideological fields of ethics, speaks to a narrow-minded, self-interested stance that at least in some quarters, if not in the majority, defines contemporary archaeologists.

Though Matthews (2009: 81) is referring to quite specific contexts such as looting, the commodification of the past and a questioning of what he sees as the 'immutable archaeological record', he, along with Pyburn, Nicholls and Hamilakis, amongst others, draws attention towards the necessity for considering ethical engagements in a much broader context: social *life*. To do otherwise, to persevere with unreflexive and under-theorised notions of not only what 'research engagement' is but 'community' too runs the risk of allowing peoples' lives to be governed, exploited and colonised by the research process. Nowhere is this issue made more strikingly clear than in the policy arena, where notions of community tend to oscillate between two distinct and limiting conceptualisations: those that circulate with convivial and overwhelmingly positive underpinnings and those that construct the notion around places of exclusion, disfunction and disappointment. As scholars attempt to engage more and more with the notion of 'community', it seems timely that further considerations into how those studies lend themselves to thinking through wider problems and concerns need be implemented. Here, I counterbalance the positive reflections outlined above with a more cautionary seam. This is because the potential for community engagements cannot fully be realised if we continue to work with the limited notions of community that seem to animate policy and practice. Indeed, I am not as yet convinced that community-based heritage research can be as empowering as it might at first seem. This is due to the processes of misrecognition I identified at the outset of this chapter, which simultaneously draw attention to the relations of power mediating both our understanding of 'community' and our approaches to heritage and its management, which, I suggested, are parity impeding. If, for example, we accept Nancy Fraser's (1999, 2000) treatment of recognition as a question of social status, then sustained attempts within heritage studies are required that take account of the context and consequence of alternative claims for participation. In the context of this chapter, with its focus upon the ethics of community engagement, what we are being asked to examine, then, are the parameters within which a parity of participation for a fuller range of communities is being allowed for—especially when we remember that a narrow collection of cultural norms and symbols, which represent a particular social class within society, are already embedded within heritage management processes. As Fraser's model makes clear, our ethical obligation at this point— the point at which supposedly discrete research projects spill across broader social life—is to explore exactly what is at stake when communities are denied the opportunity to interact as full partners, particularly with those communities of expertise that have traditionally enjoyed a position of dominance. This denial is a consequence not only of '*institutionalised* patterns of cultural value that constitute one as comparatively unworthy of respect of esteem' but of the very ways in which we have traditionally conceptualised communities in the first place (Fraser 1999: 35, emphasis in original). Indeed, as Matthews makes clear above, this has seen communities of expertise operating from a position of relative worth *over* other communities of interest, both in terms of their aspirations and identities. Importantly, these processes of misrecognition continue to be sustained through administrative codes and institutionalised patterns of heritage management, which sees heritage as something that is best attended to—and understood—by experts.

It is in this vein that the chapter takes up an explicitly political mantel and attempts to feed into vigorous debates ongoing within a wider cultural life, where talk has focused upon systemic issues preventing the development of a more rounded and dialogically sound research enterprise. Here, we are forced to ask what is it about culture and heritage—and the way we perceive it—that makes it a predominantly white, middle-class exercise? The crux of this issue draws us to wider notions of power, in which attention is placed on the particular 'rules of the game' (Richardson 2007: 31) that limit opportunities for groups to influence and engage with heritage and the management process. A great deal of work still needs to be done. Foremost, we need to find ways of embedding genuine aspirations for a community-based practice within the current processes of management. This will be an uneasy and uncomfortable project, as to do so we need to address the key question of how we approach those groups, communities and public formations that are different from ourselves. How do we disarm the self-referential structural arrangements that allow us to summarily dismiss some community formations over others? How do we negotiate the asymmetrical and recursive power relations that impede a parity of participation? These are big questions. And while we are beginning to understand better the nature of difference, self-conscious efforts still need to be made if we are to promote and produce a richer form of community life within the field of heritage studies.

Added to this are the newer spaces provided by the Internet, which complicate further an already complex situation by providing different architectures of space capable of sustaining both the weak and strong ties that cut across many offline community engagements (Wellman and Gulia 1999: 188). The problem to date, however, is that groups forming online are comprised of the same sorts of people that already dominate heritage and cultural practices in 'real' life. These public formations predominantly emerge from the professional class of archaeologists, heritage managers and museum professionals, which are themselves most often defined along the social and ethnic lines of the white middle classes (Waterton 2010). Although groups like Ligali (a Pan-African organisation agitating for more accurate representations of African people and culture), BlackPlanet (an online community for African Americans) and several small-scale groupings have emerged, all of which utilise the Internet for self-expression, affirmation and promoting oppositional understandings of culture and heritage, exposing their network to a more diverse social world, wider information and shared interests, they are still, to all intents and purposes, in the minority. Within these instances, such self-identified community groups still struggle to find legitimacy as 'authentic' and 'trustworthy' voices, particularly as they are *heard* through a medium conventionally dismissed as either seemingly or potentially false. Thus, while the Internet offers a new venue for community proliferation and engagement, it brings with it a range of tensions and instances of misrecognition that cumulatively—and unsatisfactorily—render it unhelpful.

Conclusion

As may have become clear, this chapter has been somewhat disingenuously put together. In it, I have used the idiom of 'community' to make some quite specific statements about how I see the state of heritage and its associated practices of cultural engagement. This is because, as a growing field of academic enquiry, I think heritage scholars have a responsibility to continuously re-examine the rules of their 'game' and renegotiate their position within the management process, thereby lessening the risks of alienation, misrecognition and delegitimisation. At the outset, then, this paper was set up as an attempt not only to examine the validity and relevance of community engagements but to create a platform from which to examine the insidious potency of misrecognition as a key ethical issue. In the process, it has not been my intention to romanticise the diverse ways in which 'community' is imagined and used to satisfy our needs nor propose a single characterisation for the term. Quite the opposite, my point has simply been to demonstrate that the possibilities for people to experience and engage with each other around the issue of heritage, in a way that fosters a sense of connection, continue to be hampered by ill-fitting conceptualisations that themselves work to impede participation. If nothing else, my purpose has been to agitate for casting of a reflective gaze over the field of heritage studies, in a bid to understand how more nuanced understandings of communities can be theorised and legitimised.

Theoretically, then, this chapter has sought to contribute to ongoing debates about the meaning of community. While the phrase was vitalised some time ago within the field, the various impressions offered by heritage scholars and policymakers do not yet add up to any kind of coherent whole. Rather, they are frequently based upon different imaginings of the term, with a nebulous and tidy conceptualisation of community often pitted against the realities of heterogeneous networks that are replete with differences. Added to this are online or virtual interactions, which bring yet another layer of complexity to the conceptualisations of community engagement developing in the field. Quite how the term is understood has been central to this chapter, which I hope has shown a more nuanced (and critical) account than some of us are used to thinking about: something altogether messier, but no less real, enmeshed within a mixture of politics, power plays, social cues and cultural affiliations, and bound up with complex nests of feelings and familiarity.

The chapter has also attempted to make a contribution in terms of thinking through methodologies. Here, I see a lot of importance in continually stripping bare the practices we engage in and reminding ourselves that there are so many other 'communities' with which to engage beyond that of the academy. This agenda simultaneously requires us to reflect on issues of privilege and power and think about the room we make available for dissonant and subordinated voices within the heritage management process. As such, while this chapter has ostensibly revolved around community engagement, a significant seam running through its argument has been cautionary because these are areas dominated by particular groups of people and their cultural experiences. To talk of ethics, then, also requires reflection upon the broader issues of human rights and social justice, issues that entered the international policy lexicon at least 60 years ago with the 1948 Universal Declaration of Human Rights. This has been my reason for including the third, political, dimension to the chapter, which taps into Seyla Benhabib's (1992: 8) aspiration for a 'moral conversation in which the capacity to reverse perspectives, that is, the willingness to reason from the others' point of view, and the sensitivity to their voices is paramount'. To better understand this, Nancy Fraser's 'politics of recognition' was drawn upon as a theoretical framing arguing that if dominant patterns of cultural value (both institutional and societal) prevent some communities from participating on a par, as peers, with others in social life, we can speak of misrecognition. Following from this, I suggested that dominant patterns of cultural value operative within the field of heritage—*and more broadly*—currently constitute some communities as comparatively more worthy than others. This, too, is a question of ethics. The agenda of the chapter thus became twofold: exploring the ethical conduct of research with community groups while also questioning in whose interest, and for what purpose, that research is being done. The key ethical issue for both of these parts is challenging relations of power, in both research and wider society.

References

Aas, C., Ladkin, A., & Fletcher, J. (2005). Stakeholder collaboration and heritage management. *Annals of Tourism Research, 32*(1), 28–48.

Alexander, C., Edwards, R., & Temple, B. (2007). Contesting cultural communities: Language, ethnicity and citizenship in Britain. *Journal of Ethnic and Migration Studies, 33*(5), 783–800.

Anderson, B. (1983). *Imagined communities: Reflections on the origin and spread of nationalism*. London: Verso.

Askins, K. (2009). 'That's just what I do': Placing emotion in academic activism. *Emotion, Space and Society, 2*(1), 4–13.

Bauman, Z. (2001). *Community: Seeking safety in an insecure world.* Cambridge: Polity Press.

Bell, D. (2001). *An introduction to cybercultures.* London: Routledge.

Bell, C., & Newby, H. (1971). *Community studies.* London: Unwin.

Benhabib, S. (1992). *Situating the self: Gender, community and postmodernism in contemporary ethics.* New York: Routledge.

Benwell, B., & Stokoe, E. (2006). *Discourse and identity.* Edinburgh: Edinburgh University Press.

Brown, D. (2007). Te Ahua Hiko: Digital cultural heritage and Indigenous objects, people and environments. In F. Cameron & S. Kenderdine (Eds.), *Theorizing digital cultural heritage: A critical discourse* (pp. 77–91). Cambridge: MIT.

Burkett, I. (2001). Traversing the swampy terrain of postmodern communities: Towards theoretical revisionings of community development. *European Journal of Social Work, 4*(3), 233–246.

Clarke, A. (2002). The ideal and the real: Cultural and personal transformations of archaeological research on Groote Eylandt, Northern Australia. *World Archaeology, 34*(2), 249–264.

Clarke, A., & Faulkner, P. (2005). Living archaeology in the Madarrpa homeland of Yilpara. In J. Lydon & T. Ireland (Eds.), *Object lessons: Archaeology and heritage in Australia* (pp. 225–242). Melbourne: Australian Scholarly Publishing.

Cohen, A. (1985). *The symbolic construction of community.* London: Routledge.

Crooke, E. (2010). The politics of community heritage: Motivations, authority and control. *International Journal of Heritage Studies, 16*(1–2), 16–29.

Crouch, D. (2010). The perpetual performance and emergence of heritage. In E. Waterton & S. Watson (Eds.), *Culture, heritage and representation: Perspectives on visuality and the past* (pp. 57–71). Farnham: Ashgate.

Crow, G., & Allen, G. (1994). *Community life: An introduction to local social relations.* London: Harvester Wheatsheaf.

Dicks, B. (2000). *Heritage, place and community.* Cardiff: University of Wales Press.

Dicks, B. (2003). *Culture on display: The production of contemporary visitability.* Maidenhead: Open University Press.

Fox, K. A. (1968). Agricultural policy in an urban society. *American Journal of Agricultural Economics, 50*(5), 1135–1148.

Fraser, N. (1999). Social justice in the age of identity politics: Redistribution, recognition, and participation. In L. Ray & A. Sayer (Eds.), *Culture and economy after the cultural turn* (pp. 25–52). London: Sage.

Fraser, N. (2000, May/June). Rethinking recognition. *New Left Review* 3:107–120.

Greer, S. (2010). Heritage and empowerment: Community-based Indigenous cultural heritage in northern Australia. *International Journal of Heritage Studies, 16*(1–2), 45–58.

Greer, S., Harrison, R., & McIntyre-Tamwoy, S. (2002). Community-based archaeology in Australia. *World Archaeology, 34*(2), 265–287.

Hamilakis, Y. (2007). From ethics to politics. In Y. Hamilakis & P. Duke (Eds.), *Archaeology and capitalism: From ethics to politics* (pp. 15–40). Walnut Creek: Left Coast Press.

Hoggett, P. (1997). *Contested communities: Experiences, struggles, policies.* Bristol: Polity Press.

Koster, R., Baccar, K., & Harvey Lemelin, R. (2012). Moving on from research ON, to research WITH and FOR Indigenous communities: A critical reflection on community-based participatory research. *Canadian Geographer, 56*(2), 195–210.

Kumar, C. (2005). Revisiting 'community' in community-based natural resource management. *Community Development Journal, 40*(3), 275–285.

Larsen, P. B. (2012). IUCN, World Heritage and evaluation processes related to communities and rights: An independent review, prepared for the IUCN World Heritage process.

MacGregor, S. (2001). The problematic community. In M. May, R. Page, & E. Brunsdon (Eds.), *Understanding social problems: Issues in social policy* (pp. 187–204). Oxford: Blackwell.

Markham, A. (1998). *Life online: Researching real experience in virtual space.* Walnut Creek: AltaMira.

Marshall, Y. (2002). What is community archaeology? *World Archaeology, 34*(2), 211–219.

Matthews, C. N. (2009). Is archaeology political? Transformative praxis within and against the boundaries of archaeology. *The Public Historian, 31*(2), 79–90.

McDavid, C. (2003). Collaboration, power and the internet: The public archaeology of the Levi Jordan Plantation. In L. Derry & M. Malloy (Eds.), *Archaeologists and local communities: Partners in exploring the past* (pp. 31–66). Washington, DC: Society for American Archaeology.

McDavid, C. (2004). From 'traditional' archaeology to public archaeology to community action. In P. A. Shackel & E. J. Chambers (Eds.), *Places in mind: Public archaeology as applied anthropology* (pp. 35–56). New York: Routledge.

McIver, W. (2004). A human rights perspective on the digital divide. In P. Day & D. Schuler (Eds.), *Community practice in the network society: Local action/global interaction* (pp. 155–169). London: Routledge.

Meskell, L. (2007). Heritage ethics for a present imperfect. *Archaeologies, 3*(3), 441–445.

Nakamura, L. (2000). Race in/for cyberspace: Identity tourism and racial passing on the internet. In D. Bell & B. M. Kennedy (Eds.), *The cybercultures reader* (pp. 712–720). London: Routledge.

Neal, S., & Walters, S. (2008). Rural be/longing and rural social organizations: Conviviality and community-making in the English countryside. *Sociology, 42*(2), 279–297.

Nicholls, R. (2009). Research and Indigenous participation: Critical reflexive methods. *International Journal of Social Research Methodology, 12*(2), 117–126.

Putnam, R. (2000). *Bowling alone: The collapse and revival of American community*. New York: Simon and Schuster.

Pyburn, A. (2007). Archaeology as activism. In H. Silverman & F. Ruggles (Eds.), *Cultural heritage and human rights* (pp. 172–183). New York: Springer.

Pyburn, A. (2011). Engaged archaeology: Whose community? Whose public? In K. Okamura & A. Matsuda (Eds.), *New perspectives in global public archaeology* (pp. 29–41). New York: Springer.

Quan-Haase, A., Wellman, B. and Witte, J. (2002) Capitalizing on the net: Social contact, civic engagement and sense of community, http://publish.uwo.ca/~aquanhaa/Quan-Haase_2002.pdf. Accessed September 9, 2009.

Rheingold, H. (1993). *The virtual community: Homesteading on the electronic frontier*. Reading, MA: Addison-Wesley.

Richardson, J. (2007). *Analysing newspapers: An approach from critical discourse analysis*. London: Routledge.

Ronayne, M. (2007). The culture of caring and its destruction in the Middle East: Women's work, water, war and archaeology. In Y. Hamilakis & P. Duke (Eds.), *Archaeology and capitalism: From ethics to politics* (pp. 247–265). Walnut Creek: Left Coast Press.

Ronayne, M. (2008). Commitment, objectivity and accountability to communities: Priorities for 21st-century archaeology. *Conservation and Management of Archaeological Sites, 10*(4), 367–381.

Rountree, K. (2007). Archaeologists and goddess feminists at Catalhoyuk. *Journal of Feminist Studies in Religion, 23*(3), 7–26.

Smith, L. (1940). Trends in community organization and life. *American Sociological Review, 5*(3), 325–334.

Smith, L. T. (1999). *Decolonizing methodologies: Research and indigenous peoples*. London: Zed Books.

Smith, L., & Waterton, E. (2009). *Heritage, archaeology and communities*. London: Duckworth.

Thrift, N. (2005). But malice aforethought: Cities and the natural history of hatred. *Transaction of the Institute of British Geographers, 30*(2), 133–150.

Tully, G. (2007). Community archaeology: General methods and standards of practice. *Public Archaeology, 6*(3), 155–187.

Warren, R. (1956). Toward a reformulation of community theory. *Human Organization, 15*(2), 8–11.

Waterton, E. (2010). *Politics, policy and the discourses of heritage in Britain*. Basingstoke: Palgrave Macmillan.

Waterton, E., & Smith, L. (2010). The recognition and misrecognition of community heritage. *International Journal of Heritage Studies, 16*(1–2), 4–15.

Watson, S., & Waterton, E. (2011). Heritage and community engagement: Finding a new agenda. In E. Waterton & S. Watson (Eds.), *Heritage and community engagement: Collaboration or contestation* (pp. 1–11). London: Routledge.

Wellman, B., & Gulia, M. (1999). Virtual communities as communities. In M. Smith & P. Kollock (Eds.), *Communities in cyberspace* (pp. 167–194). London: Routledge.

Williams, R. (1976). *Keywords: A vocabulary of culture and society*. London: Fontana.

Willson, M. (1997). Community in the abstract: A political and ethical dilemma? In D. Holmes (Ed.), *Virtual politics: Identity and community in cyberspace* (pp. 145–162). London: Routledge.

Chapter 5
Ethics, Conservation and Climate Change

Susan McIntyre-Tamwoy, Susan Barr, and John Hurd

Introduction

Regardless of whichever side of the 'climate wars' one might sit, there is general acceptance that the world's climate is changing, and change gives rise to new challenges to which we must adapt or which will overwhelm us. Predictions have been made regarding anticipated climate changes that include rising sea levels, more frequent storm activity of greater intensity, longer and hotter drought conditions and increased temperatures. Some attention has recently been paid to how such changes might affect lifeways, particularly in relation to vulnerable communities such as Pacific Islanders and indigenous peoples generally (Lefale 2010; Farbotko 2005, 2010). The changes in cultural practices of urban populations in affluent nations have also been considered, such as proposals to regulate for native gardens in cities, reducing individual preferences for water-reliant species as a water conservation strategy (Garden 2011; Morgan 2012) and increasing regulation regarding water usage and water play. While such studies have relevance to a consideration of impacts on cultural heritage, particularly intangible aspects such as traditional practices, there has as yet been little attention specifically focussed on the

S. McIntyre-Tamwoy (✉)
James Cook University and Archaeological and Heritage Management Solutions Pty Ltd.,
2/729 Elizabeth Street, Waterloo, NSW 2017, Australia
e-mail: SMcintyre-Tamwoy@ahms.com.au

S. Barr
Directorate for Cultural Heritage, 8196 Dep, N-0034 Oslo, Norway
e-mail: susan.barr@ra.no

J. Hurd
ICOMOS ISCEAH, London, UK
e-mail: john.hurd@icomos.org

© Springer Science+Business Media New York 2015
T. Ireland, J. Schofield (eds.), *The Ethics of Cultural Heritage*,
Ethical Archaeologies: The Politics of Social Justice 4,
DOI 10.1007/978-1-4939-1649-8_5

implications that such change may have on the range (both geographic and typo-logical) of cultural heritage places in the world (although see Cassar 2005; Cassar and Pender 2005). In relation to impacts on society, the point has repeatedly been made that it is likely that people with the least capability to mitigate and adapt to future changes in the environment will suffer the most serious consequences (Green 2009; Altman and Jordan 2008; Macchi et al. 2008; McIntyre-Tamwoy et al. 2013; McIntyre-Tamwoy and Buhrich 2012b). What does this mean in terms of cultural heritage? What are the conservation challenges that face communities, regulators and heritage professionals? What might be the ethical dimensions of the range of responses to these challenges? These are large questions, and an exhaustive consid-eration is beyond the scope of this paper. Instead we will focus on a series of case studies and through them explore the ethical issues that arise.

First, we look at the Australian context characterised by a number of issues such as dwindling government financial support for heritage conservation generally an extensive, often low-lying coastline and a diverse range of site types from indige-nous archaeological (prehistoric) sites to large cultural landscapes such as Uluru-Kata Tjuta National Park World Heritage site to modern built heritage forms such as the Sydney Opera House. Second, we consider the case of the high deserts of Asia and elsewhere where archaeological sites are already suffering in the face of chang-ing climatic conditions. Thirdly, we shift our gaze further northwards to the once-frozen landscape of Svalbard in the High Arctic, where until recently the inhospitable climate had in effect conserved cultural heritage places through isolation from the pressures of tourism and high visitation which are major conservation threats in many parts of the world. In each of these three cases, we briefly describe the sites and the issues they face, consider what if any research or conservation work is cur-rently being done and what is needed. In the final part of this paper, we begin to articulate the ethical challenges that emerge from a consideration of both the impacts on cultural heritage and current and future responses.

Cultural Heritage and Climate Change Issues and Examples in Australia

Australia is a country with a variety of climates and ecosystems. It already experi-ences a range of climate challenges to its bio-cultural diversity, and some of these will be radically exacerbated by projected changes to climate over the next 40 years. In particular, extreme climatic events such as increased severity of storms, wildfires and rising sea levels have been identified as major threats. Cultural heritage in Australia is also very diverse, encompassing a range of settler heritage sites often constructed with rather vulnerable building materials and indigenous sites ranging from ephemeral traces of past and current cultural practices to more robust con-structed sites such as stone arrangements and modified landscapes.

Climate change is likely to affect many sites in Australia in a variety of ways. Changes to hydrology and salt regimes will affect many cultural landscapes including the freshwater swamps of Kakadu that have supported not only a diversity of wildlife but also the lifestyles of the indigenous owners and which have inspired some of the world-renowned Kakadu rock paintings. In parts of Australia, change to humidity and salt regimes is also likely to threaten rock art itself. Such changes will also create challenges for the historic sandstone buildings dating to Australia's early colonial period in major capital cities. The extension of the viable environmental range for pests such as termites is predicted to threaten historic vernacular structures in areas where these have not previously been a problem, and in other areas, mosses, moulds and invasive plant species are likely to cause localised but significant management issues (e.g. Gold et al. 2011). The predicted increase in severity of storm events and cyclones is difficult to mitigate and is likely to cause damage and at times complete and rapid destruction of sites as is also the case with increased wildfires.

Perhaps the most obvious impact however and to some extent the most predictable is the impact from rising sea levels. Australia has a very large coastline and not only is the coastline the point of entry into the continent for settler Australians but it was also the point of entry, albeit many millennia earlier, for Indigenous Australians. There are literally tens of thousands of indigenous sites around the Australian coastline. Some of these are sites of contemporary use and practices, and others are sites that attest to Aboriginal and Torres Strait Islander life over the long-time depth of their occupation of the continent. The degree to which these sites will be affected ranges, depending on a number of local site factors such as the coastal topography, elevation and the topography of the seabed. However, it is clear that many sites in many areas of the coastline will be negatively impacted, and it would be a conservative estimate to suggest that thousands of sites will be lost as they are inundated by rising sea levels or lost to storm surge, erosion and bank and cliff collapse. The implications of this in terms of lost scientific (archaeological) knowledge, impacts on indigenous identity, cultural practice and community well-being have not been assessed, and detailed modelling of coastal impacts that would allow a more accurate quantification of risk/loss has not been undertaken (McIntyre-Tamwoy and Buhrich 2012b, 2013). To date there has been no attempt to estimate reliably the quantum of lost 'knowledge' that this will involve. In part this is because there has never been a systematic assessment of all indigenous sites by the government. The comprehensiveness of state databases in relation to Aboriginal site distributions and documentation varies widely from state to state; however, it is universally acknowledged that in all cases heritage databases in Australia are far from comprehensive. There has also been no systematic Australia-wide attempt to identify what social impacts this loss of cultural sites is likely to cause, including impacts to both individual and community identity and community well-being (although for localised consideration of community impacts on indigenous health and well-being, see Green et al. 2009a, b, and for impacts on indigenous identity McIntyre-Tamwoy and Buhrich 2012b). In the following section, the indigenous cultural landscape in Northern Cape York Peninsula, Queensland, and the case of Fort Denison in Sydney Harbour, New South Wales, are discussed as a means of illustrating the issues facing cultural heritage sites in Australia.

Indigenous Heritage in Northern Cape York Peninsula, Qld

In Cape York Peninsula at the northernmost tip of Australia, Aboriginal communities continue to live on traditional lands. They rely heavily on the bounty of their natural environment both for sustenance and to maintain their vibrant culture. The climate is tropical, and there is a marked seasonal division between monsoonal 'wet' season and 'dry' season. While the Aboriginal and Torres Strait Islander people in this area have a long history of forest use (Fell et al. 2009), they are characterised by their long-standing traditional and historic relationships with the coastal and marine environment. While people do use inland resources, there is a strong coastal focus and an emphasis on the resources of the sea and of coastal forests and rainforest thickets (Fig. 5.1).

For this region it is predicted that temperatures and sea levels will rise, and the intensity of storm events will increase. Some sites are already affected by seasonal storm surges, although, as the climate is monsoonal, it is difficult for traditional owners to separate what is unusual but seasonal and therefore 'normal' and what is a result of climatic change. In a study recently undertaken (McIntyre-Tamwoy and Buhrich 2012b, 2013), it was clear that local indigenous communities and specifically their community rangers (Fig. 5.2) feel that they do not have access to enough information about climate change, how it will affect them and what steps they can

Fig. 5.1 People in Northern Cape York rely on resources from the sea, littoral zone and coastal dune forests. Traditional owner Meun Lifu with granddaughters Noreena and Moeisha collecting oysters. Photograph S. McIntyre-Tamwoy

Fig. 5.2 Aboriginal rangers discussing historic graves less than 40 cm above current high tide in Cape York Peninsula. Photograph S. McIntyre-Tamwoy

take to build the resilience of their community, cultural practices and cultural sites. Strong community understanding and action are essential in remote areas as there is no active 'government' action to conserve cultural sites. For communities such as this to have a chance of adapting to climate change impacts, identifying threatened heritage places and prioritising conservation or salvage efforts, a number of things need to occur urgently. In relation to cultural heritage, these include:

- *Better communication and education* about climate change and predicted impacts on cultural heritage places.
- *Knowledge sharing* amongst scientists, governments and communities about climate change impacts. Aboriginal people living on their traditional land are early observers of environmental changes; however, this knowledge is not being effectively utilised by governments due to lack of formal communication channels.
- *Collaborative decision-making* in formulating climate change policy and responses. To date indigenous communities have not been adequately involved in the development of climate change policy.
- *Research partnerships between communities, archaeologists* and cultural heritage specialists that focus on more accurate predictions of climate change impacts, management of cultural heritage impacts and development of mitigation strategies including salvage excavation. There is an urgent need for projects to consider the potential impacts on cultural heritage places and values and the implications

of such impacts on indigenous people. Similarly research is needed to identify the range and nature of sites that might be impacted and to develop priorities for protection, documentation and/or salvage in partnership with local communities.

Australia's Colonial Heritage Sites, Fort Denison NSW

Settler Australian sites along the coastline include a range of important sites at state and local level. These include towns, port facilities, jetties and sites of indigenous settler resistance and/or conquest. These sites, as is the case with similar sites around the world, are under threat from rising sea levels, increases in salt regimes, changes in the range of pests and increased storm severity and coastal erosion.

Fort Denison is valued as an iconic feature of the Sydney Harbour cultural landscape. It is managed by NSW National Parks and Wildlife Service and is listed on the NSW State Heritage Register, as an item of State significance reflecting its heritage values for the people of New South Wales. Heritage values of Fort Denison relate to the colonial and convict fabric (Fig. 5.3) and it also has Aboriginal significance as a place where Aboriginal people were recorded harvesting oysters in the early colonial period. Watson and Lord (2008) used IPCC sea-level rise predictions of 20–100 cm in 2100, aerial photography and GIS modelling to examine the potential impacts on the heritage fabric of the fort. They identified two primary vulnerabilities at Fort Denison—the western terrace entry point, which is the lowest point on Fort Denison and vulnerable to high tide events, sea-level rise and boat wash, and the subfloor

Fig. 5.3 Pinchgut [i.e. Fort Denison], Sydney undated [pre-1885], Sydney Harbour, NSW. Photographer unknown/Source: National Archives of Australia

supporting structures which are already prone to submerging at high tides. The adaptations needed to mitigate impacts from sea-level rise include blocking the western terrace access point and using alternative access to the Fort, sealing foundations and external blockwork to prevent saltwater seepage into the subfloor and installing wave deflector caps to minimise the impacts of boat wash and high tides. They note that existing records at Fort Denison from 1992 to 2008 show a sea-level rise of 3.1 mm a year, which is the upper limit of IPCC predictions (Watson and Lord 2008:30).

The importance of monitoring impacts and understanding the latest scientific climate change projections cannot be overemphasised for Fort Denison. Watson and Lord recommended updating management plans at not more than 10-year intervals (2008:44; 2009:47). The detailed predictions made for Fort Denison present an excellent framework for understanding the implications of sea-level rise to heritage assets in Sydney. However, in a confidential survey of heritage practitioners undertaken in 2012, concerns were raised that there is pressure from heritage agencies to restrict information from the public domain rather than use this information to begin open discussions about the long-term viability and management of cultural assets around Sydney and Sydney Harbour (McIntyre-Tamwoy and Buhrich 2012a). In an environment of dwindling government resources for heritage conservation and increased conservation pressure brought about by climate change, public complacency about government responsibilities and track record relating to the conservation of the nation's heritage is dangerous. In Australia the conservation of heritage places has moved from being an area of active community agency to the domain of professionals and bureaucrats. The 1960s, 1970s and early 1980s were a time of activism, and indeed, most of the heritage legislation across the country has its foundations in this period of activism. However, once legislation was enacted, there began a process of professionalisation of the sector and a growing complacency on the part of the community predicated on their assumption that heritage conservation was now safely in the hands of government. There is of course an implied assumption that the government as custodian on behalf of the people will adequately manage the nation's cultural heritage and act transparently in relation to emerging threats. However, there is little evidence that heritage managers and governments are meeting this responsibility (although see for NSW McIntyre-Tamwoy and Buhrich (2012a), Watson and Lord (2009) and Watson et al. (2009), and for the Commonwealth ANU (2009)). It is indeed possible that government agencies in many parts of Australia no longer have the capacity necessary to meet such challenges as the trend over the past decade has been a shift from employing specialists (such as archaeologists and conservation architects) to generalist project officers who manage planning and development compliance processes rather than provide technical or strategic focus on emerging issues.

Climate Change and the Arid High Deserts

The impacts of climate change on arid high deserts are arguably greater and more visible than in most other areas, especially regarding the effects of violent and unpredictable flash floods which are frequently followed by landslides. Rogue storms and

Fig. 5.4 The fragile and vulnerable earthen World Heritage Site of Ksar Ait ben Haddou, Maroc. Photograph J. Hurd

flash flooding in deserts have always been a risk, but these events have historically been rare. In the last two decades, the regularity of such events has shown an almost exponential increase in all regions of the world, they are becoming a norm.

In locations where human settlement and habitation have developed above the tree line, heritage places are particularly vulnerable to flash floods because there is a lack of vegetation to assist in binding together the friable sands, soils and clays. Here water flows readily, picking up fine materials and other soils, and the resulting slurries flow down the valleys and gullies with the mechanical damage from water being magnified by the presence of smaller rocks and mud slurries which simply sweep away man-made structures. This is especially the case since the most common building materials in high deserts are earth and stone, which tend to be the most accessible materials, but are also the most fragile when in composite and very climate vulnerable (Fig. 5.4). In high desert contexts, adobe brick or rammed earth walling, decorated with friable, unbound paints and plasters, is often the most common structural and finishing material.

During the night of 2 August 2010, a cloudburst followed by heavy rain hit villages along tributaries of the upper Indus River in Ladakh, India. Eyewitnesses report that the violent storm, lasting no more than 2 min and followed by heavy rain for a further few minutes, caused watery slurries to race down the valleys of Indus tributaries in which most of the villages are built and almost all of the villages took heavy but very local damage (Fig. 5.5). During this short but intensely violent storm, more than 200 people were reported killed, with many more missing, in the worst storm to hit Ladakh in living memory (INTACH 2010).

Fig. 5.5 Damage in the village of Igu Ladakh. Photograph J. Hurd

Similar storms have increased in regularity across the world with reports of such events from Central Asia, North Africa, China and elsewhere. In the last decade, violent storms and flash flooding in high deserts have accounted for the loss of thousands of lives and the loss or severe damage of thousands of heritage structures and moveable objects, together with extensive regions of the intangible imprint of diverse cultural traditions in high desert cultures.

Cultural Heritage Responses

Loss of life is clearly the first concern in such events, but in terms of cultural heritage, the loss of heritage buildings and the traditions from which they have emerged need urgent research to mitigate the damage done. While it might seem that a simple solution would be to change the construction materials used in the future, substituting stronger cement, stabilised earth and so on, such solutions will eliminate rich cultural traditions, cultural landscapes and all of the less tangible traditions associated with the buildings typologies and their cultural contexts in high desert regions. Unfortunately, this is already happening across the world where local populations are taking survival measures, largely unassisted by external relief funding. In many cases this involves the demolition of traditional structures and replacement with new materials and typologies which may or may not have greater resistance to flash flooding but will certainly change the traditions in which the populations live.

In many cases small villages of exceptional cultural significance are simply being abandoned with populations moving to towns and urban centres. Little thought has been given to safe location or planning of new structures for those who remain, and almost no consideration has been given to strategies for retrofitting of traditional structures or relocation to safer areas.

It is a difficult question for state parties with large and diffuse heritage assets in high desert regions. Populations may no longer be content with earth and stone structures and often in isolated regions, such changes represent the destruction of a whole cultural tradition. There is no great international fund to help high desert cultural heritage survival, and the regions tend to be economically poor and remote. State parties are facing the ethical question of prioritisation of the sites earmarked for conservation and development budgets: how do you assess values and decide which examples deserve the budgetary focus? In many cases the lure of possible economic return from tourism is a deciding factor. It is so often a case of where the tourists can easily reach, and these places easily become cash cows. They may, if they are lucky, receive a reinvestment of part of the income raised, but many such projects suffer from the dilemma of risking eventual ruin by the weight of increasingly heavy visitor numbers.

What alternative strategies are there for people living in these regions? Prediction of storms is not fully practical since they are very local and at best 1–6 h warning may be achieved through ALERT (automated local emergency response in real time) systems, but in isolated high deserts, we are years away from any effective warning systems (Hancock et al. 2000). Therefore, there is a need for three principal mitigation measures to be implemented now:

1. Efficient and continual maintenance of water drainage and diversion infrastructure, river walls, bridges, rainwater goods and control systems in buildings, roofs and so on. In places where structures are of great age and significance, these need more than simple maintenance and may be sheltered by the application of coats of sacrificial material or sheltered by purpose-built groundworks or structures. These measures may require prioritisation of scarce funding and drive states towards listing sites in an order of significance. This in itself is fraught with practical and ethical pitfalls, where it may be hard to select protection for a wide range of sites, reflecting all of the cultures and religious expressions in a country, over the whole of its history.
2. Maintenance and construction of flood-resistant sea walls, river banks and levees designed with practical access for civil defence response, while attempting to preserve the identity of cultural life in the margins between land and water.
3. Mobilisation and training of civil society in disaster preparedness and response; working with schools and colleges, societies and interest groups in civil society, towards active cooperation in the monitoring of climatic conditions in culturally historic places; and generally spreading regional awareness on the impact of climate change and the risks that it carries, at a very clear level, raising and interpreting essential data for future response.

In historic periods, maintenance was an important social tradition and habit, with communities working cooperatively to maintain general village infrastructure and conditions in individual houses and public buildings. In more recent times, these traditions have tended to decline partly through the loss of younger populations who migrate to livelier urban centres and partly due to improved roads, which allow tradespersons to travel over wider regions.

The travel range of craftspeople is also wearing down the local nature of the architectural language in details of construction and decoration. Ideas are spread and cross-pollinate in regions which tend to water down traditional local dialects within the cultural language. These changes have had a large impact on the general social patterns of maintenance activity in formerly isolated villages. Just 50 years ago, it was possible to identify both country and region, even village, when examining vernacular structures, through an intimate knowledge of local, structural or decorative tradition. Now, even in sustainable technologies of building, using traditional materials, the accent is usually 'contemporary' rather than 'traditional'; most of the structures have lost their local character.

Civil defence, especially over the last 20 years, has also changed in similar ways, with reliance on fire and emergency services travelling from far distances. However, in the aftermath of flash floods, and other examples of climate change, the very infrastructure which has encouraged these changes is severely impaired for travelling to remote locations. It therefore follows that civil defence needs to be supported by organisations formed within a civil society to plug the hole that exists within emergency protection and response activity; this allows government and people to grow and learn together the nature and rate of the changes that are occurring, whatever their cause may be.

Cultural Heritage in the Arctic

The Arctic is a geographic point, the North Pole, surrounded by an ocean which in turn is surrounded by land masses. These land masses are for the most part adjoined to large continents (North America and the northern rim of Asia) but also include the world's largest island (Greenland) and smaller islands and archipelagos. The varying nature of the geographic areas makes it difficult to state exactly the southern boundary of the Arctic, and the concept is defined in various ways which take their starting point in such parameters as mean annual temperature, vegetation zones and even political considerations. The examples in this paper are taken from what can be called the High Arctic, the coldest and most northerly zone where the ground is permanently frozen (permafrost) apart from the upper level which thaws in the summer and where vegetation is scarce and fragile.

The cultural heritage of the High Arctic has broadly speaking two main categories: the indigenous (comprising the heritage of Inuit and various other native peoples) and the heritage which has its origins in cultures further south, usually individuals or smaller groups which moved north for shorter or longer periods mainly in order to exploit the natural resources through hunting, trapping, fishing, whaling and mining, but also for other purposes such as exploration and social work (Barr 2004). The flora and fauna of the High Arctic are dependent either directly or indirectly on the sea. Those that do not actually live in or feed off the sea receive life-giving nourishment from the excrements and other organic matter brought in to the land by seabirds, either directly to the land plants or through these to other birds and mammals. Lush vegetation under seabird-nesting cliffs illustrates this point in a vivid manner. Further inland from the sea, the High Arctic areas are either permanently ice-covered or are lacking in sufficient natural resources to sustain more than the occasional passing group of individuals. As a result of this and the transportation opportunities provided by the sea in the summer and sea ice in the winter, the main bulk of heritage sites in the High Arctic are to be found around the coasts.

The primary forms of threats to this cultural heritage have been from the harsh nature itself. This has included strong winds which can rip planks off the simple wooden buildings, erosion of the shoreline and thus the coastal heritage sites, polar bears which often smash their way into wooden cabins out of curiosity or because they can smell stored food, freeze and thaw cycles which split stone and other materials and chemical degradation caused by the salts blown in from the sea. Rot and mould action have also been known in microclimatic zones where, for example, the summer sun shines on to a sheltered corner or interior of a wooden structure. Traditionally the High Arctic sites have been protected from serious impacts of human action (particularly visitation) where summer sea ice has caused barriers to certain areas. In addition the polar areas were not considered typical tourism areas. This has changed in later years. The climate change that now can be seen around the world has hit the Arctic particularly hard, and sea ice in the Arctic Ocean has decreased alarmingly in both extent and thickness (http://www.arctic.noaa.gov/detect/iceseaice.shtml). Shorelines exposed to erosion are now even more at risk, and visitation to previously sheltered heritage sites has increased rapidly. The two case studies below are taken from the Norwegian High Arctic archipelago of Svalbard, which lies between 74° and 81° N. Although Svalbard does not have an indigenous population, the examples are representative for the general situation in the circum-High Arctic.

A Case of Erosion

Fredheim is a particularly famous trapping station on Svalbard's main island of Spitsbergen. The main cabin there was erected in 1924, but an older hut (Danielbua) from 1911 stands nearby (Fig. 5.6). In addition there is a small storage shed behind the main cabin and a small outhouse near the beach. This trapping station lies on a strandflat of loose gravel material only 1.5–2.5 m a.s.l. The sea edge of the strandflat is very exposed to erosion from sea waves, and measurements of the erosion rate have been made since 1987.[1] These measurements show that the main cabin stood

---

[1] An erosion project at the University Centre in Svalbard is currently running. The data here are from the governor of Svalbard, but originate in this project. See also Flyen 2010.

Fig. 5.6 Fredheim in 2011, with the main cabin in the foreground and the older hut behind. Photograph S. Barr

in 1987 17.7 m from the erosion edge and that this edge has moved towards the cabin at an average rate of 37 cm a year since then. However, from 2010 to 2011, the erosion rate was 57 cm, and in 2011 it was 67 cm. In 2001 Danielbua stood only 3 m from the erosion edge, and it was then moved inland 6 m by the heritage authorities. The main cabin is now only 8 m from the edge, and various methods of protecting the edge from further erosion have been considered, such as barriers of stone or rolls of geosynthetic material filled with sand/gravel. Such methods are, however, complicated to manage and would detract seriously from the impression of the natural landscape. Nor are they considered sufficiently effective. The heritage authorities are therefore considering moving the entire complex to a site further inland on the strandflat—a drastic action, but one which hopefully will preserve the structures without changing their situation in the landscape more than necessary.

Archaeological heritage, such as structural remains, middens and graves, cannot be moved in this way, and the alternatives are emergency excavation to secure information or simply documentation of the object before it is lost. Around 2000 heritage sites in Svalbard are catalogued in the national database of Norwegian cultural heritage, Askeladden, and it is recognised in the management of Svalbard's cultural heritage that not all objects can be maintained (Governor of Svarlbard 2012). Many are documented and allowed to degrade naturally. A site is seldom completely lost before erosion, fire, or other disasters erase it.

Visitation to Fragile Heritage Sites

Before the early 1990s, tourism to Svalbard was neither particularly encouraged nor systemised, although not forbidden. At the beginning of this decade, however, the Norwegian parliament named tourism as one of the three fields of activity for Svalbard in the near future (in addition to education and the traditional coal mining). After this the number of visitor days in the main settlement of Longyearbyen increased from ca. 23,000 in 1993 to 84,643 in 2012.[2] In the same period, the number of cruise passengers doubled. The number of tourist landings at sites of interest around Svalbard has increased from ca. 40,000 in 1996 to ca. 100,000 in 2010,[3] and the number of sites visited around the archipelago has increased from 52 in 1996 to ca. 240 in 2012.[4] Although many of the sites may be promoted for their natural qualities (flora, fauna, geology), the majority also contain cultural heritage sites since the historic use of the land concerned exploitation of natural resources. Similar increases in tourist visitation can be seen in many other areas of the High Arctic (e.g. Horejsova and Paris 2013; MOSJ).

The High Arctic is at the very edge of the climatic comfort zone for vegetation. The fragile plants that manage to grow there gain extra nourishment from organic materials connected with heritage sites, and the vegetation growth in turn helps to protect and contain archaeological sites. It takes very little impact from visitors' boots before the vegetation is damaged and removed, and regrowth may never occur (Fig. 5.7). Thus, the dilemma arises which is familiar to many managers of heritage sites: the sites can become 'loved to death'. Visitors who have no desire to damage or destroy either vegetation or heritage sites may do just that either by unwitting tramping on building remains and artefacts or by contributing to the formation of paths and other vegetation-free areas around the sites.

Mitigation with Regard to Threatened Arctic Heritage Sites

Heritage sites in the High Arctic do not represent only one nation or one cultural group. First and foremost, there has been indigenous presence for thousands of years in many parts of the Arctic. In addition and as mentioned above, explorers and others from many countries travelled to the Arctic on their various missions and left behind material evidence of their presence. It is therefore an obligation for national authorities to take this aspect into consideration in evaluations of climate change impacts on the heritage of their area and in related discussions of mitigation and prioritisation.

---

[2] http://www.sysselmannen.no/Documents/Sysselmannen_dok/Informasjon/REISELIVSS TATISTIKK%20FOR%20SVALBARD%202012.pdf (In Norwegian. Accessed August 2013)

[3] http://fylker.miljostatus.no/Svalbard/Tema-A-A/Bosetting-og-naringsvirksomhet/ Reiseliv/#tilstand (In Norwegian. Accessed August 2013)

[4] See footnote 2.

Fig. 5.7 A path worn by
visitors on what might be
thought to be 'nonimpactable'
ground. Photograph S. Barr

With increasing tourism and possibilities of negative human impact in mind, the heritage authorities in 2010 regulated access to nine particularly important heritage sites which were chosen both for their heritage values and for the fact that they had so far been little visited and not overly impacted. Other sites may be added if necessary, and the state of the regulated sites will be monitored. Other sites that are still on the cruise visitor schedules will inevitably be impacted, but this is offset as far as possible through education courses for tourist guides, information brochures and lectures and guidelines for visitation to sites published in print and online by both the authorities and the Association of Arctic Expedition Cruise Operators.[5]

Moving buildings threatened by increasing erosion has been mentioned above and has also been carried out at other sites in the Arctic such as Herschel Island in North Canada, which is on Canada's Tentative List for World Heritage status. This is, however, a remedy which is suitable for only a small number of particularly significant heritage sites.

---

[5] http://cruise-handbook.npolar.no/en/index.html and http://www.aeco.no/guidelines/

In most cases, mitigation at heritage sites in the Arctic will involve similar measures to those taken in other areas—sufficient maintenance of buildings to keep them as weatherproof as possible on the one hand and on the other hand recognition of the fact that sites will be lost and that detailed documentation needs to be made before it is too late to secure a record of the heritage values.

Ethical Issues Arising from the Case Studies

The examples discussed above are geographically, culturally and climatically diverse, and they raise a number of specific as well as universal issues relating to climate change impacts and mitigation in relation to cultural heritage.

In Australia we have seen that there will inevitably be a loss of coastal Aboriginal sites with the combined effects of sea-level rise, increased wave wash and more extreme weather events. The bureaucratic tradition of managing Aboriginal prehistoric sites as part of an essentially natural landscape means that the default management position/conservation response may be to assume that this loss is inevitable, respond with resigned complacency and do nothing to redress this loss. However, this gives rise to questions such as 'who gets to make those decisions', 'who stands to lose the most from this approach' and 'what are the consequences of this essentially 'do nothing' approach'. Ethical issues arise over the timely dissemination of information and the meaningful engagement with indigenous people in terms of developing mitigation strategies and responses that are culturally appropriate and made with free, prior and informed consent.

In contrast to the examples from Australia that look at incremental changes over a number of years, the ones we have looked at in the high desert areas of the world relate to the dramatic and localised impacts of extreme weather events that are likely to increase as climate change accelerates. In the high deserts of Asia as elsewhere, there is the large ethical question of the protection of traditional lifestyles and cultural traditions. These are not only the mechanisms of social cohesion and identity but also in many cases the principal earnings potential for small communities, through tourism, craft manufacture tradition and traditional trade practices. These questions also impact on pride of place, self-respect and thereby peaceful and productive lives for populations.

In many cases flash flooding not only damages the roads and access infrastructure and the built environment but also destroys the sustainability of fields, terraces and agriculture in general, a disaster that can take decades to recover from. Many governments see merit in encouraging the movement of populations to other locations, partly to centralise administration and partly to focus the expense of renewal into urban centres rather than remote areas. These considerations make the need for better defence and preparedness against climatic disaster, all the more urgent and in regard to the protection of all aspects of cultural heritage, a vital and immediate need. Already tour operators in India are organising tours of abandoned heritage ruins, a tragic and perhaps inevitable product of the general trends in disaster response. One year after the terrible tsunami that hit Japan in 2011, tour buses were diverting to the damaged wastelands, a tourism trend that seems set to increase.

The archipelago of Svalbard has never had an indigenous population. Instead visitors from further south have travelled north to the islands through the past 400 years, mainly to exploit the natural resources. They have come and gone and left behind them an international heritage that is probably unique in its variation. The archipelago is in fact on Norway's Tentative List for World Heritage status. In many cases, the material remains, including graves, contain information which is no longer found in the country of origin, for example, the clothes of seventeenth-century workers which have been found in preserved graves. The total cultural heritage of Svalbard can be considered to be a limited and endangered population, comparable to populations of fauna. However, with care and effort, a decreasing biological population may increase again given the right conditions, while cultural heritage places destroyed are lost forever.

Increasingly we are locked into binary and emotive discussions that are illogical at best. One example is the dismissal of calls to conserve cultural heritage by weighing this against the need to conserve species. Of course these things cannot be compared, and strategies to address both are necessary. However, it would seem that polar bears are more important to those worried by climate change in the Arctic than either cultural heritage or indigenous lifestyles are. Polar bears are iconic and exciting. They are highest on the want-to-see lists of tourists to the Arctic than anything else. While concern for threatened species is understandable, the fate of nonrenewable cultural heritage resources needs also to be considered. It may be that specific species in this region such as polar bears can 'adapt back again' as their ice habitat diminishes. Loss of cultural heritage is, however, permanent. We cannot bring back what has rotted away or eroded into the sea. Should we not therefore expect an urgent consideration for cultural heritage issues in the discussions concerning global climate change?

When ice limited access to polar sites which heritage authorities prioritised for preservation, the question was often heard as to why resources should be spent on heritage sites that 'no one would see anyway'. Many of these sites have now become favourite destinations that tour operators have in their promotional brochures. Yet the question must now be asked as to whether everyone has a right to visit everywhere. As tourists we can love sites to death, and in the Arctic this process can progress quickly. Although the impact from natural forces can be harsh, protection of some sites from human impact will give them the chance to exist further into the future than they might have done otherwise.

Another side of the ethical discussion is promoted by nature conservationists who would like to see the Arctic nature returned to a pristine wilderness state. They can see no reason for historic 'rubbish' to remain as an eyesore on the tundra. This is even more piquant in Svalbard where all artefacts and fixed heritage remains predating 1946 are automatically protected by law (The Environmental Law for Svalbard, 2001/ revised 2010). So pre-1946 rusty tin cans and abandoned mine workings are not rubbish, but protected heritage. To be able to accept this, it needs to be realised that the wilderness is not untouched and has not been for several centuries and that removing the historic remains will not return the tundra to a prehuman state. The answer is to lift one's gaze and see how little significance the small sites of previous human activity have in the all-encompassing nature around them. And not least, to be able to recognise that cultural heritage has as much a right to exist as natural elements.

Conclusion

The ethical considerations that emerge from a consideration of climate change impacts on the world's cultural heritage are varied, although it seems not as self-evident in the way that research on climate change impacts has been framed around economic interest and direct threats to human life and other species. Nevertheless, it is clear that there are a number of ethical issues that will arise from our collective response—including our lack of response to the issue. They can be summarised as:

- *Governance*—governments and heritage agencies have a responsibility to anticipate, explore and respond to emerging threats to the varied cultural heritage that they are charged with protecting.
- *Transparency*—there is a growing recognition that the sustainable conservation of cultural heritage requires a partnership between heritage managers, communities and others with a direct relationship to the cultural heritage. For communities to be able to exercise agency, there is arguably a need for greater transparency around threats, funding limits, research needs, development of funding priorities, etc.
- *Differential impacts of climate change on communities*, especially Pacific Island states, low socio-economic communities and indigenous peoples.
- *Interrelated and cumulative impacts* such as increased accessibility of certain sites hitherto protected through isolation and/or inaccessibility.
- *Research focus*—there is a need for researchers to reframe their research focus to a community-based approach and broker partnerships between communities, researchers and funding bodies to address some of these urgent issues including identification, impact assessment, salvage and mitigation.

Finally we leave the reader with some questions that we maintain need urgent and vocal consideration such as: Whose heritage will be most impacted? Is there a risk that mitigation measures which require large financial inputs will be focussed on monumental heritage at the expense of other forms of cultural heritage? If so, what impact will there be on the heritage of hunter-gatherer societies and small rural and remote communities? Further, given that the major anthropogenic contributors to climate change have been concentrated in the more affluent nations and yet the impact on the world's cultural heritage will be felt by many others and perhaps most severely by less affluent communities in the Pacific, by Inuit communities in the Arctic and in remote communities in marginal land in the world's high deserts, what responsibility do the affluent nations have to assist in the mitigation and salvage of cultural heritage in those places? Should tourism be allowed to increase in previously isolated areas at the risk of overrunning the local culture and cultural heritage and at the same time contributing to climate change factors?

References

Altman, J., & Jordan, K. (2008). *Impact of climate change on indigenous Australians: Submission to the Garnaut climate change review* (CAEPR Topical Issue No. 3/2008). Canberra: Australian National University.

Australian National University. (2009). *Implications of climate change for Australia's World Heritage properties: A preliminary assessment.* A report to the Department of Climate Change and the Department of the Environment, Water, Heritage and the Arts by the Fenner School of Environment and Society, the Australian National University.

Barr, S. (2004). Arctic monuments and sites. In S. Barr & P. Chaplin (Eds.), *Cultural heritage in the Arctic and Antarctic regions* (pp. 13–23). Oslo: ICOMOS IPHC.

Cassar, M. (2005). *Climate change and the historic environment* (London Centre for Sustainable Heritage University College London with support from English Heritage and the UK Climate Impact Programme). London: London Centre for Sustainable Heritage.

Cassar, M., & Pender, R., (2005). The impact of climate change on cultural heritage: Evidence and response. In I. Verger (Ed.), *14th triennial meeting*, The Hague, 12–16 September 2005 (Preprints Vol. 2, pp. 610–616). London: James & James.

Farbotko, C. (2005). Tuvalu and climate change: Constructions of environmental displacement in the Sydney Morning Herald. *Georafiska Annaler Series B – Human Geography, 87B*(4), 279–293.

Farbotko, C. (2010). Wishful sinking: Disappearing islands, climate refugees and cosmopolitan experimentation. *Asia Pacific Viewpoint, 51*(1), 47–60.

Fell, D., Lifu, M., McIntyre-Tamwoy, S., Roberts, C., Lynch, J., Leung, L., Charlie, B. & Lifu, T. (2009). *Significant species and habitats of Greater Lockerbie Scrub: Cape York Peninsula, Queensland.* Report to the Department of Environment and Resource Management, Queensland.

Flyen, A-C. (2010). *Svalbard—kulturminner og stranderosjon* (NIKU oppdragsrapport 86/2009). Oslo: Norwegian Institute for Cultural Heritage Research.

Garden, D. (2011). Gardening in a changing climate. *Australian Garden History, 22*(4), 3–4.

Gold, A., Ramp, D., & Laffan, S. (2011). Potential lantana invasion of the Greater Blue Mountains World Heritage Area under climate change. *Pacific Conservation Biology, 17*(1), 54–67.

Governor of Svalbard. (2012). *Management plan for Nordaust-Svalbard and Søraust-Svalbard nature reserves. Draft proposals for amendments to the protection regulations.* Oslo: Department of Environmental Protection.

Green, D. (2009). Opal waters, rising seas: How socio-cultural inequality reduces resilience to climate change among Indigenous Australians. In S. Crate & M. Nuttal (Eds.), *Anthropology and climate change: From encounters to action* (pp. 218–227). Walnut Creek: Left Coast Press.

Green, D., Jackson, S., & Morrison, J. (2009a). *Risks from climate change to indigenous communities in the tropical North of Australia.* Canberra: Department of Climate Change and Energy Efficiency.

Green, D., King, U., & Morrison, J. (2009b). Disproportionate burdens: The multidimensional impacts of climate change on the health of Indigenous Australians. *Medical Journal of Australia, 190*(1), 4–5.

Hancock, P., Skinner, B., & Dineley, D. (2000). *The Oxford companion to the earth.* Oxford: Oxford University Press.

Horejsova, T., & Paris, C. M. (2013). Tourism and the challenge of Arctic governance. *International Journal of Tourism Policy, 5*(1–2), 113–127.

INTACH. (2010, October). *Post flood damage assessment of heritage sites in Ladakh.* INTACH (Indian National Trust for Art and Cultural Heritage) Ladakh Chapter.

Lefale, P. F. (2010). *Ua'afa le Aso:* Stormy weather today. Traditional ecological knowledge of weather and climate: The Samoa experience. *Climatic Change, 100*, 317–335.

Macchi, M., Oviedo, G., Gotheil, S., Cross, K., Boedhihartono, A., Wolfangel, C., & Howell, M., (2008). *Indigenous and traditional peoples and climate change* (Issues Paper). Gland, Switzerland: IUCN (International Union for the Conservation of Nature).

McIntyre-Tamwoy, S., & Buhrich, A. (2012a). *The cultural assets & climate change literature review and research synthesis'*. Report to the Office of Environment and Heritage, New South Wales.

McIntyre-Tamwoy, S., & Buhrich, A. (2012b). Lost in the wash: Predicting the impact of losing aboriginal coastal sites in Australia. *The International Journal of Climate Change: Impacts and Responses*, 3(1). http://www.Climate-Journal.com

McIntyre-Tamwoy, S., Fuary, M., & Buhrich, A. (2013). Understanding climate, adapting to change: Indigenous understandings of climate and future climate change impacts in North Queensland. *Local Environment, 18*(1), 91–109.

Morgan, R. (2012). Water dreaming: Water supply and Australian garden history. *Australian Garden History, 23*(3), 4–7.

MOSJ. http://mosj.npolar.no/en/influence/traffic/indicators/cruiseturisme.html?

Watson, P. & Lord, D. (2009). Goat Island sea level rise vulnerability, a report prepared by the Coastal Unit, NSW Department of Environment and Climate Change, Sydney.

Watson, P., Lord, D., & Snelgrove, C., (2009). *Sydney harbour sea level rise vulnerability studies*. Paper presented at the 18th NSW Coastal Conference. http://coastalconference.com/2009/

Watson, P., & Lord., D. (2008). *Fort Denison sea level rise vulnerability study*. Coastal Unit, NSW Department of Environment and Climate Change. Sydney.

Chapter 6
Repatriating Human Remains: Searching for an Acceptable Ethics

Adam B. Dickerson and Erika R. Ceeney

Introduction

This chapter assesses the key ethical arguments surrounding the issue of the repatriation of human remains from cultural heritage institutions. The world's cultural heritage institutions hold large collections of remains belonging to human beings—ranging in age from some who died tens of thousands of years ago to those who died within the last century. Over the past 30 years or so, there have been increasingly organised and high-profile demands from various indigenous communities for culturally affiliated remains to be repatriated to them for care and safekeeping. This is seen by these communities as an important part of reclaiming their cultural heritage and autonomy. It is also seen as a crucial step towards righting the wrong that was done during colonial times through the desecration of indigenous burial and grave sites and the removal of remains from their culturally appropriate resting places (Green and Gordon 2010). Whilst this demand for repatriation of indigenous remains has now largely been accepted in some countries (such as the United States, Canada and Australia), it is still resisted by some key cultural heritage institutions that insist that these remains are an irreplaceable scientific resource that should remain accessible to researchers.

In this chapter, we examine the key ethical issues raised by the debate over the repatriation of human remains. We begin by providing a brief historical context discussing the origins of these collections and the ethically suspect manner in which many (if not most) were obtained. We then assess how the value of the knowledge that could be obtained from having the remains publicly accessible to science ought to be balanced against the harms that may be done as a result of such retention.

A.B. Dickerson (✉) • E.R. Ceeney
International Studies, Faculty of Arts and Design, University of Canberra,
Bruce, ACT 2601, Australia
e-mail: adam.dickerson@canberra.edu.au

© Springer Science+Business Media New York 2015
T. Ireland, J. Schofield (eds.), *The Ethics of Cultural Heritage*,
Ethical Archaeologies: The Politics of Social Justice 4,
DOI 10.1007/978-1-4939-1649-8_6

It should be noted that we approach this issue as philosophers engaged in normative ethics rather than, say, as legal scholars or cultural heritage professionals. That is, we do not proceed via an analysis and assessment of existing conventions, accords, laws, policies and procedures. Instead, we attempt to provide an account of the ethical considerations that should underpin the construction of appropriate public and institutional policies for the repatriation of human remains.

Historical Context

In this section, we provide a brief overview of the history of the collection of human remains: how they were obtained and for what purpose, the rise of the movement towards repatriation and some of the key international statements and landmark policies that have resulted. The purpose of this is to provide a context for the main focus of this chapter, which is the analysis of the ethical considerations involved in the repatriation debate.

Cultural heritage institutions around the world hold very large numbers of human remains in their collections. The biggest proportion of these remains were collected during the colonial period and belonged to indigenous people. The largest numbers are held in the most prestigious institutions such as the Smithsonian and the British Museum; but many others are held in various smaller collections. To give a sense of the numbers involved, it has, for example, been estimated that more than 10,000 Indigenous Australian remains are held in various institutions around the world (see Cubillo 2010; Atkinson 2010). In some cases, these remains play a part in important research and educational projects, whilst many others have lain in boxes in storage for decades.

Most of these remains were collected in the eighteenth and nineteenth centuries, and the key reasons for their collection included the curiosity of individual collectors and, particularly in the nineteenth century, scientific interest in human development (Fforde 2002; Riding In 1992; Atkinson 2010; Green and Gordon 2010). The rise of Social Darwinist theories in anthropology and other human sciences led to a widespread view of humanity as divided into biologically distinct racial groups, each with their own essential physiological nature, and organised into an 'evolutionary' hierarchy. Culture was seen simply as an epiphenomenon that flowed from this underlying physiology. Given this theory, in order to understand the different races and their appropriate 'rankings' in this hierarchy, a comparative quantitative understanding of their physiology was required (Fforde 2002). A famous (or perhaps infamous) example of this 'science' is Samuel G. Morton's *Crania Americana*, first published in 1839, which based its racial theorising on cranial capacity measurements drawn from the skulls of various indigenous peoples. From a contemporary perspective, it is clear that this 'science' of race functioned mainly as an ideology for colonialism. For it made the 'white race' the pinnacle of human development and therefore justified various forms of paternalism in the treatment of 'lower races' (Jones and Harris 1998; Gonzalez-Ruibal 2010).

To modern eyes, not only were the key motivations for collecting these indigenous remains thus deeply racist, but the methods used in collecting them were equally unethical. There was systematic desecration and violation of grave sites, the surreptitious removal of bodies from morgues (Fforde 2004; Riding In 1992), and, in some cases, it even appears that murders were committed in order to obtain bodies and body parts [for one poignant example, see Fforde (2002)]. It is apparent then that on the whole there was little or no attempt to obtain consent from either individuals or communities to the collection of human remains for whatever purpose the 'collector' had in mind. Indeed, the 'collectors' were acutely aware of the indigenous communities' resistance to the desecration of their ancestors' burial sites. As Fforde (2002: 27) notes, '[r]esistance to collecting by local people appears to have been so frequent that this activity was recognized as hazardous'. In sum, as Australian Indigenous activist Henry Atkinson (2010: 16) remarks,

> The remains of my people were collected like one collects stamps or swap cards. It was what I call the 'ivory trade' of my people, the first stolen generation. However, my people were not elephants. They were parents and children, all belonging to a family just like yours.

From our (contemporary) perspective, the conclusion to be drawn from this historical record seems inescapable: these collections of human remains were largely obtained in the service of pseudoscience and racist ideology and by means that were grossly unethical and disrespectful. It is, then, hardly surprising that the presence of these human remains in various institutions was, and continues to be, a source of deep distress, anger and humiliation for many indigenous people around the world.

Since the 1970s, with the international growth in the public profile of indigenous activism and increasingly influential demands for forms of self-determination, the repatriation of human remains has become widely recognised as an important step towards reconciliation. This recognition has resulted in a series of significant policy and legislative changes. One of the earliest sympathetic repatriation policies was implemented by the NSW Australian Museum Trust in 1974 (Green and Gordon 2010). However, it was not until the 1980s that this issue gained a significant international profile (in part, because of the influence of Australian Indigenous activists) (Turnbull 2010; Cubillo 2010). This indigenous activism, combined with the rise of a new 'socially conscious' archaeology that had emerged from the critique of positivism in the 1960s, helped to bring the issue of repatriation—and as a consequence the idea of indigenous groups' rights to control their own cultural patrimony—to the forefront of governmental legislative concerns and institutional policy making.

Perhaps the most influential document to emerge from this rise to international prominence of the repatriation issue is the 1989 Vermillion Accord on Human Remains. Adopted by the World Archaeological Congress (WAC) in 1989, the Accord consists of six statements, the first of which is 'Respect for the mortal remains of the dead shall be accorded to all, irrespective of origin, race, religion, nationality, custom and tradition'. As Turnbull (2010: 118) remarks, '[t]he accord implicitly recognise[s] that demands by Indigenous peoples for the return of remains reflected the survival and continuing vitality of their cultures and systems of customary law'. There is no doubt that the Vermillion Accord was thus an important step forward because it insisted that science take into account the 'legitimate concerns' of indigenous communities with regard to research into human remains. However, it remains unclear in the Accord just how much weight such concerns should be given and whose concept and practices of respect should be accorded priority (cf. Tarlow 2001).

Subsequent to the adoption of the Vermillion Accord by the WAC, two landmark and internationally influential acts of legislation were passed in the United States. These are the National Museum of the American Indian (NMAI) Act of 1989 and the Native American Graves Protection and Repatriation Act (NAGPRA) of 1990. The former Act created the NMAI within the Smithsonian Institute, as a museum devoted exclusively to the history and culture of native American Indians. The NMAI Act clearly sets out the museum's purpose as being a holding place for remains so that research may be conducted in order to determine the provenance of remains and funerary objects so that appropriate tribes/groups may be notified and arrangements for repatriation made, should this be desired. In other words, the key purpose of the NMAI is to facilitate the repatriation of human remains. The latter act, NAGPRA, sets out legal rights to human remains. It confers the responsibility for, and ownership of, human remains found on a given piece of land to the lineal descendants of the cultural group or tribe that used to occupy that land.

Despite such important legislative and policy shifts towards repatriation of human remains, as well as changing attitudes amongst cultural heritage profession-als, the issue continues to be contentious. Institutions in the United Kingdom, for example, which hold many indigenous human remains, have tended to be slower and more resistant to facilitating or responding to repatriation requests. The status of very ancient remains is also highly contested. In general, it remains unclear just how the key ethical issue should be resolved—that is, how the competing claims of science and indigenous descendants should be weighed against each other.

Ethical Analysis

The previous section provided a very brief overview of the historical context of the debate over the repatriation of human remains. This overview had no pretences to be either detailed or systematic; its purpose was simply to provide a frame for this section of the chapter, which is an attempt to clarify the ethical issues at stake in the debate. To put it another way, this is an attempt to answer the questions: Ought cultural heritage institutions agree to demands for the repatriation of human remains? And if so, or if not, on what sorts of ethical grounds should the answer to that question depend?

Before we even begin, an objection might be raised to the very project which we have set ourselves. What is the point, it might be said, of trying to 'answer' these questions through reasoned ethical discussion? The ethics of repatriation must depend crucially upon the views one holds about such things as: the meaning of death and the relation of the human body to that meaning; what constitutes respectful treatment of the dead; the relationships between death, place and cultural memory. These views about death vary greatly between cultures—particularly between the secular culture of the 'West' and many indigenous worldviews. Hence, there can be no neutral or impartial perspective on this matter, and any particular ethical answer one gives must depend upon a prior commitment to some worldview or other. Are we not thus faced, the objection concludes, with an irreconcilable conflict of values, which cannot be resolved through 'reasoned discussion' but only via political struggle?

It is worth discussing this challenge in more detail, as that will help to reveal some important constraints on any useful approach to the ethics of repatriation. We can exemplify the sort of issue to which this objection is pointing, by drawing on an influential paper by Tim Mulgan (1999). In this paper, Mulgan suggests a schematic, but nonetheless useful, twofold categorisation of views of death. There are views of death which make the *Dead-Are-Gone Assumption*, and there are those that instead make the *Dead-Are-With-Us Assumption*. The former is the view that, [t]hose who are no longer living have no morally relevant interest in the contemporary polity", whilst the latter is the view that "[s]ome of those who are no longer living are affected by the fate, actions and life-styles of their descendants, and thus have a morally relevant interest in the contemporary polity (Mulgan 1999: 54), As an example of the latter assumption, let us take the claim made by some Indigenous Australians that "the spirits of the dead cannot rest until [their remains are] returned to their 'Country'" (Truscott 2006). If this claim were correct, then it would follow that the failure to repatriate Indigenous Australian remains is wrong. It would be wrong, because the spirits of the dead have morally relevant interests in the fate of their remains, and curating those remains in a museum or other institution (outside their 'Country') would constitute a failure to respect those interests and, consequently, cause serious harm to those spirits. For those who believe this claim (an example of the Dead-Are-With-Us Assumption), this is a compelling argument for repatriation. However, for those who instead take the view that, at death, the person no longer exists (i.e., for those who make the assumption that the Dead-Are-Gone), this argument will not be persuasive at all—for in that case, it seems that there would be no subjects to take an interest in the fate of their remains or to suffer any harms.

This is thus an example of the objection given above, in which the answer to our question about the ethics of repatriation seems to depend entirely upon the religious–metaphysical view of death to which one is committed. In the face of this, what can reasoned discussion hope to achieve? The traditional task of philosophical ethics is to seek the *truth* of the matter—to end with a position that states 'this is right, and this is wrong'. In this case, that would seem to require a demonstration, from some ground acceptable to both sides of the discussion, that one of those assumptions about death was true and the other false. This already sounds like an utterly hopeless task. Hence, the pessimistic conclusion that there is no place for reasoned discussion here.

However, we argue that this pessimism is unwarranted and is the result of a failure to distinguish *public* morality from *private* morality (a distinction which we take from Warnock 2004; cf. Benhabib 2002, Chap. 5). The collections of human remains that are the focus of repatriation demands are not in the keeping of private individuals but in that of large public, or at least quasi-public, institutions within secular, liberal democracies. Now, a private individual must make moral decisions on the basis of what she believes to be right and wrong. That is, she must make those decisions on the basis of what she believes to be the truth about the moral obligations that she has, even if she cannot always articulate and justify these moral obligations in terms that are acceptable to others ('I just feel that I must do this', she might say, or 'I just know that this is the right thing to do'; see Warnock 2004: 24–26). In contrast, however, a public institution must be seen to make decisions on the basis of explicitly articulated reasons that can be embedded in policies and public statements and that are publicly *acceptable* as reasons for those decisions. As Warnock (2004: 76–77) writes:

> In public issues where there is a radical difference of moral opinion … and where no compromise is possible, the concept of the acceptable is a useful and indeed indispensable one… in that it may set the best goal possible in the circumstances.

In other words, a discussion of the ethics of repatriation needs to be constrained to a search for the acceptable rather than the true. And what this means is seeing whether arguments can be mounted which rely only on premises that are broadly acceptable to those with widely varying views about the meaning of death and the forms of respect that are owed to human remains. These arguments are unlikely to be fully satisfying to all people in the debate, but they must at least be something that they can 'live with'.

What we mean by this can be illustrated by returning to our example from above. It seems clear that it would not be acceptable for a public cultural heritage institution (in a secular liberal democracy, at least) to justify a repatriation policy on the grounds that *if we do not return these remains to their 'Country', the spirits of the dead will be unable to rest*—any more than it would be acceptable for such a public institution to justify a policy on the basis of any other equally contentious religious–metaphysical view. However, it would be possible for an institution to base such a policy on a related but still very different claim, namely, *it is the strong belief of many indigenous people that, if these remains are not returned, the spirits of the dead will be unable to rest; and it is important that the policies of this institution* respect *that belief*. What has shifted here is that, instead of the reason for the decision being the claim that *the spirits of the dead will be unable to rest unless …* (etc.), it has become the claim that *we ought to respect the belief that the spirits of the dead …* (etc.). In turn, the sort of justification required has shifted from the need to demonstrate the truth of a deeply contentious view about death to a need to demonstrate that certain indigenous beliefs are owed a certain kind of respect by public institutions (and where the truth or falsity of those beliefs are beside the point). Of course, this shift is not cost-free. The former claim about the dead may be seen by those who hold to it as an inescapable obligation, with a deontological force that trumps many other values; the latter claim, on the other hand, may well be seen as lacking that 'trumping' force and be just one value that needs to be balanced against others in a more consequentialist fashion. This diminution in its moral force may well be disappointing to those that hold that belief about the spirits of the dead (for they may feel that their view, although 'respected', is somehow not being taken altogether 'seriously'), but nonetheless it is the latter claim and not the former that potentially offers a way towards a publicly acceptable moral argument for repatriation.

It should be noted that none of this is to claim that public morality in a liberal democracy is *impartial* between competing moral viewpoints and that it somehow represents a neutral 'framework' within which all competing views of the good can flourish. It is simply the pragmatic point that in order for policies and legislation (i.e. public morality) to be politically achievable and sustainable, they cannot be seen to depend upon any views that are considered highly contentious. And this in turn is to remind ourselves that liberal democracy is primarily a pragmatic solution to a real problem: the problem of how people can live in a community together despite disagreeing about fundamental values (cf., Shklar 1989). Of course, what is considered 'acceptable' and what 'contentious' within a given polity is contingent and subject to change (e.g. because of successful political activism and persuasion). However, it remains the case that *respecting* different cultural worldviews is very different from accepting one of those worldviews as *true*.

Let us sum up the conclusions of this 'methodological' discussion. The fundamental point is that the debate over the repatriation of human remains is a matter of public, rather than private, morality. This in turn means that any (useful) discussion of it is subject to certain constraints. First, it is of the nature of public morality in contentious areas to be a consequentialist, balancing of the benefits and the harms of various courses of action—and thus talk of moral 'trump cards' (such as appeals to 'rights') is unlikely to be helpful. Second, the case that there are such benefits and harms must be based on reasons that will be publicly acceptable in a pluralist society—for example, on appeals to broad liberal norms such as equality, fairness, autonomy and mutual respect (cf. Williams, 2005). Some of the ways in which this second constraint operates will become evident in the course of our discussion below.

Possible Benefits

Given that the form of this debate must, as stated, be a weighing of benefits against harms, we begin our discussion by examining the main possible benefit of retaining these human remains in public cultural heritage institutions, namely, the value to science of such retention. This is the suggestion that curating such remains will ensure that they are available as a research resource to appropriately qualified experts, which will in turn tend to produce an important public good—scientific knowledge. As Baker et al. (2001: 69) write, human remains possess 'enormous value … for understanding our collective past and facing our future'. Through the study of human remains, it is possible to discover various things about the human past, such as evidence about migration patterns, past cultural practices and their meaning, diet, prevalence of illnesses and so on and so forth. Such knowledge potentially has instrumental value, in that it can lead to technical advances that may improve human welfare in various ways (e.g. developments in the treatment of disease; see Baker et al. 2001: 73–75 for examples). But, perhaps more importantly, it could also be seen as having intrinsic value, on the grounds that knowing and understanding more about the world and ourselves is an end in itself. These are arguments all based on an appeal to the *universal* value of such knowledge. A supplementary or alternative argument could argue that such knowledge derived from the remains of indigenous people is particularly valuable for the indigenous cultures themselves, as it provides a way of recovering important facts about their history and cultural heritage that would otherwise have remained unknown.

Let us evaluate this argument and its presuppositions. Even if the claim that the study of human remains can produce scientific knowledge that is (widely considered to be) valuable is granted, anyone putting forward this line of argument needs to answer two objections. First, why must the human remains *continue* to be held by these institutions? For, it may be objected, the remains were collected decades or even centuries ago, and surely this has been enough time to perform whatever research can productively be done on them; in which case, there can be no further value in retaining the remains, and they ought to be repatriated. Second, why must the human remains continue to be held in these *public* institutions rather than held under the custodianship of the communities that are culturally affiliated with those remains? For there seems no reason why, in some cases, the communities should not permit various kinds of research on the remains to continue—in which case, the remains could be repatriated without any loss of their value to science.

The standard (and perhaps only possible) answer to the first objection is that, because new methods of research are constantly being developed, the same human remains will continue to generate new knowledge indefinitely. As Baker et al. (2001: 75–76) write, '[m]ethods continue to improve and change, questions and problems expand, and the ability to restudy populations means that new information can be cumulative and complementary'. This reasonable expectation that knowledge will continue to be produced from the remains, it is claimed, thus justifies their indefinite retention.

The weakness of this argument—with its appeal to an unknown future—should be emphasised. It is one thing to argue that some human remains need to be retained for a certain limited period of time, because that will allow us to apply a particular analytical technique, which we are in a position to apply and which we have good reason to believe will produce knowledge of a particular kind and value. In such a case, we would be in a position to make a judgement about the potential benefits of this way of proceeding, which could then be weighed against the potential harms. It is quite another thing to claim that, because we may at some point in the future develop an analytical technique (we know not what), which may produce some sort of knowledge (we know not what), an institution is entitled to retain these remains *forever*. (It should be noted that this claim is *one* part of the justification that underpins the very idea of the universal museum and its permanent retention of cultural materials; however, exploration of this broader debate is beyond the scope of this paper.) Compare the following: it is one thing to perform an invasive autopsy on the body of a murder victim in order to discover the cause of death (a very important piece of knowledge); it is quite another thing to discover this fact and then pickle the victim's body and store it indefinitely—against the family's objections—on the grounds that 'people in the future may be able to discover something important from these remains'.

In response to this, it could be said that, serendipitously, we do sometimes discover very valuable things which we could not have expected to discover and that this possibility should be sufficient to permit such exploratory investigation of the human remains to continue. For example, we could point to the case of Henrietta Lacks, where a biopsy of her tumour was used without her knowledge or permission, and this tissue sample then played a crucial role in the development of treatments for polio (Zielinski 2010). Here is a case, it seems, where the harm from the unethical behaviour (the taking and using of the biopsy without consent) is outweighed by the great good that, by chance, this resulted in. It might then be concluded that this supports the case for allowing continued research on human remains, despite the unethical way in which those remains were acquired, and the further possible harms that retention of them may cause. However, to draw such a conclusion is to confuse private with public morality. It is certainly possible that research on these remains could produce a good so great that it would outweigh all the other harms that such research involves—in which case, that research would have been a good thing. However, it simply does not follow from the fact that this is a possible outcome, that we should therefore *permit* such research as a matter of legislation or institutional policy.

The strongest answer to the second objection—the claim that the same knowledge could be extracted from the remains if they were repatriated and held under indigenous custodianship—proceeds along rather different lines. This argument begins from the premise that *open inquiry* is a very important public good (e.g. Goldman 1999). That is, the public availability of information produces great social goods: it is a key value of science (for it facilitates the spread of new ideas and thus their critique and further development) and of an open democratic culture, with an informed and reflective citizenry. Open inquiry is, in other words, an important good independent of whether any particular exercise of it produces valuable knowledge; rather like we might hold free speech to be an important good, independently of whether any particular exercise of that speech produced anything especially valuable. Now (the argument proceeds), if research materials were to be placed under the control of particular groups (e.g. cultural groups), rather than being publicly available to any researcher, then this value of open inquiry would be seriously undermined. Such undermining could happen in two ways. First, it would be possible for those groups to make the knowledge derived from 'their' research materials, available only to people of their choosing (e.g. by refusing to allow publication of research results and insisting on them being disseminated only to the group or certain members of the group) (cf. Joyce 2002). Second, it would be possible for those groups to insist that only researchers with certain beliefs or theoretical commitments be allowed to study the research materials in question—which could have a damaging effect on the open critique that is so essential to the evaluation of knowledge claims. And proponents of this line of argument could go further, pointing out that if indigenous custodianship of indigenous human remains was morally required, then, via an all-too-easy slippery slope, would not this same reasoning apply to *all* cultural materials? In which case, it might be suggested, we would end with a situation in which each cultural group could prevent the study of its own cultural materials by any 'outsider'—a result which would surely be as bad in its own way as the total commercialisation (and hence privatisation) of such knowledge.

This argument thus reaches a similar conclusion to the argument from the idea that cultural heritage is a resource that is of universal importance (i.e. is important to *all*), which therefore needs to be held under the stewardship of a profession dedicated to such universalism (i.e. cultural heritage professionals). However, it lacks that latter argument's problematic commitment to the idea of 'universal significance' and replaces it with a much more defensible concept of 'open inquiry' and its value. Despite this, it should be remarked that the dire consequences of repatriation to which the argument appeals need not be the case. How we decide the answer to the question of the repatriation of human remains need not determine the answer to the repatriation of cultural objects more generally, as there is a clear distinction between them. Nor, from experiences where certain groups have taken custodianship of cultural materials, need that necessarily lead to damaging restrictions on academic research, as there have been many cases of beneficial cooperation between cultural heritage professionals and indigenous communities (see some of the examples given in Meskell 2009).

In conclusion, whilst these arguments in favour of retaining human remains in public institutions as a research resource cannot be dismissed out of hand, they also cannot be considered as being in any way conclusive. The fact that something is valuable to science and the production of knowledge cannot itself be seen as 'trumping' other ethical concerns about such retention. Scientific research, like any field of human activity, is subject to ethical constraints, and the goods it undoubtedly produces must be balanced against the harms it can cause in the pursuit of such goods. Hence, it is important to examine the other side of this balance and to look at the types of harm which the refusal to repatriate may cause.

Actual Harms

There are two forms of harm that the refusal to repatriate may be seen as causing. First, it could harm the *dead* in various ways; second, it could harm the *living* in various ways. We will examine these in turn.

In order to make a case that the failure to repatriate harms the dead, we need to find some acceptable premises that would support this conclusion. One well-supported premise which might appear promising in this connection is the following: we know that, in most cases, the indigenous people whose remains these are had strong interests (when alive) in not having their bodies treated in this way (cf. Bahn 1984; Truganini is a famous example—see Onsman 2004). That is, we know that had these people known that their graves were destined to be treated in a way that they would have seen as desecration, and their remains removed from what they considered to be their proper resting places, to be taken to an institution of a foreign culture, where they would be retained as an object of scientific inquiry or educational display, they would almost certainly have been horrified and appalled. We know this because of the deep importance most of these cultures attached to human remains being treated in appropriate ways and laid to rest in appropriate places, and to the beliefs that they had as to the relation between the fate of their remains and the fate of their spirit. As Scarre (2003: 239) remarks, in many of these cultures 'interfering with a person's buried remains is thus [considered to be] as bad as doing him a serious injury while alive. Removing his bones to a laboratory or museum is positively harmful to his spirit'.

Suppose that, for these reasons, we grant the claim that curating these remains rather than repatriating goes against the deeply held wishes and interests of those whose remains they are; there is then still a difficulty in moving from this premise to the conclusion that therefore such a failure to repatriate harms the dead. Certainly, if we make the assumption that the Dead-Are-With-Us, then we can indeed draw that conclusion. For in this case (as in the remark just quoted from Scarre 2003), there is still a person (as spirit, soul or shade) who has preferences about how her remains should be treated and who can be harmed in some way (e.g. delayed in her travel to the spirit world or be unable to rest) by the frustration of those preferences. However, if we instead make the assumption that the Dead-Are-Gone, then we face an obvious problem. If death is seen as the end of the person, then after death there is no subject who can be harmed—no one who can, for example, feel pain or frustration that her preferences about the treatment of her remains are being flouted. That is, there is no doubt that a person, whilst she is alive, can have preferences (perhaps very strong ones) about how she wishes things to go after her death; however, if death is the end of that person's existence, then if those preferences are not fulfilled after her death, then she cannot be harmed by that failure, for she no longer exists. In other words, if death is the end of the subject, and harm requires a subject, then the dead cannot be harmed.

A number of philosophers have explored ways of avoiding this conclusion—that is, the intuitive thought that, if we make the Dead-Are-Gone assumption, then events that occur after a person's death cannot harm that person (for she no longer exists) (see, e.g. Pitcher 1984; Wilkinson 2002; Scarre 2003, 2006). The core of these suggestions is that it is the *living* person who is harmed by what occurs after his or her death. So, for example, when Tutankhamun's tomb was opened and dismantled by Howard Carter (which presumably would have run directly counter to Tutankhamun's own wishes about his tomb), then it is the *living* pharaoh who is harmed (during his lifetime, 3,500 years ago) by those actions. This is because, as Scarre (2003: 241) writes, '[e]ven if disturbance of an [ancient] Egyptian's burial is not genuinely harmful to his soul or spirit, it renders null and void a project that mattered greatly to him in life'. Hence, the suggestion is, when we treat the remains of a person in ways contrary to what that person would have wanted that treatment to be, there is a prima facie case for the claim that we are thereby acting with disrespect towards that person—and thus 'harming the dead'.

There is no doubting the philosophical interest of these arguments; however, there are profound difficulties with attempting to turn them into a basis for publicly acceptable policies about repatriation. In part, this is because the arguments for the claim that the dead can be harmed by a failure to repatriate their remains are either highly contentious (because reliant on the assumption that the Dead-Are-With-Us) or deeply paradoxical in appearance (despite the philosophical ingenuity expended in trying to defuse such apparent paradox). However, even if these problems could (somehow) be overcome, there remains the issue of just how much weight should be accorded to the interests and preferences of the dead, when weighing them against the interests and preferences of the living. After all, the dead did not simply have preferences about how their remains should be treated—many of the long dead would, for example, almost certainly have been horrified and appalled by moves towards the equality of women in our society. If ignoring the wishes of the dead with respect to the treatment of their remains constitutes a harm, then so does ignoring their wishes about how women ought to be treated. Should this then be weighed on the balance against the benefits we see in such changing policies and attitudes? And, if so, how might such a 'weighing' proceed? We suggest that the public unacceptability of such arguments in a modern pluralist society is obvious. In sum, the notion of harming the dead is too problematic to form part of an acceptable argument for the repatriation of human remains. This means that if we are to find such an argument, we must look instead at the harms to the living that the failure to repatriate is responsible for.

Such harms to the living are obvious enough and do not require sophisticated arguments to demonstrate their reality. For many indigenous communities, the retention of their ancestors' remains as research materials in cultural heritage institutions is deeply distressing. Of course, there are many differences in spiritual and cultural beliefs between various indigenous cultures around the world, but three attitudes towards the dead that are widely shared across these cultures help to explain this distress and humiliation (see Vines 1999). First, for many of these cultures the *place* in which an ancestor's remains lie is of crucial significance. For example, for many Indigenous Australians, ancestors' bodies need to be placed in the proper site in their own 'Country' and that place then takes on a sacred significance as a locus of cultural memory (long after the bodies have been reabsorbed into the earth). Hence, for some ancestors' remains not to rest in that site is, as it were, for those ancestors to be alienated from their own culture. Second, the connection to one's ancestors tends to extend much *further into the past* in these cultures than, say, is typically the case in the secular culture of the 'West'. That is, whilst 'Westerners' typically would know little of their families past a generation or two, for many indigenous cultures, there is a strong connection, embedded in oral history, that goes back many generations. Third, the connection to ancestors in such communities tends to be very *broad*—in that a very wide range of people would be considered close 'kin' to the dead and thereby to have a strong interest in, and responsibility for, the treatment of their remains. Given these three characteristics, the distress felt by many indigenous communities is unsurprising. The remains held are not being treated in accordance with the forms of respect of their own culture—perhaps most importantly, are not located in the *place* that is considered fitting for them—and this is of concern despite the age of many of the remains, and not simply to those who might claim some direct family link to the remains, but to the many people in that community who claim broader kinds of kinship with those ancestors.

The failure to repatriate their dead is not only distressing to many indigenous communities (for the reasons just discussed) but could also reasonably be considered to be a humiliating insult by those communities. As discussed in the first section of this chapter, it seems clear that the initial collecting of many of these remains should be regarded by us, now, as a shameful historical wrong—consisting, as it did, of actions which demonstrated the colonisers' contemptuous disregard for the culture and beliefs of the indigenous peoples of the colonised nations. Given this historical context, it is all too easy for a refusal to repatriate to look like a continuation of this contemptuous disregard—and thus as a continuation of colonialism itself. That is because it seems not merely to be a failure to make amends for that past wrong but a refusal even to recognise that it *was* a wrong—which, in turn, constitutes a continued refusal to recognise or respect the beliefs of those indigenous cultures [on the ethical importance of such recognition see Taylor (1994)].

Alongside these obvious harms of distress and humiliation, there is a further harm: that in denying a cultural group the freedom to treat their dead according to their own canons of respect, these institutions are denying that cultural group a basic kind of autonomy to which they are entitled. After all, it is an important liberal value that different cultures and religions within a polity should have freedom (within reasonable grounds) to pursue their own cultural, spiritual and religious practices without interference. This is important, because such freedom is crucial for those cultural groups (and hence the individuals that comprise them) to pursue and construct their own identity without interference. Of course, such a freedom is not absolute, because some cultural or religious practices (e.g. female genital mutilation, religious blasphemy laws) are clearly not 'private' matters, when they clash with other important public values about individual autonomy, and how to resolve such clashes is a vexed question (see, e.g. Benhabib 2002). However, the desire to see the human remains of people one is culturally affiliated with returned to one's community for treatment that is decent and appropriate (in the eyes of that community) does not seem to involve any such clashes. Hence, if a cultural heritage institution is preventing this, by its refusal to repatriate remains, then it looks to be infringing on a group's cultural autonomy and thereby denying *justice* to that group.

Conclusion

From this discussion of the important benefits and harms that need to be weighed in a consideration of the repatriation issue, it can be seen that this is in some ways a tragic state of affairs, in which ethics does not dictate an obvious answer. On the one hand, there is no doubting the distress and humiliation that the failure to repatriate these remains has caused, and is causing, to many Indigenous communities.

However, we also need to take seriously the value of these remains for scientific inquiry. After all, we can only know the past through the traces of it that exist in the present—and thus these collections of remains are one of our windows into the human past; a point of access which, if destroyed, is gone forever. Of course, it is not the case that everything ought to be known, but such a loss would be a genuine harm, just as the distress and humiliation are also genuine harms. Nonetheless, the considerations above strongly suggest that the strength of the argument lies on the side of repatriation and that custodianship and control of the remains should lie with the appropriate Indigenous communities. This does not mean that no research into those remains can occur; but it does entail that those who wish to carry out such research require the informed consent of that community. In turn, this means that the justification of proposed research could not rest on vague claims that '[h]uman remains … have the potential to make a contribution to the public good, through research, teaching and, in some cases, display' (DCMS 2005: 7). Rather, any request would need to articulate precisely what kind of research was proposed, the sort of knowledge that could reasonably be expected to result from that research, how valuable this knowledge was likely to be, and to whom, and how this knowledge would be disseminated. The decision on whether or not to permit such research would then belong to the indigenous community. What this suggests, in other words, is that there is not such a great distance between the ethics of research undertaken on human remains and the ethics of research on living human subjects.

It should be noted that, throughout this discussion, we have made the simplifying assumption that there is a single, clear-cut community of 'descendants' who are clearly linked via cultural affiliation to the human remains under consideration and who are thereby entitled to request repatriation of those remains. As a final point, we will end with some brief remarks about the more problematic cases, where the link between the remains and an existing cultural group are contested. Famous examples of this are cases of very ancient remains, such as the 'Kow Swamp' remains and the 'Kennewick Man' [for discussion, see, e.g. Mulvaney (1991), Haller (2007)]. In these cases, we have remains that, according to the scientific evidence, have no direct genetic link to existing indigenous groups. It has thus been argued that, in such cases, those groups are not descendants of the ancient people whose remains these are, and hence, those groups have no valid ground to demand any special say in what happens to the remains. A few comments are worth making in regard to this. To begin with, this issue has sometimes been posed as a question of how to resolve a clash between the claims of science and the oral tradition of such groups (a tradition which may claim links between a cultural group and a place that are far longer than are in fact supported by the scientific data). But this way of construing the issue is not forced on us, for whilst direct descent may be sufficient to give an individual or a group reasonable grounds for being morally concerned about some human remains, it is clearly not a necessary condition. To take a simple example, we could recognise that an adopted child may feel a strong moral responsibility for her adoptive parents' remains and their fate and that this responsibility ought to be respected by others—a clear case in which genetic links between the parties are irrelevant. In a similar fashion, when indigenous people claim certain ancient remains as the remains of their 'ancestors', perhaps this is best construed as a moral claim (to be responsible for the fate of those remains) rather than a claim about the facts of genetic descent (which is thus competitive with the claims of science). One way of thinking of this is in terms of hospitality. If someone were to die in a foreign country, their remains might well be treated according to the forms of respect of that country—and to offer such respect is part of being hospitable to a stranger. In a similar way, an indigenous person might say: these ancient remains are found in what is really *our* country (i.e. we have the first right to offer such hospitality) and are thus deserving of being treated according to *our* forms of respect, not *yours*. If this suggestion is correct, then it means that the answer to the question about the appropriate treatment of very ancient remains is not one that can be resolved by ethics, or by science, but is inseparable from broader political processes of indigenous reconciliation and recognition.

References

Atkinson, H. (2010). The meanings and values of repatriation. In P. Turnbull & M. Pickering (Eds.), *The long way home: The meaning and values of repatriation* (pp. 15–19). New York: Berghahn.

Bahn, P. (1984). Do not disturb? Archaeology and the rights of the dead. *Journal of Applied Philosophy, 1*(2), 213–225.

Baker, B., Varney, T., Wilkinson, R., Anderson, L., & Liston, M. (2001). Repatriation and the study of human remains. In T. Bray (Ed.), *The future of the past: Archaeologists, native Americans and repatriation* (pp. 69–82). New York: Garland.

Benhabib, S. (2002). *The claims of culture: Equality and diversity in the global era*. Princeton, NJ: Princeton University Press.

Cubillo, F. (2010). Repatriating our ancestors: Who will speak for the dead? In P. Turnbull & M. Pickering (Eds.), *The long way home: The meaning and values of repatriation* (pp. 20–26). New York: Berghahn.

Department for Culture, Media and Sport, UK. (2005). *Guidance for the care of human remains in museums*. London: DCMS.

Fforde, C. (2002). Collection, repatriation and identity. In C. Fforde, J. Hubert, & P. Turnbull (Eds.), *The dead and their possessions: Repatriation in principle, policy and practice* (pp. 25–46). London: Routledge.

Fforde, C. (2004). *Collecting the dead: Archaeology and the reburial issue*. London: Duckworth.

Goldman, A. (1999). *Knowledge in a social world*. Oxford: Oxford University Press.

Gonzalez-Ruibal, A. (2010). Colonialism and European archaeology. In J. Lydon & U. Z. Rizvi (Eds.), *Handbook of postcolonial archaeology* (pp. 39–50). Walnut Creek: Left Coast Press.

Green, M., & Gordon, P. (2010). Repatriation: Australian perspectives. In J. Lydon & U. Z. Rizvi (Eds.), *Handbook of postcolonial archaeology* (pp. 257–265). Walnut Creek: Left Coast Press.

Haller, S. (2007). Grave concerns: Concepts of self and respect for the dead. *International Journal of Applied Philosophy, 21*(2), 195–212.

Jones, G., & Harris, R. (1998). Archaeological human remains: Scientific, cultural, and ethical considerations. *Current Anthropology, 39*(2), 253–264.

Joyce, R. (2002). Academic freedom, stewardship and cultural heritage: Weighing the interests of stakeholders in crafting repatriation approaches. In C. Fforde, J. Hubert, & P. Turnbull (Eds.), *The dead and their possessions: Repatriation in principle, policy and practice* (pp. 99–107). London: Routledge.

Meskell, L. (Ed.). (2009). *Cosmopolitan archaeologies*. Durham: Duke University Press.

Moreton, S. (1839). *Crania Americana: A comparative view of the skulls of various aboriginal nations of North and South America. To which is prefixed an essay on the varieties of the human species*. London: Simpkin, Marshall and Co. Available at http://archive.org/details/cihm_38366

Mulgan, T. (1999). The place of the dead in liberal political philosophy. *Journal of Political Philosophy, 7*(1), 52–70.

Mulvaney, J. (1991). Past regained, future lost: The Kow Swamp Pleistocene burials. *Antiquity, 65*, 12–21.

Onsman, A. (2004). Truganini's funeral. *Island, 96*(Autumn), 38–52.

Pitcher, G. (1984). The misfortunes of the dead. *American Philosophical Quarterly, 21*(2), 183–188.

Riding In, J. (1992). Without ethics and morality: A historical overview of imperial archaeology and American Indians. *Arizona State Law Journal, 24*, 11–34.

Scarre, G. (2003). Archaeology and respect for the dead. *Journal of Applied Philosophy, 20*(3), 237–249.

Scarre, G. (2006). Can archaeology harm the dead? In C. Scarre & G. Scarre (Eds.), *The ethics of archaeology: Philosophical perspectives on archaeological practice* (pp. 181–198). Cambridge: Cambridge University Press.

Shklar, J. (1989). The liberalism of fear. In N. Rosenblum (Ed.), *Liberalism and the moral life* (pp. 21–38). Cambridge: Harvard University Press.

Tarlow, S. (2001). Decoding ethics. *Public Archaeology, 1*, 245–259.

Taylor, C. (1994). The politics of recognition. In A. Gutmann (Ed.), *Multiculturalism: Examining the politics of recognition* (pp. 25–74). Princeton, NJ: Princeton University Press.

Truscott, M. C. (2006). *Repatriation of Indigenous cultural property*. Paper prepared for the 2006 Australian State of the Environment Committee, Department of the Environment and Heritage, Canberra, at http://www.deh.gov.au/soe/2006/emerging/repatriation/index.html

Turnbull, P. (2010). The Vermillion Accord and the significance of the history of the scientific procurement and use of Indigenous Australian bodily remains. In P. Turnbull & M. Pickering (Eds.), *The long way home: The meaning and values of repatriation* (pp. 117–134). New York: Berghahn.

Vines, P. (1999). Bodily remains in the cemetery and the burial ground: A comparative anthropology of law and death or how long can I stay? In D. Manderson (Ed.), *Courting death: The law of mortality* (pp. 111–127). London: Pluto.

Warnock, M. (2004). *An intelligent person's guide to ethics*. London: Duckworth Overlook.

Wilkinson, T. M. (2002). Last rights: The ethics of research on the dead. *Journal of Applied Philosophy, 19*(1), 31–41.

Williams, B. (2005). Modernity and ethical life. In G. Hawthorn (Ed.), *In the beginning was the deed: Realism and moralism in political argument* (pp. 40–51). Princeton, NJ: Princeton University Press.

Zielinski, S. (2010). *Henrietta Lacks' 'immortal' cells*. Smithsonian.com, at http://www.smithsonianmag.com/science-nature/Henrietta-Lacks-Immortal-Cells.html

Chapter 7
The Ethics of Visibility: Archaeology, Conservation and Memories of Settler Colonialism

Tracy Ireland

Introduction

In this chapter, I explore some of the ethical implications of the practices and products of heritage conservation and historical archaeology in the context of settler colonialism. Archaeological excavation, followed by the conservation in situ of archaeological remains, are practices and processes that make particular things visible, therefore providing the opportunity for 'memory-matter engagements', activated by the affective qualities of archaeological traces (Rose and Tolia-Kelly 2012:5). My focus here is on how urban heritage conservation takes these made-visible vestiges out of the realm of archaeological research and transforms them into a city's curated past in a conscious heritage, place and memory-making project. The products of this process—historic sites, conserved objects and in situ remains—can corroborate the veracity of shared memories of colonial history and national birth, but they also allow for creative uses by diverse communities in identity and locality building and in the production of counter-memory (Hall 2006).

However, a tension is created in the way this archaeological and conservation process privileges the material aspects of the past and reinforces a perception of the invisibility of the pasts of indigenous and other marginalised groups and perpetuates their absence from the representational and symbolic spaces of the city. While there are now numerous examples of ethical and decolonising approaches that aim to correct the absence of indigenous and other groups in the archaeology and heritage of periods since colonisation (e.g. Lydon and Rivzi 2010), the extent to which these approaches have transformed the heritage spaces/places of settler cities, or the legal and operational structures of heritage management, remains open to question (Byrne 2003; Joyce 2006; Lydon 2005; Smith 2006a, b).

T. Ireland (✉)
Faculty of Arts and Design, University of Canberra, Bruce, ACT 2601, Australia
e-mail: tracy.ireland@canberra.edu.au

© Springer Science+Business Media New York 2015
T. Ireland, J. Schofield (eds.), *The Ethics of Cultural Heritage*,
Ethical Archaeologies: The Politics of Social Justice 4,
DOI 10.1007/978-1-4939-1649-8_7

This chapter draws on a broader research project which explores how and why urban archaeological remains have been conserved in settler cities, considering examples from Australia, New Zealand, Quebec in Canada and the northeastern United States (Ireland 2012a, b, c). In this research, I approach archaeological conservation as a socially embedded creative practice, rather than a politically neutral scientific technique, which responds to desires for heritage and commemoration by employing a distinctive aesthetic vocabulary. Central to this aesthetic are the affective and sensory qualities of archaeological remains: drawing on cultural memories of romantic ruins, and their potential to provide alternative renderings of history, these 'ruins of colonialism' provide embodied experiences of authenticity, place and identity while at the same time evoking the 'old world' of Europe and its richly layered urban landscapes (Hetherington 2010). Significant examples of these types of settler archaeological places include Pointe-à-Callière in Montreal (Montreal Museum of Archaeology and History), the recently opened St-Louis Forts and Châteaux National Historic Site in Quebec City, the President's House in Philadelphia (USA), Te Aro Pa in Wellington, New Zealand, and the Big Dig site at the Sydney Harbour Youth Hostel in Sydney (Figs. 7.1–7.4). Alongside these elaborate conserved and curated displays are numerous smaller-scale examples where fragments of the settler past are conserved in situ or where interpretations or representations of the past have been created in urban locations marking or commemorating sites where archaeological excavations have taken place (Figs. 7.5–7.7). These inscriptions on the urban landscape materialise evidence of progressive history, performing rhetorical work for the settler nation, speaking for its legitimacy and its successful development from remote col-

Fig. 7.1 Pointe-à-Callière, the Montreal Museum of Archaeology and History, photograph by the author 2011

Fig. 7.2 The President's House Site, Philadelphia, USA. Photograph by the author 2011

Fig. 7.3 Te Aro Pa archaeological site display in central Wellington, New Zealand. Photograph by the author 2013

ony to modern nation. But through their material endurance and visibility, these places also provide opportunities for individuals and groups to seek ethical experiences of reconciliation, recognition and respect in terms of their own particular social justice concerns and identity politics (Ireland 2014).

Fig. 7.4 Artefact display within the Sydney Harbour Youth Hostel which incorporates the Cumberland and Gloucester Street archaeological site and the Big Dig Archaeological Education Centre, Sydney, Australia. Photograph by the author 2012

Fig. 7.5 Windows looking into the basement archaeological display of the Windmill Street Cottages in Millers Point, Sydney, Australia. Photograph by the author 2012

Fig. 7.6 Towns Place precinct incorporating archaeological remains and artefact displays in Walsh Bay, Sydney, Australia. Photograph by the author 2012

Fig. 7.7 Parramatta Justice Precinct display of archaeological remains of colonial hospital site, in Parramatta, Australia. Photograph by the author 2011

Discussions about these kinds of settler archaeological heritage places have tended to centre on their educational potential and the means used to interpret them and present their cultural significance to the 'public'. In the important example of the African American Burial Ground in New York, the conservation and commemoration of the site and the individuals interred there followed as a result of intense public and professional debates about archaeological ethics, relationships with stakeholder communities and the politics of identity and recognition—debates which had a significant impact upon the way historical archaeology, conservation and commemoration have since been practised (e.g. La Roche and Blakey 1997; Jeppson 2011). Indeed, many of these urban archaeological places have been conserved as a result of struggles between competing communities of interest, drawn into sharp opposition because of the visibility of these contests in meaning-laden urban space (Ireland 2012a). In shifting the focus here to 'visibility', I aim to move away from the now more familiar discussions of the ethics of stakeholder consultation, stewardship and preservation, to a consideration of the ethical and political implications of how things are made visible, responding to calls for a more careful analysis in heritage studies of the link between visibility, materiality and power (Smith 2006a, b:61; Rose and Tolia-Kelly 2012:9).

Ethics, Theory and Practice

In archaeological and heritage conservation literature there is a tendency to separate ethics into their own domain, generally concerned, as I have just mentioned, with stewardship, professionalism and the discipline's relationships with and responsibilities to outsiders, including non-experts, 'communities' and 'stakeholders' (Beaudry 2009; Zimmerman et al. 2003). I approach ethics as embedded in all aspects and at all levels of archaeological and heritage conservation theory and practice. Often, however, the ethical underpinnings of theory and practice are not made explicit, either because of their normative function as disciplinary standards reflecting universal, modernist concepts of heritage and conservation or because they are interpreted not as ethics, but as allegiance to a particular body of theory or practice that offers the possibility of producing either more accurate or inclusive representations of the past or engagements with communities in the present. This last theme is particularly prominent in historical archaeology in the settler world, where social justice issues deriving from, for instance, indigenous dispossession, forced migration, slavery, the expansion of capitalism and extractive industries, environmental degradation, etc., are central to the histories of settler nations, their cities and urbanised areas.

Debates about the relationship between theory and practice in archaeology and heritage conservation often project a dichotomy between theory-driven and practice-driven perspectives. Otero-Pailos claims that parts of the American conservation profession have been deeply anti-intellectual and antagonistic towards theorised approaches in conservation (Otero-Pailos 2007a:viii), while Laurajane

Smith (2006b:314) described how in Australian archaeology those who debate theory are often criticised as failing to really 'do' archaeology. In both cases, intellectual work is seen as a dereliction of the ethical duty to just get on and do the necessary physical work of conserving or excavating archaeological material. This polarisation can also be seen as influenced by implicit, competing ethics—on the one hand, a kind of 'muscular' ethic that values 'doing', 'work' and concrete outcomes, and on the other hand, a self-reflective stance that condemns non-reflective practitioners as naively supporting structures of inequality through their failure to critique the link between power and knowledge, or to acknowledge the implications of critical insights which challenge disciplinary authority and its power structures, such as the heritage management system itself (e.g. Smith and Waterton 2009). It is therefore helpful to approach these discussions, which are often interpreted as about the importance or relevance of theory in archaeology and conservation, as actually about contested values and ethical positions. My study of how settler pasts are made visible in urban environments moves towards a more reflective practice of heritage management, first by problematising conservation, which is generally simply accepted as inherently ethical and good (Otero-Pailos 2004:6), and then by producing a clearer understanding of the ethical aims and blind spots of the historical archaeological and heritage management theories and practices that have produced these materials and places, as well as some of the narratives and cultural memories that structure people's experience of them.

Visibility

...visibility is not only an effect of power but also its condition of possibility.

Gordon (2002:132)

Just as there are visible and invisible ethics in archaeology and heritage management, there are ongoing ethical implications derived from how these processes create visibility/invisibility and how their visible products are consumed, experienced and mobilised in cultural politics, and from the ongoing material existence and changing use of these things and places. Watson and Waterton have recently discussed the visual representations through which heritage is consumed, showing how these representations can appear to naturally inhere in material culture, masking how meaning has been constructed through the processes of heritage and conservation and also through the changes made by successive generations of conservation activities: 'This sees the reification of the social relations that create, sustain and reproduce heritage objects as autonomous things that tell their own story about the past, which is expressed, limited and satisfied by their very materiality' (Waterton and Watson 2010:2).

Considering the relationship between visibility and power highlights the recursive nature of material culture and the urban landscape, as both a reflection of and a material agent influencing the practice and performance of social relationships, memory and identity. This of course has been a prominent research theme in archae-ology, cultural geography and other disciplines, building on a Foucauldian concept of power, as well as the insights of thinkers concerned with place and space such as Lefebvre (1991) and de Certeau (1984). However, archaeological remains them-selves often appear to evade ideology and theory, self-authenticating through their materiality, their embeddedness in place and their apparent rarity, survival and endurance through time. Archaeological conservation in situ is not a neutral act but a process that monumentalises these materials, creating cultural and economic val-ues and shaping practices of place by imprinting particular memories and narra-tives. In situ conservation is a form of historicity, a way of visibly representing the past, its potential for recovery and its relationship to the present.

While archaeological excavation is designed to recover the faintest remaining traces of human occupation through its increasingly forensic methods, archaeolo-gy's foundational doctrine of stratigraphy tends to reinforce concepts of linear suc-cessions and replacements, rather than complex forms of continuity (Rubertone 2008:19). In discussing the American tradition of 'inventive placemaking' by pres-ervationists who have reconstructed sites using archaeological evidence, Patricia Rubertone concluded that such reconstructions are aimed at an audience who seek (or are assumed to need) education and entertainment, rather than demonstrating the belonging or continuity of contemporary Indigenous communities, who often, in fact, continue to live nearby (Rubertone 2008:19). In a similar vein, writing about Latin America, Gustavo Verdesio (2010:351) claims that Western eyes are precon-ditioned to the 'ruin' as the expected signature of the human past, suggesting that archaeologists have been culpable in allowing pre-Columbian pasts to remain invis-ible, leading, he argues, to the 'ruin' of archaeology itself.

In many settler contexts, the concept of the cultural landscape has been enthusi-astically taken up as a more useful frame for approaching the complexities of colo-nial cultural exchange and enduring forms of cultural practice and interaction between people and environments. The landscape approach has produced a rich array of insights in archaeology and heritage management but, as scholars that work with these concepts have highlighted, this approach risks once again the con-flation of indigenous people with nature and landscape, rather than with contempo-rary urban realities. In urban contexts, the evolved and designed spaces of settler cities are both evidence of, and metaphors for, the transformation and modernisa-tion of colonial frontiers. The urban fabric of the city appears to foreclose on opportunities to experience or visualise the material record of prior indigenous occupations. The sometimes elusive and fragile nature of the archaeological traces of the pasts of indigenous, oppressed or impoverished groups, when they are miraculously discovered in an urban location, means that while their survival or antiquity may be briefly marvelled at, they rarely possess the visible, material qualities that can be rendered stable, legible and permanent through the processes of heritage conservation. While many historians, geographers and archaeologists have worked on recovering indigenous history and memory in urban contexts (e.g. Edmonds 2010; Gelder and Jacobs 1998; Karskens 2009; Silliman 2010), the conserved and displayed material origins of settler nations and cities reproduces the logic of 'colonialist evolutionism—a march towards the ultimate in urbanity and 'civilisation" (Herzfeld 2006:128). In fact, this retrospective nationalising of settler histories has created a new form of invisibility for the colonial past, subsuming it into national histories of inevitable development and progress. For instance, the term 'colonial' is rarely used in Australian heritage management, and in my own published work, I have often been encouraged by reviewers to substitute the terms 'Australian' or 'historical' when referring to archaeological sites dating to the colonial period.

One of the distinctive aspects of the city that is of importance in this consideration of ethics, visibility and heritage is the close relationship between urban space and political power (Wells 2007:139). The incorporation of archaeological remains into the way a city displays its heritage is obviously one of a range of practices of monument and memory creation that support the nation-state and its imagined community (Herzfeld 2006:129; Hamilakis 2007). Governments, corporations, communities and individuals compete in the urban arena with their overlapping and interwoven agendas—from maintaining and demonstrating the legitimacy of state power through to the recognition of more marginal identity claims. Thus, the case histories of urban archaeological conservation projects—which groups support conservation, the role of governments, the role of capital and corporations and the arguments made by experts such as archaeologists, historians and heritage specialists—become object lessons in how interest groups compete for visibility and how visibility is necessary for strategies of not only social control but also of resistance (Gordon 2002:132).

Perhaps one form of intervention in heritage's insistent focus on the visible and material has been the rise in scholarly and popular interest in haunting and ghosts (e.g. Cameron 2008; Edensor 2008). Analyses of colonial and postcolonial geography and literature discuss the ghost as a means of expressing settler guilt and moral burden and have sought to expose and name these colonial ghosts, giving a form of visibility to suppressed histories (Gelder and Jacobs 1998). However, Emilie Cameron has suggested that while the prevalence of haunting tropes in the literature and cultural studies of Canada, the United States and Australia seems to be an attempt to conceptualise what cannot easily be seen and to acknowledge colonial trauma, this tendency can have unintended, negative political consequences. 'The Aboriginal ghost has been used to evoke a generalised sense of history in the Canadian landscape, but always with a sense of linearity and succession' (Cameron 2008:384). She suggests that 'confining the Indigenous to the ghostly also has the potential to reinscribe the interests of the powerful upon the meanings and memories of place' and urges the development of approaches to the phenomenology of place, and to the sensual, affective qualities of material, that are more politically aware and less self-referential (Cameron 2008:390). Despite my scepticism about the efficacy and ethics of calling on the ghostly as a way of acknowledging invisible histories, it is important to remain open to new ways of seeing and the possibilities for altering perceptions through continuing engagement with visualities and materialities. Jane Lydon has recently argued that although colonial photographs of Indigenous people in Australia have usually been interpreted as evidence of the 'othering' of Indigenous subjects, they also, at specific historical moments, provided a form of visibility for remote Aboriginal people that allowed 'stories of injustice to take hold of the popular imagination'. She concludes that 'invisibility is the ultimate form of racism' (Lydon 2012:17).

Conservation Ethics

As Frank Matero (2006:57) has neatly summarised, archaeological sites are made, not found. In situ conservation is the term used in archaeological heritage management for conservation processes that preserve and retain archaeological remains in the place where they were found. An underpinning premise of in situ conservation is that it is only ethical to expose and display remains if their long-term preservation can be assured. In situ conservation therefore implies a range of long-term technical and ethical challenges—remains that were once buried in a stable environment are exposed to an unstable one where changes in light, heat, moisture and temperature may affect different materials in different ways, often causing their accelerated deterioration. The ethical premise of in situ conservation is that it will preserve context and authenticity in historical, environmental and archaeological research terms, as opposed to the loss of authenticity that occurs if remains are removed and reconstructed in more convenient locations, as often occurred before the professionalisation of heritage conservation (e.g. Lyon 2007). In situ conservation is therefore a technique whereby archaeological remains are not only made visible in the urban landscape but also a means by which they visibly testify to their authenticity—these remains are not monuments that commemorate past events but are traces of the event itself. Archaeological remains have therefore been seen as challenging modernist concepts of 'progressive sequential time' (Hamilakis 2011:409). However, in situ archaeological remains in the city also display evidence of stratigraphy and their exposure through excavation, reinforcing the fact that unlike romantic ruins that have been eroded slowly by time, these remains were once erased by progress and politics.

Archaeological conservation has a particular history, and the concept of in situ conservation has gained increased momentum in recent decades with the formalisation of a number of charters, such as the ICOMOS Charter for the Protection and Management of the Archaeological Heritage and the European Convention on the Protection of the Archaeological Heritage (Willems 2008), and by the growing number of international examples of this genre (e.g. Matero 2000:74; Nixon 2004; Keily 2008). While these European charters have clearly influenced archaeological heritage management policy and practice in Australia, New Zealand, the United States and Canada, it is also important to understand the different historical trajectories and social and political contexts of these regional traditions of archaeology and conservation. Heritage management literature tends to explain the growing use of conservation in situ as evidence of the 'maturing' or 'development' of settler societies masking the complexity of the local and global political, economic and cultural factors at play in this process.

As I have noted above, conservation is often portrayed as inherently ethical. Only in recent analyses of heritage have the implications of the uncritical acceptance of this position been discussed (e.g. Harrison 2013; Russell 2012). Harrison suggests that continuing to conserve an ever-broadening material heritage is not only economically unsustainable but also avoids critical analyses of how collective memory is produced in the social relations between conserved traces and absences. In a similar vein, Russell suggests that archaeologists need a deeper, self-reflective engagement with what he terms the 'archaeological choice' and its ethical implications, moving towards a form of 'posthumanist' ethics that value the recognition of nonhuman agency in the processes of decay (Russell 2012:264). However, the mechanics via which we might operationalise an ethical form of forgetting remain obscure as we continue to see the ever-increasing use of heritage by communities in the sociopolitics of identity and recognition (e.g. Graham and Howard 2008).

A central principle of conservation ethics as they developed through the twentieth century is that of expertly defined 'authenticity' (Jokilehto 2009). The notion of a universal standard of heritage authenticity, exemplified by the World Heritage concept, has long been challenged by the postmodern focus on cultures and diversity and the influence of postcolonial theory across a range of disciplines. In terms of in situ archaeological conservation, I have already discussed how authenticity is demonstrated at one level through the location of remains in place, below the later developments of the city. Authenticity is also produced in this context through the distinctive aesthetics of in situ conservation. Jorge Otero-Pailos has discussed how the practice of the total reconstruction of colonial buildings on the basis of fragmentary remains, which had been very popular in America from the 1920s, was criticised in the 1970s as being elitist because professionals provided the public with a complete, fixed interpretation of the past (2007b:iii). He cites as a key example of the critique of the total reconstruction process, and a turning point for historical archaeological sites conservation, the famous 1976 Venturi and Rausch design known as the 'ghost house', on the site of Benjamin Franklin's former residence in Philadelphia (Fig. 7.8). This design has since been emulated on many archaeological sites around the world, including Australia (Fig. 7.9).

The more recently excavated site of the President's House, also in Philadelphia, is where the remains of the house occupied by the nation's first president, George Washington, are conserved within a 'monument' (in the sense that it is a structure designed to evoke the memory of the absent building) that echoes the premise of Venturi and Rausch's 1970s design. The 'monument' takes the form of an architectural rendering of the plan and elevations of the house. It is a less radical design than the Venturi and Rausch 'ghost house', but replicates the aesthetics of the earlier monument in terms of its evocation of absence rather than attempting to fill the

Fig. 7.8 The Venturi and Rausch designed 'ghost house' (1976) Franklin Court, above the archaeological remains of Benjamin Franklin's demolished residence, Philadelphia, USA. Photograph by the author 2011

historical void with a reconstruction (Levin 2011). At the Museum of Sydney, opened in 1995, where the archaeological remains of the first Government House built by the British in 1788 are preserved, a similar conservation aesthetic also prevailed, directly emulating the pavement plan and periscopes of Philadelphia's 'ghost house' site (Fig. 7.8). Otero-Pailos suggests that this 'new conservation poetic involved striving towards an aesthetic that made its own making visible' (Otero-Pailos et al. 2010:76). The ethical imperative here relates to the perceived democratisation of heritage conservation by employing transparency and truthfulness about what is really known about the past. Venturi and Rausch's radical, artistic vision has now become a form of orthodoxy for urban archaeological sites—the fragmentary remains and ghostly evocations of past structures stand for the truthfulness and reliability of the heritage conservation process, thus establishing authenticity.

Fig. 7.9 Foundation Park in the Rocks Sydney, Australia. Archaeological remains of terrace houses built against a steep rock escarpment. Photograph by the author 2011

Visibility and Memory

The catalyst for authentic encounters with a past made visible and tangible through archaeology and conservation is memory. Archaeological remains provide a distinctive kind of aesthetic resource for memory production and are frequently thought of as allowing direct access to the past, as a form of material memory. These archaeological places are rather theatres of memory—a stage where rituals of memory are improvised, rehearsed and performed. Authenticity, as we have just seen, is not something that places and things 'just have', it is an effect constructed through the discourse of heritage and the 'rhetorical work' that a place performs (Blair et al. 2010:27). I have suggested that archaeological remains conserved in situ encode their authenticity through their location in place, their unreconstructed, fragmentary form, and through the way in which they are produced by archaeology—a practice defined by its promise of trustworthy, scientific knowledge of the past. But perhaps what is most interesting about these archaeological memory places is the moment when their perceived authenticity allows particular memories or narratives to 'stick' to them. We can see that archaeology, in uncovering lost remains, allows new forms of public memory to be performed, and that the conservation of these material touchstones becomes imperative when particular 'affective intensities', such as belonging, pride, desire for recognition, desire for restorative justice, empathy and compassion, are associated with or invested in these places (Blair et al. 2010:16).

Settler nations are particularly self-conscious about the legitimacy of their 'birth', and archaeology has provided memory places animated by the affective intensities of pride, belonging and desire for recognition. For example, Pointe-à-Callière in Montreal makes visible the origins of francophone 'civilisation' in North America, while the remains of the first acts of British colonisation in Australia are seen at the Museum of Sydney. However, the narrative that 'stuck' to the remains made visible by archaeology at the President's House site in Philadelphia, while they are also clearly associated with the 'birth of the nation', was that related to the enslaved Africans who had been part of George Washington's household (Levin 2011; Ireland 2014). One of the community groups formed to lobby for the conservation of this site, called the 'Avenging the Ancestors Coalition', sought to give visibility to the enslaved individuals who had once lived on the site, as well as to the issues of slavery and race that had been absent from the National Parks Services' plans to interpret the historic Liberty Bell Centre precinct prior to the excavation of the house site. In this case, the uncovering of the tangible foundations of slave quarters gave a physical focus for tentative and difficult discussions between visitors, archaeologists and others about race and slavery. Archaeologist Jed Levin suggests 'Somehow the physicality of the remains made it harder to deny or avoid this history. The archaeological uncovering was also the uncovering of something that had been hidden…, the remains themselves were unexpected - they were like the past reaching up to people and jolting them out of the predictability of American life' (Ireland 2014).

The Ethics of Historical Archaeology

> One of the key themes that does hold historical archaeology together is that we walk in a uniquely dangerous space of the human past, a space between often very powerful 'master narratives' of cultural and social identity and much smaller, stranger, potentially subversive narratives of archaeological material.
>
> Johnson (1999:34)

If the conditions of possibility for the practice of archaeology include the discovery of the 'otherness' of the past, 'the recognition of differences within what is similar', as claimed by Olivier (2004:206), then the point of emergence of archaeologies of the colonial past of settler societies is of particular interest. It is not deep time that is perceived as separating settler societies from their colonial, archaeological past— this past is admittedly shallow. It is rather the perception that the colonial past is over, left behind and replaced by a more mature state of modernity and nationhood that gives rise to these kinds of history, heritage and memory-making activities. Historical archaeology in Canada and the United States commenced in the nineteenth century as a process closely tied to nationalistic causes and implicitly understood as 'useful' in contributing to civic society and patriotism, in contrast to the more rationalised, scientific approach to the so-called prehistoric archaeology of the past of Native American peoples (Dawdy 2009:134). Similarly in Australia, archaeology's founding figure, John Mulvaney, was a staunch advocate for the establishment of historical archaeology and heritage legislation from the 1970s, but on a different footing from research into 'prehistory' and the antiquity of human occupation of the Australian continent. In essays such as *The Heritage Value of Historical Relics*: *A Plea for Romantic Intellectualism* (first published in 1979), he referred to the evocative character of historic sites, their role in giving pleasure and their importance for understanding Australian cultural identity (Mulvaney 1991). At a time when approaches derived from processual or the 'New Archaeology' dominated cultural heritage management in Australia, Mulvaney argued for heritage management techniques that appreciated the romantic, experiential values of historic sites and their role in building what was seen as much-needed shared historical narratives.

Historical archaeology's potential role as a 'democratising force', in both giving a past to 'people without history' and in revealing history's systematic erasure or distortion of events, has been broadly proclaimed since the 1970s. The American folklorist Henry Glassie (1977:29) articulated this as historical archaeology's potential to act against the 'superficial and elitist tales of viciousness' which formed 'myths for the contemporary power structure'. These aims have been a driving force for developments in the theory and practice of historical archaeology around the settler world. They arise from a diverse array of empathies and philosophical approaches, but they share a focus on contemporary social inequalities and a sense of moral responsibility for the burden of the past in the present.

Concern for the oppressed had been a central theme in American historical archaeology concerning race, class and gender (Little 1994:10), while studies of slavery and colonialism also aimed to 'give back history' (e.g. Orser 1996). The work of the American historical archaeologist Mark Leone has consistently focused on the historical archaeologist's responsibility to challenge the way capitalism uses 'biology and history' to fix essential identities (Leone and Potter 1999:viii). In 1973, Leone declared one of archaeology's major rationales to be the 'empirical substantiation of national mythology', but what he found offensive in this situation was not complicity with nationalism per se, but the naiveté of archaeologists in their lack of understanding of the operation of ideology in their practice and, consequently, in its perpetuation of the dominant ideologies which underpinned social inequality (Leone 1973:133). In 2010, Leone gave a more straightforward account of what had always underpinned his Marxist approach to historical archaeology: his emotions and feelings. 'Because we do not inherit a set of questions that are clear and well thought out, I suggest that those questions are within us, given by our experience and education, and are brought forth by our emotional reactions to our own history when we see remains and results every day' (Leone 2010:8). While the relationship between archaeology and the nation is now generally well studied by archaeologists (e.g. in relation to Australian historical archaeology and nationalism, see Ireland 2002), it's been suggested that 'American archaeology has been left almost entirely unscathed by critiques of nationalist archaeology' (Dawdy 2009:134). Certainly, capitalism has been the preeminent concern of politically and ethically engaged approaches in American historical archaeology.

In Australia and New Zealand, postcolonial critiques have been more central to the ethical aspirations of archaeologists engaging with contemporary social justice issues. While there has been widespread recognition of the way in which the historical burden of colonialism in Australia has impacted upon the archaeology of Indigenous people (previously called 'prehistory'), historical archaeology has tended to be somewhat separated from these debates about archaeological ethics. This is because they have been largely concerned with the moral responsibilities surrounding research into the past of 'others' and their descendant communities, while historical archaeology traditionally focused on the colonial origins of the collective 'us' of the imagined national community. In the 1990s there were calls for the development of a *historical archaeology* of Indigenous peoples to assist in historicising their recent experiences, include them in national narratives and make their past visible as a counter to the dominant visibility of colonial heritage in the landscape (e.g. Byrne 1996, 2003; 2003; Colley and Bickford 1996; Murray 1996). Such calls have been enthusiastically acted upon, and Indigenous historical archaeology is now a major component of Australia's historical archaeological research (e.g. Lydon 2009; Paterson 2010).

In New Zealand, the problem of archaeological invisibility has not been such a significant factor because of the tradition of interest in Maori settlements and fortifications; however, archaeological interest was traditionally focused on the reconstruction of 'precontact' Maori life (Bedford 1996). The Maoritanga, or 'Maori Renaissance', and subsequent policies of biculturalism developed since the 1980s have encouraged a research focus on past Maori cultural dynamics and adaptation in the context of colonialism (Phillips 2000). The archaeological site of Te Aro Pa (Fig. 7.3) is remarkable for its conservation of Maori cultural remains right in the centre of the capital city of Wellington. Te Aro Pa was a Maori habitation site occupied in the early colonial period from the 1820s to the 1880s, and the remains of surviving structures (whare ponga) have been conserved in the ground floor of a new apartment building. The conserved site was opened in 2008 with cultural rituals conducted by Maori people from Wellington and Taranaki which aimed to reawaken the place.

Historical archaeology's focus on a past which is directly and demonstrably involved with present social conditions means that it, more than other forms of archaeology, has long been seen to have the potential to act as what Foucault called a history to 'diagnose the present', as an 'ontology of ourselves' (Foucault 1986: 96). However, a factor that has perhaps limited the impact of the ethical aims of historical archaeology is a failure to address the teleological effects of the modernist project in which it finds itself doubly enfolded—if we accept the proposition that historical archaeology emerges out of modernity's (and thus also nationalism's) self-conscious historicism, but also takes capitalist modernity as its central object of study (Dawdy 2010:763). This has led to current ethical concerns about the ever-expanding use of archaeology to produce a visible material heritage for particular groups to use in the politics of identity and recognition (Dawdy 2009; Matthews 2006; Waterton and Smith 2009). Dawdy has written of how her experiences of doing cultural heritage assessment work in New Orleans in the aftermath of Hurricane Katrina made her question the role of archaeology in producing 'heritage', calling for a more ethical archaeology in the service of contemporary problems, such as climate change, disaster and recovery or alternative forms of energy and resource management. She expresses scepticism about the possibility of doing meaningful community archaeology because the agenda is inevitably set, she claims, by archaeologists rather than by community members. She calls for an ethics of honesty: 'So I am simply asking us to be honest. Most public archaeology should really be called public relations archaeology' (Dawdy 2009:138). However, discussions about 'community archaeology' which are looking more closely at how communities of interest are created, rather than reflected, through the practices of archaeology, the materials it makes visible and the narratives and emotions it links to places, offer important new directions for the development of ideas about archaeological ethics and professional responsibilities (e.g. Carman 2011; Matthews 2006; Smith and Waterton 2009).

Conclusions: Visible Ethics

I predict there will be a growing acceptance in our professions that most people in the world relate to the material past via their emotions, their imaginations, their belief in the supernatural and in the immanence of ancestors. In heritage practice it will come partly via the realization that conservation solutions that fail to mesh with local beliefs and practices are not solutions at all. It will come, in other words, when authoritarian conservation is rejected as morally unsustainable.

Byrne (2009: 249)

In this chapter, I have reviewed a number of themes that emerge from a consideration of the intertwined practices of historical archaeology and heritage conservation and how these practices have conceptualised the ways in which they give communities access to 'their heritage' by providing physical and intellectual forms of visibility to invisible, forgotten or suppressed pasts. Archaeology has been used to provide places where shared memories of the colonial past can be created, performed and contested. I have foregrounded how the ethical responsibilities entailed in creating visibility through heritage conservation and its manipulation of urban materialities have been thought of largely in terms of stewardship, the authenticity of in situ conservation, and how visibility provides recognition of identities and shared memories. Historical archaeology has often been seen as linked to claims for restorative social justice and to revealing the historical foundations for embedded social inequalities; however, the roles played by state and corporate funding in enabling the conservation of archaeological remains in the highly visible political landscapes of the city have ensured that colonial archaeological remains perform important rhetorical work for nation states.

It would be simplistic, however, to see these urban historical archaeological sites only as the 'ruins of colonialism', as monuments that continue to celebrate and bolster settler or neocolonialism—their role in the present is more complex than this. In particular, the potential of these archaeological sites and their archives to endure and outlive the particular sociopolitical contexts within which they were created means that they provide material artefacts that can subsequently be reinterrogated and reshaped in response to new questions (Jeppson 2006). These places are thus examples of what Ann Laura Stoler terms 'imperial debris'—locations where we can examine the 'political life of imperial debris, the longevity of structures of dominance, and the uneven pace with which people can extricate themselves from the colonial order of things' (Stoler 2008:193). The visibility created by archaeology and heritage conservation brings particular ethical responsibilities derived from how visibility provides the condition of possibility for strategies of power and control, but also the possibility for strategies of resistance. If we agree that 'looking is a responsibility; a visceral, ethical and historically conscious practice', then this gives us grounds to rethink how we understand the ethical implications of archaeology and conservation (Rose and Tolia-Kelly 2012:5). We need not only visible ethics, in terms of the practice and theory of our professions, but also, more broadly, an ethics of visibility that help us to understand what it is these practices have created.

References

Beaudry, M. (2009). Ethical issues in historical archaeology. In D. Gaimster & T. Majewski (Eds.), *International handbook of historical archaeology* (pp. 17–29). New York: Springer.

Bedford, S. (1996). Post-contact Maori: The ignored component in New Zealand archaeology. *The Journal of the Polynesian Society, 105*(4), 411–439.

Blair, C., Dickinson, G., & Ott, B. L. (2010). Introduction: Rhetoric/memory/place. In G. Dickinson, C. Blair, & B. L. Ott (Eds.), *Places of public memory The rhetoric of museums and memorials* (pp. 1–54). Tuscaloosa: The University of Alabama Press.

Byrne, D. (1996). Deep nation: Australia's acquisition of an indigenous past. *Aboriginal History, 20*, 82–107.

Byrne, D. (2003). Nervous landscapes: Race and space in Australia. *Journal of Social Archaeology, 3*(2), 169–193.

Byrne, D. (2009). A critique of unfeeling heritage. In L. Smith & N. Akagawa (Eds.), *Intangible heritage* (pp. 229–252). London and New York: Routledge.

Cameron, E. (2008). Indigenous spectrality and the politics of postcolonial ghost stories. *Cultural Geographies, 15*, 383–393.

Carman, J. (2011). Stories we tell: Myths at the heart of 'community archaeology'. *Archaeologies, 7*(3), 490–501.

Colley, S., & Bickford, A. (1996). 'Real' aborigines and 'Real' Archaeology: Aboriginal places and Australian historical archaeology. *World Archaeological Bulletin, 7*, 5–21.

Dawdy, S. L. (2009). Millennial archaeology. Locating the discipline in the age of insecurity. *Archaeological Dialogues, 16*(2), 131–142.

Dawdy, S. L. (2010). Clockpunk anthropology and the ruins of modernity. Current Anthropology, 51(6), 761–93.

de Certeau, M. (1984). *The practice of everyday life* (S. Rendall, Trans). Berkeley: University of California Press.

Edensor, T. (2008). Mundane hauntings: Commuting through the phantasmagoric working-class spaces of Manchester, England. *Cultural Geographies, 15*, 313–333.

Edmonds, P. (2010). Unpacking settler colonialism's urban strategies: Indigenous peoples in Victoria, British Columbia, and the transition to a settler-colonial city. *Urban History Review, 38*(2), 4–20.

Foucault, M. (1986). Kant on revolution and enlightenment. *Economy and Society, 15*(1), 88–96.

Gelder, K., & Jacobs, J. (1998). *Uncanny Australia: Sacredness and identity in a postcolonial nation.* Melbourne: Melbourne University Press.

Glassie, H. (1977). Archaeology and folklore: Common anxieties, common hopes. In L. Ferguson (Ed.), *Archaeology and the importance of material things* (pp. 23–35). Society for Historical Archaeology.

Gordon, N. (2002). On visibility and power: An Arendtian corrective of foucault. *Human Studies, 25*, 125–145.

Graham, B., & Howard, P. (Eds.). (2008). *The Ashgate research companion to heritage and identity.* Farnham, Surrey, England: Ashgate.

Hall, M. (2006). Identity, memory and counter memory: The archaeology of an urban landscape. *Journal of Material Culture, 11*(1/2), 189–209.

Hamilakis, Y. (2007). *The nation and its ruins: Antiquity, archaeology, and national imagination in Greece.* Oxford: Oxford University Press.

Hamilakis, Y. (2011). Archaeological ethnography: a multitemporal meeting ground for archaeology and anthropology. Annual Review of Anthropology, 40, 399–414.

Harrison, R. (2013). Forgetting to remember, remembering to forget: late modern heritage practices, sustainability, and the 'crisis' of accumulation of the past'. *International Journal of Heritage Studies, 19*(6), 579–595.

Herzfeld, M. (2006). Spatial cleansing: Monumental vacuity and the idea of the West. *Journal of Material Culture, 11*(1/2), 127–149.

Hetherington, K. (2010). The ruin revisited. In G. Pye & S. Schroth (Eds.), *Trash culture: Objects and obsolescence in cultural perspective* (pp. 27–49). Oxford, New York: Peter Lang.

Ireland, T. (2002). Giving value to the Australian historic past: Archaeology, heritage and nationalism. *Australasian Historical Archaeology, 20*, 15–25.

Ireland, T. (2012a). Excavating globalisation from the ruins of colonialism: Archaeological heritage management responses to cultural change. In E. Negussie (Ed.), *Changing world, changing views of heritage: The impact of global change on cultural heritage. Proceedings of the ICOMOS Scientific Symposium 2010* (pp. 18–29). Paris: ICOMOS.

Ireland, T. (2012b). Grounding identity: Exploring perceptions of urban archaeological sites in Australia and New Zealand. *Historic Environment, 24*(3), 19–27.

Ireland, T. (2012c). 'I felt connected to a past world': A survey of visitors to colonial archaeological sites conserved *in situ* in Australia and New Zealand. *Conservation and Management of Archaeological Sites, 14*(1–4), 458–468.

Ireland, T. (2014). Archaeological traces and memory places. In P. Ashton & J. Z. Wilson (Eds.), *Silent system: Forgotten Australians and the institutionalization of women and children* (pp. 89–102). Melbourne: Australian Scholarly Publishing.

Jeppson, P. (2006). Which Benjamin Franklin: Yours or mine? Examining responses to a new story from the historical archaeology site of Franklin court. *Archaeologies, 2*(2), 24–51.

Jeppson, P. (2011). The dynamics of inclusion at the dynamics of inclusion in public archaeology workshop public event. *Archaeologies, 7*(3), 635–656.

Johnson, M. (1999). Rethinking historical archaeology. In P. Paulo, A. Funari, M. Hall & S. Jones (Eds.), *Historical archaeology: Back from the edge* (pp. 23–36). London: Routledge.

Jokilehto, J. (2009). Conservation principles in the international context. In A. Richmond & A. Bracker (Eds.), *Conservation principles, dilemmas and uncomfortable truths* (pp. 73–83). London: Butterworth-Heinemann & Victoria and Albert Museum.

Joyce, R. (2006). The monumental and the trace: Archaeological conservation and the materiality of the past. In N. Agnew & J. Bridgland (Eds.), *Of the past, for the future: Integrating archaeology and conservation: Proceedings of the conservation theme at the 5th World Archaeological Congress, Washington, DC, 22–26 June 2003* (pp. 13–18). Los Angeles: Getty Publications.

Karskens, G. (2009). *The colony: A history of early Sydney.* Sydney: Allen and Unwin.

Keily, J. (2008). Taking the site to the people: Displays of archaeological material in non-museum locations. *Conservation and Management of Archaeological Sites, 10*(1), 30–40.

La Roche, C. & M. Blakey (1997). Seizing intellectual power: The dialogue at the New York African burial ground. *Historical Archaeology, 31*(3), 84–106.

Lefebvre, H. (1991). *The production of space.* Oxford: Blackwell.

Leone, M. (1973). Archaeology as the science of technology: Mormon town plans and fences. In C. Redman (Ed.), *Research and theory in current archaeology* (pp. 125–150). New York: Wiley.

Leone, M. (2010). *Critical historical archaeology.* Walnut Creek: Left Coast Press.

Leone, M., & Potter, P. (Eds.). (1999). *Historical archaeologies of capitalism. Contributions to global historical archaeology.* New York: Plenum.

Levin, J. (2011). Activism leads to excavation: The power of place and the power of the people at the president's house in Philadelphia. *Archaeologies, 7*(3), 596–618.

Little, B. (1994). People with history: An update on historical archaeology in the United States. *Journal of Archaeological Method and Theory, 1*(1), 5–40.

Lydon, J. (2005). Driving by: Visiting Australian colonial monuments. *Journal of Social Archaeology, 5*(1), 108–134.

Lydon, J. (2009). *Fantastic dreaming: The archaeology of an aboriginal mission.* Lanham: Altamira.

Lydon, J. (2012). *The flash of recognition: Photography and the emergence of indigenous rights.* Sydney: New South.

Lydon, J., & Rivzi, U. Z. (2010). *Handbook of postcolonial archaeology.* Walnut Creek: Left Coast Press.

Lyon, J. (2007). The Temple of Mithras: Changing heritage values in the city of London 1954-2006. *Conservation and Management of Archaeological Sites, 9*(1), 5–37.

Matero, F. (2000). The conservation of an excavated past. In I. Hodder (Ed.), *Towards reflexive method in archaeology: the example of Catalhöyük* (BIAA Monograph No. 28, pp. 71–88). Ankara: British Institute of Archaeology.

Matero, F. (2006). Making archaeological sites: Conservation as interpretation of an excavated past. In N. Agnew & J. Bridgland (Eds.), *Of the past, for the future: integrating archaeology and conservation: Proceedings of the conservation theme at the 5th World* Archaeological Congress, Washington, DC, 22–26 June 2003 (pp. 55–63). Los Angeles, CA: Getty Publications.

Matthews, C. (2006). The idea of the site: History, heritage, and locality in community archaeology. In L. Lozny (Ed.), *Landscapes under pressure: History, heritage and locality in community archaeology* (pp. 75–91). New York: Springer.

Mulvaney, J. (1991). The heritage value of historical relics: a plea for romantic intellectualism. In *Prehistory and heritage. The writings of John Mulvaney* (pp. 266–271). Canberra: The Australian National University.

Murray, T. (1996). Creating a post-Mabo archaeology of Australia. In B. Attwood (Ed.), *In the age of Mabo* (pp. 73–86). Sydney: Allen and Unwin.

Nixon, T. (2004). *Preserving archaeological remains in situ? Proceedings of the 2nd conference, 12–14 September 2001.* London: Museum of London Archaeology Service.

Olivier, L. (2004). The past of the present. Archaeological memory and time. *Archaeological Dialogues, 10*(2), 204–213.

Orser, C. (1996). *An historical archaeology of the modern world.* New York: Plenum Press.

Otero Pailos, J. (2004). Now is the future anterior for advancing historic preservation scholarship. *Future Anterior, I*(1), 6–8.

Otero Pailos, Jorge (2007b). Preservation's anonymous lament. *Future Anterior, IV*(2):iii-vii.

Otero-Pailos, J. (2007a). Conservation cleaning/cleaning conservation. *Future Anterior, IV*(1), iii–viii.

Otero-Pailos, J., Gaiger, J., & West, S. (2010). Heritage values. In S. West (Ed.), *Understanding heritage in practice* (pp. 47–87). Manchester: Manchester University Press.

Paterson, A. (2010). The archaeology of historical indigenous Australia. In J. Lydon & U. Rizvi (Eds.), *Handbook of postcolonial archaeology* (pp. 165–184). Walnut Creek California: Left Coast Press.

Phillips, C. (2000). Post-contact landscapes of change in Hauriki, New Zealand. In R. Torrence & A. Clarke (Eds.), *The archaeology of difference: Negotiating cross-cultural engagements in Oceania* (pp. 79–103). London: Routledge.

Rose, G., & Tolia-Kelly, D. (2012). Visuality/materiality: Introducing a manifesto for practice. In G. Rose & D. P. Tolia-Kelly (Eds.), *Visuality/materiality images, objects and practices* (pp. 1–11). Farnham: Ashgate.

Rubertone, P. (2008). Engaging monuments, memories, and archaeology. In P. Rubertone (Ed.), *Archaeologies of placemaking: Monuments, memories, and engagement in native North America* (pp. 13–33). Walnut Creek: Left Coast Press.

Russell, I. (2012). Towards an ethic of oblivion and forgetting. The parallax view. *Heritage and Society, 5*(2), 249–272.

Silliman, S. (2010). Indigenous traces in colonial spaces: Archaeologies of ambiguity, origin, and practice. *Journal of Social Archaeology, 10*(1), 28–58.

Smith, L. (2006a). *Uses of heritage*. London: Routledge.

Smith, L. (2006b). Doing archaeology: Cultural heritage management and its role in identifying the link between archaeological practice and theory. *International Journal of Heritage Studies, 6*(4), 309–316.

Smith, L., & Waterton, E. (2009). *Heritage, communities and archaeology*. London: Duckworth.

Stoler, A. L. (2008). Imperial debris: Reflections on ruins and ruination. *Cultural Anthropology, 23*(2), 191–219.

Verdesio, G. (2010). Invisible at a glance: Indigenous cultures of the past, ruins, archaeological sites, and our regimes of visibility. In J. Hell & A. Schönle (Eds.), *Ruins of modernity* (pp. 339–353). Durham: Duke University Press.

Waterton, E., & Smith, L. (2009). *Taking archaeology out of heritage*. Newcastle upon Tyne: Cambridge Scholars Publishing.

Waterton, E., & Watson, S. (2010). Introduction: A visual heritage. In E. Waterton & S. Watson (Eds.), *Culture, heritage and representation: Perspectives on visuality and the past* (pp. 1–19). Farnham: Ashgate.

Wells, K. (2007). The material and visual cultures of cities. *Space and Culture, 10*(2), 136–144.

Willems, W. (2008). Archaeological resource management and preservation. *Geoarchaeological and Bioarchaeological Studies, 10*, 283–289.

Zimmerman, L., Vitelli, K., & Hollowell-Zimmer, J. (2003). *Ethical issues in archaeology*. Walnut Creek: Altamira Press.

Chapter 8
The Normative Foundations of Stewardship: Care and Respect

Andreas Pantazatos

Introduction

Ethical concerns about archaeological and heritage practice have been central to the discussion of the role of values in the development of heritage debate. The emergence of archaeological ethics can be seen as a response to the conflicts of interests primarily between archaeologists, heritage practitioners and local communities with regard to the stewardship, broadly construed, of the past material and human remains. This has led to a continually expanding debate that involves issues such as the ownership of the past, rights over the interpretation and protection of cultural heritage, cultural appropriation, treatment of human remains, repatriation of archaeological objects and the role of universal museums, the state of heritage in war zones and subsistence digging and the illicit trade of antiquities.[1]

I presented earlier versions of this paper at a workshop on the *Normativity of Stewardship* at the Centre for the Ethics of Cultural Heritage at Durham University, at the *Vulnerability of Cultural Heritage* conference at the University of Leicester and at the *Cambridge Heritage Research* seminar at the University of Cambridge. I am grateful to their audiences for helpful comments. I wish to thank David E. Cooper, Ivan Gaskell, Cornelius Holtorf, Lynn Meskell, John Schofield, Robin Skeates and Nick Zangwill for their feedback on an earlier draft of this paper. I am indebted to Geoffrey F. Scarre for discussions on the subject and his useful comments on my paper.

[1] Testament to the emergence of archaeological ethics is the amount of edited volumes and sessions of archaeological conferences that focus on the ethical practice of archaeologists and relevant practitioners such as museum curators during the last twenty years. See, for example, Zimmerman et al. (2003) and Scarre and Scarre (2006).

A. Pantazatos (✉)
Department of Philosophy, Centre for the Ethics of Cultural Heritage, Durham University,
50 Old Elvet, Durham DH1 3HN, UK
e-mail: andreas.pantazatos@durham.ac.uk

© Springer Science+Business Media New York 2015
T. Ireland, J. Schofield (eds.), *The Ethics of Cultural Heritage*,
Ethical Archaeologies: The Politics of Social Justice 4,
DOI 10.1007/978-1-4939-1649-8_8

127

This chapter will focus on what I consider a common thread of arguments in these ethical debates: the notion of stewardship. Stewardship is usually understood as the very idea that archaeologists, by virtue of their training, can become custodians of the past and its knowledge on behalf of the public. What is striking about stewardship is its presumed status as a device which provides guidance for ethical dilemmas in archaeological and heritage practice. My claim is that we cannot grasp how stewardship delineates obligations for practitioners in the field, if we do not look for the source of these obligations, which I will argue can be traced in the ethical concepts of *care* and *respect*. In what follows I will consider an ethical dilemma which calls for a closer inspection of the hydraulics of stewardship and challenges its normative foundations. John Bintliff's (2003) ethical dilemma in his excavation in Boeotia is an appropriate place to begin.

Bintliff's Ethical Dilemma

Bintliff describes the case of a local community which denies links with its heritage. Members of the community do not want their heritage to be revealed or protected in any sense. Their case defies the idea that all humans are interested in heritage and particularly in their own. In his *Ethnoarchaeology of a 'Passive' Ethnicity: The Arvanites of Central Greece*, Bintliff (2003) explains that while he was excavating in Boeotia, he came across past remains which were not typically Greek. The remains (house structures, agricultural objects) were remains of Arvanites, people who were invited to populate the regions of Attica and Corinth in the late fourteenth century AD by the Florentine dukes who were then in charge of Athens. Arvanites lived in these areas and also moved into other areas of Greece. After the war of Greek independence against the Turks, while the new Greek nation was being created, Arvanites and their heritage were not given any special identity although their language and culture were rather different from those of the rest of the Greek population at that time. According to Bintliff, their heritage and language were never preserved and were not officially acknowledged. For a long time, Arvanites were considered to be pariahs and it took them a long time to shed their special identity. The fact they could communicate in Albanian with the new immigrants who arrived in Greece from that country in the beginning of the 1990s makes them even more sensitive to their cultural differences. Arvanites do not want their heritage to be saved or protected. They do not want to highlight the identity and cultural background that makes them different from Greek people, given that it took a long time to feel socially integrated. As a result, Bintliff's excavations which brought to light traces of Arvanitic house construction were almost a threat to the cultural identity that Arvanites want to develop for themselves. Hence, Bintliff's (2003: 141) dilemma:

> For me as an archaeologist who wants to give local communities their own history—something even current Greek history syllabuses fail to do—an ethical problem does arise in privileging the very different basis from which Arvanitic villages developed. Does this rural society really want to have such a history highlighted? Would rediscovering their supposed

historical ethnicity be even disadvantageous to them, especially to their children? I am still unsure of the answer to these questions.[2]

How should this conflict be resolved? Should Bintliff ignore the wishes of the Arvanitic community and record and publish his findings for the benefit of future generations who will be able to know how Arvanites lived their lives? Or, should he respect the wishes of the Arvanitic community and bury their past and any related knowledge of that era? If stewardship were to offer ethical guidance, it should provide resolution to this dilemma. Yet one could claim that stewardship might not always be the appropriate ethical framework for archaeological and heritage dilemmas. Let me briefly respond to this point before proceeding to the main argument.

Significant aspects of stewardship are obviously compatible with archaeology. For instance, given that the primary role of a good steward is to take care of what is entrusted to him/her, archaeologists and heritage practitioners, to large extent, act in the capacity of stewards by virtue of their expertise. They are trained to interpret and study the knowledge of the past, and this enables them to be appropriate custodians of the past. On a similar note, what is central to stewardship is protection and care of what is entrusted to capable stewards. A remarkable feature of archaeology is that protection and care of past remains are also vital for the interpretation of the past. The integrity of archaeological objects and knowledge of the past cannot be guaranteed if archaeologists are not protective and careful. Moreover, the development of professional codes of ethics for archaeology has brought forward the importance of accountability, the idea that archaeologists are answerable for their practice to colleagues, institutions, local communities and the wider public. Accountability is embedded in stewardship because stewards do not own what is entrusted to them; they merely take care of it and must therefore answer for their actions to those who have entrusted them with the objects at issue. Hence, the ethic of stewardship has become a prominent component of archaeological ethics, and it has been used to provide solutions to many ethical dilemmas.

If the concept of stewardship guides ethical decision-making for archaeologists, it is worth considering whether it has generally done so successfully. Bintliff's dilemma shows that the guiding role of stewardship in archaeological and heritage practice is still an open question. A route to a more certain answer can be sought if we turn our attention to the normativity of stewardship. Given that ethics provides

---

[2] One could claim here that Bintliff's dilemma describes the so-called paradox of stewardship which Colwell-Chanthaphonh (2009) nicely describes in 'The Archaeologist as a World Citizen'. According to his explanation, stewardship leads to a paradox in which two communities express different wishes about past remains. He refers, for instance, to the case of the Bamyan Buddhas. For certain members of the communities of Pakistan, the statues of the Buddhas had to be preserved, whereas the Taliban claimed they had no relation to their heritage, and they should therefore be destroyed as being offensive to Islam. However, Bintliff's dilemma is different from Colwell-Chanthaphonh's. In the case of Bintliff's dilemmas, Arvanites accept and acknowledge their past but deny preservation for reasons that are not strictly related to heritage. They want to make this decision for the future generations of Arvanites because they think that future generations will be better off without a special cultural identity.

us with guidance about how to act, norms are central to ethics because they embody standards of guidance that justify our actions and thus provide a framework of understanding in which those actions are rendered intelligible. Ethics highlights the sources of our obligations, how these obligations should be discharged and who the beneficiaries and stakeholders of these obligations are.

Consequently, we cannot understand what we might call the 'hydraulics' of stewardship if we do not pay close attention to its normative character. Any discussion regarding the impact of stewardship which does not consider its normativity overlooks the action-guiding force of stewardship, and it cannot therefore explain very well why stewardship has been effective in ethical decision-making. Thus far, debates about the ethics of archaeological stewardship have not paid sufficient attention to its normative character but focus mainly on how current accounts of archaeological stewardship supply archaeological practice with insufficient guidance.[3]

What follows is an exploration of the normative character of stewardship and an argument that it should be understood under the concept of *care*, complemented by that of *respect*. I set two tasks to achieve this aim. The first, using as a foil for my discussion on Bintliff's dilemma (2003), is to explicate the normative character of archaeological stewardship. The second is to defend an understanding of stewardship which is grounded in a concept of respectful care inspired by Meskell's (2010) notion of 'negative heritage'.

Understanding the Normative Character of Stewardship

Ethical reflection responds to the questions: 'what should I do?' and 'how should I live my life?' Good answers to both questions identify the optional courses of actions available to us. The justification of these actions is a normative extension which evaluates whether our actions are right or wrong, as opposed to merely explaining why we performed them. Hence, the understanding of the normative standpoint is vital for ethical practice. Professional ethics, broadly speaking, deal with ethical issues that arise in different professions. Professionals seek ethical signposts when trying to make sense of their ethical obligations and decide how to discharge them. Within the realm of professional ethics, it seems difficult to separate professional practice from ethical practice. And sometimes, therefore, good professional practice

---

[3] See Groarke and Warrick (2006) and Colwell-Chanthaphonh (2009). Groarke and Warrick attack the definition of stewardship which was adopted by the Society for American Archaeologists (SAA 2000) arguing that it addresses mostly political issues for which the archaeologists should not be involved. Colwell-Chanthaphonh argues that the paradox of stewardship might be solved if we adopted the rooted cosmopolitanism viewpoint. He refers to the normativity of stewardship implicitly. Alison Wylie (2005) puts forward an argument for the normative force of stewardship and not a criticism of its application in archaeological and heritage practice. My paper is more in alignment with her quest for the normativity of stewardship.

is considered tantamount to ethical practice, or ethical practice is reduced to good professional practice (Tarlow 2001; Grigoropoulos and Pantazatos 2007). For instance, a sign of good professional archaeological practice is the accurate recording of the excavation material in accordance with rules for scientific recording. This may also double as ethical practice but not necessarily. If the archaeologist never consulted local communities about the excavation and its record, the archaeologist still fulfils the criteria of good professional practice, but whether the proposed way of conduct is ethically commendable is less clear.

Good professional practice and ethical practice are, of course, not mutually exclusive. Rather, their relationship is a complementary one. Ethical practice is a broader category because it concerns our obligations to more beneficiaries than those who might be involved in professional practice. Ethical reflection should help us realise that our professional practice has impact beyond the limits of our profession and that professional practice must not be too narrowly focused. So, the quest for the normative character of ethics within the realm of professional ethics sheds much needed light on the obscure interface between general ethical practice and good professional practice. My claim is that a satisfactory account of the normativity of stewardship should provide firm support for an ethic suitable to inform professional practice. I argue that current accounts of the archaeological stewardship ethic misunderstand the normative character of stewardship and misplace its normative standpoint. My working definition of archaeological stewardship will be the one introduced by the Society of American Archaeologists (SAA) in 2000 which tries to address issues with regard to the normative character of stewardship:

> The archaeological record, that is, in situ, archaeological material and sites, archaeological collections, records and reports, is irreplaceable. It is the responsibility of all archaeologists to work for the long-term conservation and protection of the archaeological record by practising and promoting stewardship of the archaeological record. Stewards are both caretakers of and advocates for the archaeological record for the benefit of all people; as they investigate and interpret the record, they should use the specialised knowledge they gain to promote public understanding and support for its long-term preservation.

A closer look at the ethic of archaeological stewardship adopted by the SAA reveals how this definition entails two different accounts regarding the normative core of stewardship.[4] On the first account, according to which archaeological objects are a finite resource, this suffices to generate obligations towards them. Prima facie, SAA's proposal follows the example of environmental stewardship (Wylie 2005).[5] Remains from the past, like some species of plants and animals, are a resource in danger of extinction. As a result, there is a duty to protect this resource. This account places significant weight on archaeological objects themselves as a source of ethical obligation. The assigned special status entails that for anything which is in danger,

---

[4] This definition of stewardship has its limitations. However, it fits my purpose because it provides interesting insights to the normative core of stewardship. My thanks to Lynn Meskell who pressed me on this issue.

[5] The ethic of stewardship is hardly new, given that it has been central to debates in environmental ethics reflecting Christian views about the relationship between humans and the environment.

there should be someone capable of taking good care of it. The successful caretaker has to understand the objects under her control (Berry 2006). Therefore, there is a need for stewards who have expert knowledge of the object in question. If we assign special status to an object in virtue of our concern for its possible extinction, then we eo ipso treat it as valuable. The understanding of archaeological objects as a finite resource bases the source of our obligations towards them. But does it also provide sufficiently precise ethical guidance to how we ought to treat them?

Treating archaeological objects primarily as a finite resource can lead to overlooking the overall biography of the object. Burial objects in ancient Egypt, such as canopic jars for instance, were crafted with the intention to accompany the dead in the afterlife. They were not created to be saved and displayed. Similarly, amphorae, which have been found in ancient Greek tombs and which were buried as part of the personal belongings of the dead, were not crafted to be reused or to be studied by archaeologists and art collectors. As objects travel in time and the patina of time adds more detail to their biographies, their use changes and they acquire different meanings. One could argue that treating them as a finite resource is just another stage in their narrative and contributes something new to their meaning. Although to some extent this might ring true, the assigned status of finite resources sometimes requires priority over other episodes in the objects' life in a way that distorts the objects' overall narrative.

Moreover, different cultures pursue different understandings of past material remains, and these do not necessarily include the idea that past remains have a finite character. Take, for instance, the pillars of Ashoka (MacGregor 2010), stone inscriptions giving lifestyle advice erected by King Ashoka for the benefits of the citizens of his kingdom. Local communities in places where these inscriptions are found still feel strongly about the meaning of the pillars and consider them as significant within their own life narratives. The Ashoka pillars still play a role for those communities and help them define who they are. However, I, as a westerner participating in a culture that celebrates and values written tradition, might perceive the Ashoka pillars as predominantly an example of early public message boards. I might assign a finite character to them or I might not, given that quite a few fragments of the Ashoka pillars have now been saved and are unlikely to soon disappear. In my case, the finite character of archaeological objects does not suffice to capture the normative core of stewardship because it cannot explain how objects are a source of value beyond their capacity to resist the ravages of time.

The finite character of past remains—the archaeological record broadly construed—is underpinned by the idea that what is significant about objects from the past is that they are inherently and instrumentally valuable and thus worthy of care. This view is nicely captured by Alison Wylie's discussion about the normative core of archaeological stewardship. Wylie points out that much of the debate about the normative core of archaeological stewardship focuses on what marks the value of past remains. Panhuman interest in the past and its remains are what lie at the core of stewardship because they contribute to our understanding of the past. Past objects were created for specific usage and have acquired their own features and qualities through time, as mentioned above. A closer inspection of their biographies brings to light information about humans and explains patterns of human behaviour which extend our understanding of the human condition in the past and how it is related to the present. Hence, past objects are carriers of significant epistemic value for the past, and this defines them as a source of ethical obligation. It strikes me that such an argument is subject to the old 'is-ought' objection that Hume (1975) (*Treatise*, 469–470) put forward for the first time. It is not possible to derive a prescription to do something from a descriptive claim that something is the case. For example, from the claim 'Roman terracotta lights are a source of information for Roman domestic life', I cannot logically conclude that 'I therefore should treat them with respect'.[6] The epistemic value of past remains shapes professional archaeological practice, but it is not sufficient to formulate ethical practice.

If we approach past cultural heritage, broadly construed, as a resource, supported by the idea that heritage is instrumentally valuable because it contributes to knowledge and understanding of the past, and given that knowledge is intrinsically valuable and human beings acknowledge that knowledge of the past can potentially contribute to their well-being, we can explain why heritage and past objects are worthy of protection. This approach also justifies the performing of certain acts in the name of stewardship and assumes that all (or at least many) people manifest interest in heritage and in the knowledge of the past in general. But there is a fundamental problem with this approach. Assuming that heritage is worthy of care because humans have an interest in it, the normative core of stewardship addresses only the question *why* objects should be protected without giving any adequate weight to the question of *for whom*. The normative core of stewardship should be providing a framework of understanding in which the relationship between the two questions (why should we take care of past objects and for whom should we take care of them?) can be addressed. It is only by relating these two questions that we can enlighten the different obligations that should be addressed by an ethic of stewardship, if the latter is going to provide useful advice in archaeological and heritage practice.

If we locate the normative core of stewardship only in the question 'why should we care for past objects?', it is difficult to provide ethical advice on some hard cases because relationships with certain stakeholders are not taken into consideration. It strikes me that Bintliff's dilemma (2003) is a good example. Bintliff's ethical dilemma highlights the problematic aspect of archaeological stewardship, according to which our obligations are rooted in the panhuman interest for the knowledge of the past. His dilemma presents a rather clear case of a community whose relation to their heritage and past is perceived as traumatic. On an ethic of stewardship which addresses primarily the question 'why should we care about objects from the past?', obligations towards the communities that Bintliff's (2003) case discusses could easily be dismissed. If panhuman interest is what drives stewardship, then advocates of

---

[6] I do not wish to imply that Wylie commits the naturalistic fallacy, given that she argues for a model of collaborative stewardship according to which panhuman interest might inform the archaeologists' ethical behaviour. But, as she clearly stipulates, it does not define the normative core of stewardship. Additionally, she points out that it is the SAA's definition of archaeological stewardship that appears to depend, primarily, on the epistemic value of past remains.

this approach should be able to argue that panhuman concern is an overriding human concern which silences the communities' wishes. And if this is the case, they should be able to offer an argument which justifies the supremacy of the authority of the panhuman interest in the past. If one accepts panhuman interest in the past as the normative core of stewardship, as what provides us with guidance on what to do, this might cause more harm than good. If an archaeologist or heritage practitioner decides to save the community's heritage and reveal its history, this has a potential impact for the social integration of the community's future generations. Hence, panhuman interest appears to advise the preservation of the objects to the detriment of the community.

More importantly, Bintliff's dilemma shows how the normative justification of stewardship on the grounds of the finite character of past objects and panhuman interest in them appears to be incomplete, because it ignores the issues that arise if panhuman and local interests in heritage disagree.

Care

Following Lowenthal's claim that we 'inherit more than goods' from the past (1998: 138), one can understand that the normative foundations of stewardship should address 'why' and 'for whom do we steward the past?' We inherit more than objects, more than monuments and more than remains. We inherit first and foremost people's association with remains from the past, resonances between communities and objects and/or monuments and a relationship between current and past communities via remains from the past. These associations should be captured by the normative foundations of stewardship because they define the steward's obligations. The competent steward should be able to understand how her obligations arise from the associations that communities have built with their past remains and what these associations mean for the communities involved.

What is striking about our understanding of the ethic of stewardship is our tendency to overlook the fundamental ethical concept which is at the core of stewarding, namely, *care*. Usually stewards are defined as custodians, guardians and caretakers. Stewards are those who have been entrusted with something that might be in need for care for a variety of reasons. However, the debate does not generally turn its attention to the ethical concept of care itself, exploring whether it can provide us with a satisfactory normative background for stewardship.[7] It makes sense then to focus here on the ethical concept of care. My claim is that care can legitimately accommodate both the questions 'why should objects be protected' and 'for whom?'

---

[7] In their recent book *Archaeology: The Discipline of Things*, Olsen et al. (2012:196-209) argue for a possible relationship between archaeology and care, but they do not address the ethical dimensions of care and its relationship to the normative core of stewardship.

Care is present in everyday discourse in numerous ways. Fisher and Tronto (Tronto 1993:103) provide a nuanced definition of care:

> On the most general level, we suggest that caring be viewed as a species activity that includes everything that we do to maintain, continue and repair our 'world' so that we can live in it as well as possible. That world includes our bodies, ourselves and our environment, all of which we seek to interweave in a complex, life-sustaining web.

Fisher and Tronto's definition portrays the phenomenology of the experience of care in everyday life. Care is usually associated with those in need, with those who call for help because they cannot maintain their own well-being. For instance, medical patients are obviously recipients of care. So are young children in need of their parents' help to survive. In this respect, care is related to vulnerability. Arguably, this understanding of care fits my purpose here, given that remains from the past can be described as 'vulnerable' because they are in danger of loss, and at the same time, communities are also 'vulnerable' to losing their ties with their heritage, if remains from the past disappear. If, however, I focused on vulnerability, I would stress the nature of past remains as a finite resource, and I have already explained why this is not the best candidate for underpinning the normative foundations of stewardship.

Care can be understood better if we replace vulnerability with the idea of dependence, as Daniel Egnster (2005) argues. Care is morally distinctive because it reminds us that we are all dependent on each other, and this is the first step to understand that we are capable of forming relationships that generate obligations. One's own life conditions depend on others' and how they conduct themselves in life. From the moment one realises this, one takes the first step in understanding that one is responsible for others and vice versa. So, an ethic of care can justify our obligations to others by acknowledging our own dependence on others. But how are we to understand this in relation to stewardship and heritage?

The ethic of care is appropriate for the normative core of stewardship because it foregrounds the relatedness of persons. According to some advocates of the ethic of care (Held 2006), our capacity to be moral beneficiaries and fulfil our obligation towards others is grounded in our capacity to form relationships with others[8]. These relationships can be with family, relatives, friends and colleagues, as well as social ties in general. Being capable of establishing and participating in a caring relationship, one should be sensitive to the needs of others. One should also be trustworthy, and there should be mutual concern between the members of the relationship. Given that a significant aspect of heritage is to reveal relations between people and past remains (between current and past generations) and also to foster relations between

---

[8] Care has been central to feminist ethics. For a detailed account of the role of care in feminist ethics see Noddings, N. (2010). *The maternal factor: Two paths to morality*. Berkeley: University of California Press, and Noddings, N. (1984). *Caring: A feminine approach to ethics & moral education*. Berkeley: University of California Press. For the relationship between care, autonomy and justice, see Clement, G. (1996). *Care, autonomy and justice: Feminism and the ethic of care*. Boulder: Westview Press. For a relationship between care and empathy, see Slote, M. (2007). *The ethics of care and empathy*. London: Routledge.

communities, competent stewardship should be able to accommodate these relationships and sustain them. The steward's obligations are defined by her capacity to form relationships with communities, understand their past and nurture their relationship with objects from the past and thereby past generations. It should be noted here that the relationship between objects and communities is both instrumental and constitutive. The communities survive via their objects and shape their current meaning, and at the same time, objects shape current communities and define their relationship with the past. The archaeologist or heritage practitioner as a steward is not just an individual who pursues research duties; she is more importantly a person who has relationships with communities. Her relationship with these communities calls for her attentiveness and responsiveness to their voices with regard to their past remains and the development of their joint concern for the past.

As mentioned earlier, care is morally distinctive once we acknowledge our dependence on others. What also marks this relationship of dependence is that we have as persons both past and history. We acknowledge our dependence on others by being historically situated, by acknowledging our and their distinct life narratives.

According to Held (2006: 131), an ethic of care 'employs a concept of the person as… historically situated'. It occurs to me that forming associations with objects from the past can be one way to situate communities historically, revealing how their relations with the past have crafted their identity and shaped their cultures. An ethic which pays attention to this dimension of the particular narratives of the person cannot exclude what plays a role in the authorship of the narrative and so cannot exclude the care of objects from the past. Recall Bintliff's dilemma. Arvanites are shaped by their past, and Bintliff is in a position to understand their demand for their heritage to remain unrevealed. Their demand makes sense once one understands how their worries about their identity have developed. An account of stewardship that is shaped by care engages with the way in which communities are historically situated and acknowledges their associations with objects from the past not merely as a bare fact but, more importantly, as grounding and shaping the obligations of stewards.

So far I have argued that we can place the normative core of stewardship in an ethic of care because the latter is in tune with the contextual nuance and the particular narratives of people. This approach does not treat communities as abstract entities which ought to follow universal claims about past remains. It also does not distinguish between 'why do we steward the past?' and 'for whom do we steward it?' because the meaning of the objects is only rendered intelligible by communities who therefore cannot be excluded from consideration. Before I pursue an objection against the idea of care as the normative foundation of stewardship, let me present a final point in support of the role of care.

A possible advantage of locating the normative core of stewardship in care is that as Held (2006: 136) claims, 'care is beyond cultural divides'; care is a universal experience and it can be understood more easily than western conceptions of universalised rights and liberal toleration. On a similar note, Groarke and Warwick (2006:236) remind us that stewardship is fundamentally a Christian concept which has been appropriated in debates of environmental ethics and archaeology. Given that stewardship of heritage is pursued in non-Christian communities, an appeal to ethical terms that can be understood by both the heritage practitioners (potentially Christians) and local non-Christian communities can make their conversation and the consequent collaboration more comfortable and fruitful. If care, as stated earlier, is fundamentally understood via dependence, the latter is an experience that all human beings independently of religion or ethnicity share and they can therefore relate to. Given that the debate over stewardship of past remains has highlighted the differences between western and non-western approaches to our relationship with the past and the treatment of its objects, this aspect of care is one that is well worth noting.[9]

So far, we can conclude that the concept of care provides stewardship with normative foundations that the finite character of past remains as resource and panhuman interest do not. But care addresses a significant aspect of the normative foundation of stewardship; care alone is not sufficient to capture the normativity of stewardship. Imagine a parent who denies her child permission to join a football team, arguing that in the long run this is not going to help him with anything important and that concentrating on his studies is far more significant in the long run. She makes this decision without letting the child play any role in the decision-making. The parent cares about the beneficiary of her actions, but she does not care about him in a respectful manner. And respect is what complements care in the normativity of stewardship.

Respect

Respect plays a highly significant role in our moral understanding. But, like care, it has not been much addressed in the discussion of the normative foundations of stewardship. According to Lowenthal (1998:220), what underpins our understanding and the ethical role of stewardship with regard to heritage is the idea rooted in the medieval European conception of family duty and inheritance. The difficult term 'heritage' denotes something hereditary—that can be inherited. We understand that if something is hereditary, there should be a legitimate successor who takes over what is handed down from her family. This leads to the idea that what should be respected is not heritage, but inheritance, and inheritance is the source of obligation. Those who are legitimate heirs inherit from their family, say an estate, which they are now 'bound' or obliged by family duty to take care of. The legitimate heir is a steward on behalf of the family, and she should act in the interests of the family so that inheritance which is entrusted to her is kept intact. She may be expected to respect the family property and the predecessors who have bequeathed it to her.

Central to evaluating the ethical status of an action is to locate the beneficiaries who are affected by that action. Either I reflect on my action in regard to the motive

---

[9]This aspect of care might also be an answer to those who claim that stewardship is not the most appropriate term to use when we think of archaeology and heritage ethics. My thanks to Neil Brodie who pressed me to think on this issue.

from which it proceeded, or the consequences that my action brought about, or from the character trait that initiated it. In each case, the designated beneficiaries of my action are people for whom I ought to feel appropriate respect. If, for instance, I have a duty to take care of my sick father, the immediate recipient of my action is my father. If, for example, I give money to charity because I believe my action will help alleviate poverty, the beneficiaries of my contribution to charity are those who are poor.

One would expect something similar in the case of cultural heritage stewardship. In the case of cultural heritage, however, we cannot claim that the source of obligation to care about heritage is any kind of hereditary entitlement. Hence, the role of inheritance in defining the obligations of stewardship has been partially replaced by a purer concept of respect. Respect determines the beneficiaries of stewardship without appealing to any hereditary entitlement. Rather, it treats everyone as equal and equally deserving of respect. A focus on respect stresses the question 'for whom do we steward past objects?', and the answer is that we do so for any person who is associated with the heritage in any way. To respect people is to acknowledge the entitlement that anyone can have to cultural heritage. Therefore care of such heritage should be executed in a way that is respectful to all.

More importantly, if morality is grounded on a relationship with each other, the concept of respect requires recognition for common membership of a moral community (Bagnoli 2007:118–123). To respect others means that one accepts that others have equal weight in the moral community and are in themselves valuable. So, respect serves as a condition that limits what we can and cannot do to others. From the time we recognise others are equals, we enter into a relationship with them, and this relationship determines the obligations which are rooted in this mutual recognition. And it is this mutual recognition that holds us accountable for our actions. In the case of stewardship, the web of obligations and beneficiaries is grounded in the complementary relationship between care and respect. Respect provides the justificatory basis for care, accommodating all possible stakeholders' associations with heritage and acknowledging them as sources of valid claims and stewards. We can now see how this complementary relationship works for stewardship in the context of what is understood as 'negative heritage'.

In her *Negative Heritage and Past Mastering in Archaeology*, Meskell (2010) describes succinctly Ground Zero in New York, where the Twin Towers were located before the 9/11 terrorist attack transformed them ultimately to a heritage and commemoration monument. She describes how developers chose materials from the remains of the destruction of the buildings to establish a museum which will commemorate the tragic events of that day. However, as Meskell points out, not everyone has been happy with this process. Founding a museum to commemorate the event with remains from the site may disturb those who lost loved ones, while others may have different associations with activities which took place here. For some of these people, it is a negative heritage, something they might think they are better off without. People who live in New York have close association with the towers and with people who used to work there or whose relatives and friends worked there. They have developed particular associations with the towers that cannot be replaced by any commemorative process. The different degrees and levels of associations that people have developed with the Twin Towers may be reasons why, for some, any commemoration is perceived as negative heritage.

Meskell's (2010) reference to negative heritage and its preservation can explain why the normative foundation of stewardship is articulated best by the complementary relationship between care and respect. If stewardship of the Twin Towers' heritage was reduced merely to care, one could claim that a competent steward is the one who cares both about the past remains of the towers and the stories which are associated with those remains and who acts accordingly. Meskell's point about negative heritage reminds us that care in this case can be performed in a respectful manner only if the sensitivity of the traumatic experiences of people who have developed associations with the Twin Towers is addressed as an equally valid claim from the perspective of stewards of the heritage. A lack of respect can be charged against those who do not take all experiences seriously. Respecting negative heritage in this case is to acknowledge the various relationships between people's lives and the fall of the towers.

Hence, the discourse of respect not only addresses the multiple beneficiaries of stewardship but also reminds us that stewards are in a mutual relationship with them. From the time they recognise beneficiaries as persons who set their own ends, they acknowledge them as a source of value. They also enter into a relationship of accountability. Respect drives accountability because we are accountable to each other from the time we accept our morally equal status and realise that your concerns should be addressed equally with mine. We are told that stewards are accountable for their actions to their beneficiaries, but their accountability is shaped by respect and by mutual recognition. As Darwall (2006) points out, we are competent to become members of the moral community because we are capable of employing the second-person standpoint. Following from this, we may choose to perform an action only if it is consistent with demands one would make of anyone from a standpoint that we can share as accountable persons. Hence, the steward is someone who has the capacity to relate to others as a member of the same moral community.[10]

Conclusion

One might suggest that the explanation offered for the normative foundations of stewardship does not provide a basis of solid practical advice for ethical dilemmas in archaeological and heritage practice. My response would be that I did not set this as a task in this instance. In this chapter, I have explained how we misconceive the

---

[10] I would like to note here that my argument is different from Wylie's approach to the normativity of stewardship. Following Tully's (1985) constitutional pluralism, she proposes a model of collaborative stewardship according to which archaeologists and communities can collaborate and act together as stewards of the past. I argue that the pair of ethical concepts, namely, care and respect, are good candidates for the normative foundations of stewardship because they can render our ethical obligations to steward the past intelligible. I wish to thank Alison Wylie for discussing her approach on stewardship with me on numerous occasions.

normative foundations of stewardship if we separate two questions that should be addressed together, namely, 'why do we steward the past?' and 'for whom do we steward the past?' I have argued that care complemented by respect can constitute the normative foundations of stewardship because their pairing captures accurately the beneficiaries of stewardship and thereby defines its obligations. Addressing the source of their obligations is fundamental for all archaeologists and heritage practitioners. Accountability entails more than a disposition to conform with definite rules of behaviour and formulas of good professional practice; it also involves holding morality in esteem (Hill 1973:99–104) and in this respect plays a central role. A closer look at what I have understood as the 'hydraulics' of stewardship reminds us that there is more to the ethics of stewardship than the finite character of past objects or communities' concerns about their heritage or compliance with professional codes of practice.

References

Bagnoli, C. (2007). Respect and membership in the moral community. *Ethical Theory and Moral Practice, 10*, 113–128.

Berry, R. J. (Ed.). (2006). *Critical perspectives: Past and present, environmental stewardship.* London: Continuum.

Bintliff, J. (2003). The ethnoarchaeology of a 'passive' ethnicity: The Arvanites of Central Greece. In K. S. Brown & Y. Hamilakis (Eds.), *The usable past: Greek metahistories* (pp. 129–144). Lanham: Lexington Books.

Clement, G. (1996). *Care, autonomy and justice: Feminism and the ethic of care.* Boulder: Westview Press.

Colwell-Chanthaphonh, C. (2009). The archaeologist as world citizen. In L. Meskell (Ed.), *Cosmopolitan Archaeologies* (pp. 140–165). Durham: Duke University Press.

Darwall, S. (2006). *The second-person standpoint: Morality, respect, and accountability.* Cambridge: Harvard University Press.

Engster, D. (2005). Rethinking care theory: the practice of caring and the obligation to care. *Hypatia, 20*, 50–74.

Grigoropoulos, D.; & Pantazatos, A. (2007). Ethics in archaeology: Paradigm or platitude? In H. Schroeder, P. Bray, P. Gardner, V. Jefferson & E. Macaulay-Lewis (Eds.), *Crossing frontiers: The opportunities and challenges of interdisciplinary approaches to archaeology* (pp. 143-152). Oxford: Oxford University Press.

Groarke, L., & Warrick, G. (2006). Stewardship gone astray? Ethics and the SAA. In C. Scarre & G. Scarre (Eds.), *The Ethics of Archaeology: Philosophical Perspectives on Archaeological Practice* (pp. 163–177). Cambridge: Cambridge University Press.

Held, V. (2006). *The ethics of care.* Oxford: Oxford University Press.

Hill, T. (1973). Servility and self-respect. *The Monist, 57*, 87–104.

Hume, D. (1975). *A treatise of human nature.* Oxford: Oxford University Press. 1739-1740.

Lowenthal, D. (1998). *The heritage crusade and the spoils of history.* Cambridge: Cambridge University Press.

MacGregor, N. (2010). *History of the world in 100 objects.* London: British Museum Press.

Meskell, L. (2010). Negative heritage and past mastering in archaeology. *Anthropological Quarterly, 75*, 557–574.

Noddings, N. (2010). *The maternal factor: Two paths to morality.* Berkeley: University of California Press.

Noddings, N. (1984). *Caring: A feminine approach to ethics & moral education*. Berkeley: University of California Press.

Olsen, B., Shanks, M., Webmoor, T., & Witmore, C. (2012). *Archaeology: The discipline of things*. Berkeley: University of California Press.

SAA Ethics in Archaeology Committee 2000:11. http://www.saa.org/. Accessed 1 March 2010.

Slote, M. (2007). *The ethics of care and empathy*. London: Routledge.

Tarlow, S. (2001). Decoding ethics. *Public Archaeology, 1*, 245–259.

Tronto, J. C. (1993). *Moral boundaries: A political argument for an ethic of care*. New York: Routledge.

Tully, J. (1985). *Strange multiplicity: Constitutionalism in an age of diversity*. Cambridge: Cambridge University Press.

Wylie, A. (2005). The promise and the perils of an ethic of stewardship. In L. Meskell & P. Pels (Eds.), *Embedding Ethics: Shifting Boundaries of the Anthropological Profession* (pp. 49–68). Oxford: Berg.

Zimmerman, L., Vitelli, K., & Hollowell-Zimmer, J. (2003). *Ethical issues in archaeology*. Walnut Creek: Altamira.

Part II
Ethics in Practice

Chapter 9
Ethics and Collecting in the 'Postmodern' Museum: A Papua New Guinea Example

Elizabeth Bonshek

Introduction

In his short description of collecting *onggi,* ceramic food bowls from the Republic of Korea for an American museum, Robert Sayers pondered, along with other museum anthropologists some 21 years ago, whether, given tightening budgets, museums should collect at all (1991:8). In describing his own experiences, he touched upon a number of concerns still current in ethnographic collecting (see also King 1982): these included the ethics of collecting in societies in which people, for a variety of reasons, did not participate fully in a mainstream cash economy. Within such an environment, establishing what might be considered a fair price both from the 'seller's' point of view and the buyer's can be problematic: this is a consideration quite apart from any issues concerning illegal activity, and falls into the arena of ethical behaviour. Sayers (1991:12) closed by saying:

> …as a foreign scholar I often found myself an awkward participant in a reciprocal gift-giving culture, the dimensions of which I did not always understand…[w]here monetary payment was warranted, I tried to arrive at a figure that was neither miserly nor patronizing – one that would reflect well on members of my discipline…[w]hether I was entirely successful in this endeavor remains to be seen.

The lack of a common understanding concerning the collecting process itself (commented upon in historical transactions by Nicholas Thomas, 1991), shifting values concerning the specific objects collected and difficulties of deciding what is

E. Bonshek (✉)
Heritage, Museums and Conservation, Faculty of Arts and Design, University of Canberra, Bruce, ACT 2601, Australia
e-mail: elizabeth.bonshek@canberra.edu.au

© Springer Science+Business Media New York 2015   145
T. Ireland, J. Schofield (eds.), *The Ethics of Cultural Heritage,*
Ethical Archaeologies: The Politics of Social Justice 4,
DOI 10.1007/978-1-4939-1649-8_9

'representative' or what exactly constitutes 'a sample' all persist and have come to dominate the day-to-day life of postmodern museum curators and collection management staff.

One of the difficulties of negotiating a 'price' for the desired object(s) relates not only to a view of the intrinsic properties of the object but to the social relations surrounding it. Here, I understand collecting to be a socially defined activity between people, not one necessarily, or only, driven by the market and market forces in a uniform way in all places and societies. This premise forms the core of my paper, and to discuss this, I bring the collecting process in a specific place and time to the fore, in a similar fashion to Sayers. It is also this dimension of collecting that has largely been overshadowed by a sizeable commentary on the history of collecting both inside and outside museums and also in studies of contemporary popular collecting. Fortunately, succinct reviews of this vast literature (e.g. MacDonald 2006; Belk 2006) identify some of the dominant themes commencing with the origins of collecting by European Renaissance collectors, the birth of scientism in the early modern period and the broad epistemological changes that transpired, and the emergence of the present 'postmodern' museum. Specific collections and collectors have been rigorously examined creating 'biographies' of both them and the objects (or collections); and various approaches, both psychological and sociological, have been used to analyse a supposed underlying 'drive' to collect. For museums today (if not individual collectors), the 'new museology' of the late twentieth and twenty-first century presents a 'democratised' museum which is, or is supposed to be, 'inclusive', incorporating a diverse cultural constituency in which 'representation' and reflexive practice are central concerns (Bennett 1995; Genoways 2006; Sandell and Nightingale 2012).

Here, I want to draw a line between institutional and private collecting in the contemporary period and focus upon making a collection for an anthropology museum. Some 40 years on, the effects of the 'new museology' (Vergo 1989) are evident in a number of concerns in contemporary museum policy: 'representation' and social inclusion of all communities, including those whose cultural heritage is held in museum collections, are foremost; legal frameworks (both international conventions and national legislation) have been established which aim to prevent illegal activity in relation to collecting (Perrot 1997; O'Keefe and Prott 2011); and at a practical level, financial considerations also restrain what is acquired (i.e. not only the availability of acquisition funds but also the associated costs of storage and the maintenance of object collections through conservation care; Weil 2002:141–150; Knell 2004).

But notwithstanding such frameworks, it is people who work in museums and museum staff (or their agents) who make collections, doing so within policy frameworks. Museum staff represent the institution and engage with those from whom they collect: and where people interact, social relationships become important.

If we assume that museum enact policy, how can they collect ethically, on the ground, within the intellectual environment of the socially focused museum? How are anthropological aims concerning research reconciled with support of community control over representation at the point of collection at a practical level, rather than at the level of abstraction—for example, collecting will be done in a 'respectful' way (Edson 1997)? MacDonald's (2006) use of the 'social practice of collecting'

and consideration of the human - object relationship as historically specific is helpful in this investigation of collecting; but in this study, the social practice of collecting is social and culturally specific in contemporary time.

The context of my enquiry is the acquisition of pottery from Wanigela, a remote
rural area in Collingwood Bay, in Papua New Guinea (PNG), for the Australian
Museum, Sydney, in 2003. Wanigela women make clay pots as both gifts and commodities for sale or exchange, depending on context. They have an accepted social
practice of acquiring pots in which one's relationship with a potter determines
whether a cash purchase is appropriate or not. Thus, immediately a potential for
tension can emerge if the museum requires its collector to determine a 'fair price' to
avoid unethical acquisitions. For museums, forms of monetary transactions (price,
fair price) are components of provenance which feed into legal ownership
(Commonwealth of Australia 2009).[1] In situations where social relationships determine outcomes, the appropriate use of money may present a challenge for the
museum. In Wanigela, as I will show, the social interactions surrounding the acquisition of particular objects determined the appropriate recompense.

I have discussed the importance of social relations in the acquisition of a museum
collection elsewhere (Bonshek 2011), but in this paper, I focus not only on the idea
of the ethics of collecting in a specific circumstance, but also why some anthropology museums still want to collect and how this process can be negotiated in an arena
where concepts such as museums, collections and collecting and the documentation
of social change over time (McLeod 1993) are not of particular concern. I also illustrate how a methodology for collecting has changed within the environment of the
post-colonial museum.

Collecting Practices

Michael O'Hanlon (1993) discussed his acquisition of material from the Wahgi
Valley, PNG, for the British Museum in the 1990s. He confronted questions in
deciding what exactly anthropology's conception of 'material culture' was and what
constituted a Wahgi 'artefact'. Echoing Sayers, the introduction of objects and parts
of objects that were not made by the Wahgi but were used by them raised questions
about what objects could reflect Wahgi and their neighbours with whom they interacted. Here, cross-cultural interactions, not cultural isolation, typified aspects of
Wahgi life. And rather than dominate in interactions concerning price, O'Hanlon
found himself to be a junior partner in acquisitions, receiving direction not only
about materials to be collected, but their price. Thus, price itself came to materialise
his relationships with the Wahgi.

My own experience of collecting for museums in Melanesia reinforces the view
of the activity as socially defined (2010). Indeed, museum collecting and museology itself is a particularly, socially and historically defined way of doing things

---

[1] Henrietta Lidchi (2012) presents an interesting examination of the ethics of collecting contemporary
Native American jewellery bought in pawnshops.

(see Stanley 2007 for a discussion on alternate modes and the indigenisation of museums in the Pacific). Thus, when museum professionals and commentators such as Simon Knell (2004) and Steven Conn (2010) discuss the range of museums' activities as occurring on an axis of disciplinary museum vis-à-vis community/ social identity museums, the former tends to occlude social practice. This divide supposedly rests on differing approaches to museum objects: while community/ social identity museums use objects to support statements about social identity, disciplinary museums attribute qualities to the physical nature of the object. Knell refers to these as 'sets of attributes' which include 'authorship, research rigour, connoisseurship, tradition and a range of knowledge structures' (Knell 2004:23):

> To this [disciplinary] world, a museum built purely on personal meaning making [community museum] would be entirely worthless unless it conformed to disciplinary requirements for selection and data capture. The act of collecting can then become a point of tension between the self-creation of meaning by the group which is its subject and that academic 'other' which hopes to understand that group on its own terms.

Knell's comments were perhaps more directly aimed at an attempt to redefine the process of collecting than to reinforce divisions in the ways different museums interpret objects. In his commentary on the collection development policies and practices of museums, he suggests that institutions should no longer hang on to unquestioned orthodoxies such as collections being held in perpetuity; the valuing of objects on the basis of age, rarity or uniqueness; the necessity to fill collection gaps; an object's monetary value; and the fetishisation of the object as a 'museum object'. Knell suggests a revaluing of collections on the basis of what knowledge they can provide and embraces new technologies and their potential to record context about an object's manufacture and use which may result in the three-dimensional object being left un-acquired (in essence, the collection of intangible heritage). But, and as Knell acknowledges, these two approaches, at first glance apparently diametrically opposed, do overlap and are often intertwined.

In museums in Australia, New Zealand, Canada and the USA (the 'new world' museums), indigenous people have been vocal in demanding access to and authority over the representation of objects collected from their ancestors in the past. Today, indigenous and community consultation has become mainstream in many museums, and it is no longer the case that these two approaches need *necessarily* be in opposition to one another (see Allen and Hamby 2012; Peers and Brown 2003). The development of museum policy in Australia certainly testifies to this significant shift from an emphasis on 'access' (Council of Australian Museums Association 1993) to one of 'responsibilities' (Museums Australia 2005).

Contemporary Museums and International Policy Frameworks

The 'ICOM Code of Ethics for Museums' (2013) presents the minimum standards of museum practice including acquisition. Eight guiding principles establish the purpose and role of the museum and include (italics my emphasis): (1) the *preservation*, interpretation and promotion of the cultural and natural inheritance of

humanity; (2) the benefit and development of society through collection maintenance; (3) the consideration of objects *as primary evidence for establishing and
developing knowledge;* (4) the provision of opportunities to appreciate, develop and
manage the cultural and natural heritage; (5) the provision of opportunities and
benefits for other public services through the museum's resources; (6) *the collaboration with the communities from whence collections originated* as well as the communities that they serve; (7) the operation of the museum in a *legal* manner; and (8)
the operation of the museum and staff in a *professional* manner.

The requirement to collect objects is contained within the second principle:
wherein museums have a 'duty to acquire' objects/collections, governed by a collection policy, as well as maintain collections and care for them following good
collection management practices (which in this section emphasise legal title, the
importance of provenance and the recognition of culturally sensitive material
amongst other concerns) ICOM 2013. The museum should also ensure 'collection
continuity' (point 2.18, ICOM 2013:5) through appropriate provision of information about its collections, and this information should be made available to future
generations.

Of particular relevance to the subject in hand is 'field collecting', Principle 3,
point 3.3:

> Museums undertaking field collecting should develop policies consistent with academic
> standards and applicable national and international laws and treaty obligations. Fieldwork
> should only be undertaken with respect and consideration for the views of local communi-
> ties, their environmental resources and cultural practices as well as efforts to enhance the
> cultural and natural heritage (ICOM 2013:6).

And lastly, Principle 6 encourages collaboration with communities from whence
collections originate:

> Museum collections reflect the cultural and natural heritage of the communities from which
> they have been derived. As such, they have a character beyond that of ordinary property,
> which may include strong affinities with national, regional, local, ethnic, religious or politi-
> cal identity. It is important therefore that museum policy is responsive to this situation
> (ICOM 2013:10).

Furthermore:

> Where museum activities involve a contemporary community or its heritage, acquisitions
> should only be made based on informed and mutual consent without exploitation of the
> owner or informants. Respect for the wishes of the community involved should be para-
> mount (point 6.5, ICOM 2013:10).

Thus the use and, by extension, acquisition of objects should be 'respectful for
human dignity and the traditions and cultures that use such material' and thus promote
'multi-social, multicultural and multilingual expression' (point 6.7, ICOM 2013:11).

Issues of social justice have become key to museum ethics. Museums are charged
with ensuring social and moral accountability which includes finding a balance
between providing access, both physical and intellectual, to collections (virtual
access is increasingly used to facilitate access and meet these requirements) and
respecting specific social significance. These might include restrictions concerning
object handling, storage and display (e.g. of secret sacred materials or human

remains), as well as a duty of care to acquire only firmly provenanced material. Deaccessioning is a contested arena, separating as it does those objects worthy of being held permanently and those which are considered expendable and also potentially saleable. In today's museum, staff are required to respond to complex situations which encapsulate human relationships across space and across past, present and future time (Besterman 2006:432). As Hein has commented, changes in ethical standards reflect changes in society and what society has come to value (Hein 2000:93; Besterman 2006).

But having set out the guiding principles for museums, the ICOM Code of Ethics for museums leaves the specifics of acquisition to individual museums which have their separate collection histories and aims in developing their collections.

Why Collect? A Disciplinary/Anthropological Response

While I was carrying out my doctoral fieldwork in Wanigela, PNG, between 2001 and 2003, I made a collection for the Australian Museum. At that time, the museum's acquisition policy was outlined in *Policies and Principles of Collection Management* (Australian Museum 1989).[2] The museum sought acquisitions which protected and preserved artefacts of national and international cultural heritage, that developed research collections and that documented social change (1989:3).[3] Thus, the museum perceived a 'diachronic perspective' as necessary and sought to collect contemporary arts and crafts in 'increasingly larger proportion' for its collections. It was not concerned to purposefully seek out older material, but did acquire such material if it became available (1989:4).

Within its budgetary constraints, the museum sought to build upon its existing collection strengths, to acquire well-documented objects and collect objects which represented the full range of material culture, including objects that incorporated introduced materials and which reflected 'conceptual modification' and that where possible collections would be made in the context of research programmes (1989:4). Any acquisition (and access to collections) would 'take into account...the ongoing feelings of the community of origin of such material concerning its appropriate use, storage and disposal', and the museum would make attempts to 'avoid or reconcile conflicts of interest between the Museum's scientific and educational role and its role as an aware and responsible custodian of such material' (1989:7). The quality of associated documentation was specifically mentioned and indeed the museum had already carried out significant field documentation on parts of its existing collections. The museum also sought to establish 'mutually productive working relationships with indigenous makers and users of cultural material' (1989:7).

---

[2] This document was updated in 2008 (Australian Museum 2008), most recently in 2014 (Australian Museum 2014).

[3] I have selected those aspects of the document that are relevant to this paper. The document includes other attributes not discussed here.

The Pacific Acquisitions Policy (Australian Museum 1989:17–18) briefly described the range and scope of the Pacific collections and identified priority areas for active acquisition strategy. Thus material from Melanesia, especially PNG, was identified as top priority for strengthening the collections; the extension of the period of time encompassed by the collections was stipulated again:

> Where significant collections made in earlier decades (and especially at the turn of the century) occur, the Museum seeks to acquire contemporary material to document change over time. By preference the Museum seeks to acquire Melanesian material by making field collections in the context of anthropological research programmes (Australian Museum 1989:17).

In essence, the 1989 policy was concerned with keeping the collections (1) representative across time and (2) building upon existing collections, so as (3) to make commentaries about the processes of change and continuity. Lastly, (4) ethical concerns, such as the accommodation of 'ongoing feelings of makers and users', the 'appropriate' handling of collections and the willingness to 'avoid and reconcile differences' between scientific, educational and custodial[4] roles were considered important. These were significant departures from the nineteenth-century evolutionary theory upon which museum interpretations of objects were founded (Alexander and Alexander 2008; Bennet 1995; contributions in Stocking 1985; see Specht 1979 for the specific history of the Australian Museum's anthropology department and collections).

As will become clear, judged against the criteria 1–3 above, a contemporary collection of pottery from Wanigela was an opportunity to build the collections. But, as is required of policy-level frameworks, little practical detail regarding the day-to-day aspects of obtaining a collection is included. As I describe in this example, the method of collecting in large part was determined by consideration of what might be acceptable from the Wanigela point of view: I describe my attempt to achieve the disciplinary/anthropological objectives of the museum but also accommodate not only the wishes of the local community but their expectations of how things should be done. While this approach does not alleviate the concern which questions the extent to which a museum can represent a 'culture' through a handful of objects, it does address the issue of how communities represent themselves, rather than how others choose to represent them.

---

[4] The 2008 document contains the essential points of the 1989 document (as these relate to the Pacific component) but introduces and clearly articulates a connection between the cultural and the natural environment; it continues to emphasise the continuity of collections over time, rephrased as a 'time series' (rather than 'diachronic collections'); it adds the 'unlocking' of knowledge held in the collections and specifies the nature of social change (effects of urbanisation, industrialisation, tourism, environmental change, disasters). It introduces mention of the 'origin and functions of social exchange' (Australian Museum 2008:3) and emphasises the importance of the connection between collecting and research: the document sets out a specific listing of prioritised collection areas and object types and the cultural criteria These criteria foreshadow those listed by Russell and Winkworth (2010) against which new acquisitions should be assessed.

The Concept of a 'Timeline' of Change

The proposed collection for 2003 built upon an existing pottery collection from Wanigela registered into the museum between 1904 and 1910. The collection was acquired from a lay missionary Percy Money who had been resident in Wanigela from 1901 to 1910. The Money collection provides a point for comparison of change over time from the earliest period of first contact in PNG. It was made shortly after Britain annexed British New Guinea in 1884. While the first Administrator, Sir William MacGregor, made a much bigger ethnographic collection (Quinnell 2000) including material from the Collingwood Bay area in the late 1890s, he never visited Wanigela itself and so must have acquired the pots that he collected as items that had already been removed from Wanigela.

Money was not the first missionary in Wanigela. This was Reverend Abbott (resident in Wanigela from 1898 to 1901, Wetherall 1977:334) who, as was commonly done, also made a collection but which does not appear to have included pots.[5] Reverend Arthur Kent Chignell replaced Abbott in 1907 and also made a collection which contains only one pot.[6] So, while all four men (MacGregor, Abbott, Money and Chignell) made collections, only Money accumulated a substantial pottery collection. Therefore, Money's collection can be interpreted as representing a form from which changes or continuities over time can be assessed. In letters to the museum, Money stated that he wanted to preserve the material culture of a community that he felt was fast disappearing (Bonshek 1989), a sentiment which was in accord with the scientific community of the time who were engaged in 'salvage ethnography'.

Some 50 years later, Margaret Tuckson and Patricia May made a survey collection of pottery in PNG (2000 [1982]) and deposited their collection, including pots from Wanigela, in the Australian Museum. This accession contributes to the museum's 'time series'. And, in terms of 'continuity and change', this collection was substantially different to Money's. The addition of a collection made in 2001–2003 therefore allowed for a third time series and the possibility for investigation of change and continuities in social practices over a period of nearly a century, as well as contemporary expressions of social identity.

Thus, an acquisition in 2003 extends the existing archive providing material evidence of the past and the present with which questions about the way things used to be can be asked and theories of human interaction and agency can be generated and interpreted. Questions to be addressed included developments in local regional exchange networks, continuities in designs and manufacturing techniques, and the social significance of contemporary pottery manufacture.

---

[5] Abbott collected around 100 objects which he sold to the museum in Edinburgh (now the National Museum of Scotland).

[6] Chignell served in Wanigela from 1907 to 1914 (Wetherall 1977:335). Chignell sold his collections to the British Museum (and to other museums as well).

However, because Money did not record details of his collecting methods, it is a matter of theory as to how he actually acquired his collection; however, my analysis of his pot collection (Bonshek 2012) affords room for speculation that he collected them in ways other than through the media of barter or trade (Humphrey and Hugh-Jones 1992). Money's long-term residence in Wanigela, and his ability to speak the *tok ples*[7] language, suggests that he had probably been familiar with the indigenous protocols of acquiring pots and possibly these had even been given to him as gifts.

But if Money did not bequeath to us the detail of how he collected, there is direct evidence of the 'standard' of the time at this particular period in this particular region because MacGregor has left a record which gives an insight into how he collected and his sensibilities concerning the ethics of collecting. Also, as the first Administrator of British New Guinea, MacGregor was crucial in establishing the first legislation pertaining to the treatment and export of cultural heritage from British New Guinea and also setting the ethical standards for his time for collecting in British New Guinea (see Craig 1996).

Ethics of Collecting at the Turn of the Nineteenth Century: MacGregor's Collecting Practice

Collecting objects as ethnological material during the late nineteenth century was widespread (see Craig 1996 for a detailed overview of the history of collecting in PNG). Macgregor articulated a number of concepts underlying collecting at this time (Quinnell 2000). Collecting had to be done 'before it is too late' (Quinnell 2000:83)—a state that MacGregor already feared had become a reality by 1883. MacGregor saw collecting as a responsibility of a government officer and the collection as the property of the Crown. But he also encouraged private collectors of natural history specimens, demanding a share of the materials they acquired (Quinnell 2000: 84). On the ground he was, in fact, "trading" for food to supplement rations as well as for "ethnology"(2000:84): he exchanged iron, coloured cotton cloth, clothing, mirrors, beads, plane irons, hoop iron and hatchets for artefacts. Often, his interchanges were mediated by the indigenous men recruited into the Native Constabulary, who accompanied MacGregor on exploratory missions (Quinnell 2000:84–85).

MacGregor wanted his collection to be as 'complete' as possible: by which he meant 'as full a set of arms, utensils, products of different kinds &c., as would illustrate its past and present position in the future' (Quinnell 2000:90). 'Scientific' collecting in the late nineteenth century focused upon two sets of ideas: representativeness and completeness (MacDonald 2006) which in turn involved concepts such as 'duplicates' and 'gaps'. But obtaining a representative sample of the complete range

---

[7] PNG has three national languages: Tok Pisin, Motu and English as well as hundreds of local languages. *Tok ples* is the Tok Pisin term for the local language of an area.

of material culture was not easy: MacGregor could only collect the things that people were prepared to give him (and people did refuse to give him things). He noted the absence of women and children in his encounters and this in turn was reflected in the kinds of objects in his collection: he could not acquire a cross section of objects that related to all aspects of life (Quinnell 2008:87–88). MacGregor recorded a 300 % price rise for artefacts in some areas during his residence (Quinnell 2008:88), and he avoided these areas preferring to acquire where it was not 'too late'. His collecting ethos targeted preservation, not change. Duplicate objects from such collections were exchanged widely between museums in Britain, Europe and the colonies to fill 'gaps' in each institution's collections (King 1997).

In this model, an object's physical form held value, not the social relationships that surrounded it or that it materialised. In museums today, the social relationships surrounding a particular object might very well play a factor in the assessment of the object's value to the collection. But for MacGregor and his contemporaries, it is the 'thing' itself that was important because it manifested a stage of technological progress according to a particular understanding of social evolution (Chapman 1985).

Quinnell notes that MacGregor condemned the removal of objects by force and those who 'wantonly robbed and plundered' (2008:86). There were two cases of note at that time: D'Albertis' expedition up the Fly River in 1884 and that of the Royal Geographical Society of Australasia in 1885. MacGregor wrote:

> Of course such acts cannot be committed in the Possession now, as the actors would be dealt with in the police court, but it will take some time of fair dealing and kind treatment to efface from the native mind the impression left by carrying off those so called curiosities, which are to their native owners neither more nor less than the family jewels and heirlooms, and which they can seldom be induced to part with even for the much-coveted steel axe or new shirt (MacGregor, quoted in Quinnell 2008:86).

And so the ways in which people were collecting at that time were the subject of comment regarding an ethics of collecting.[8] MacGregor was concerned about the appropriate recompense, and decorous interactions surrounding the acquisition of objects and legislation was quickly introduced in an attempt to control the vigorous export of artefacts from the country (see Craig 1996; Busse 2000). Some 20 years later, the Government Anthropologist, F. E. Williams, wrote a report on the ethics of collecting in Papua, triggered by a report concerning the theft of ethnographic objects. Williams (1923) acknowledged in detail the significance of certain objects to local communities, emphasising their importance in ritual and religious life. Both MacGregor and Williams acknowledged an indigenous perspective regarding the human-object relationship which recognised an alternative and culturally specific significance. Legislation concerning the illegal export of cultural property was introduced early in PNG, and categories of prohibited items quickly

---

[8] Quinnell suggests that MacGregor clearly distinguished between 'collecting' through exchange and collecting via confiscation within his own collecting project. MacGregor did not, for example, incorporate the 1,563 items confiscated by him after a skirmish with locals on the Wassi Kussa River in 1896, rather he had these items destroyed (Quinnell 2000:87).

identified (see Craig 1996 for a history of the development of Cultural Heritage legislation in PNG). Pursuant to the current legislation governing cultural heritage (built upon MacGregor and Williams' legacy), pots of contemporary manufacture are not considered to be protected items of cultural heritage, and therefore, they are not prohibited from export.[9]

The Ethics of Ethnographic Collecting in the Twenty-First Century

Acknowledging the principles outlined in museum codes of practice, what constitutes ethical collecting 'on the ground'? How can ethical practice incorporate local perspectives? Or can this question be rephrased to ask, what constitutes the correct way to behave to acquire a collection of pottery in Wanigela?

In my ethnographic present of 2001–2003, pots in Wanigela could be acquired through purchase (as a commodity) or through gift, in recognition of social attachment. The emic use of clay pots in Wanigela is vital to understand which context is the appropriate one. Most older people in Wanigela say that women make pots because women are Wanigelan. Pot making distinguishes them from all the other villagers in Collingwood Bay. While metal pots and pans have largely replaced clay pots for daily cooking, older women continue to make them and some use them for presentations of cooked food at ceremonial events. In addition, pots continue as currency for exchange objects such as decorated bark cloth worn in festive dancing, for obtaining domesticated pigs for feasting and for outrigger canoes, string bags and puppies to be trained for hunting (Bonshek 1989, 2005; Egloff 1979). Established equivalences govern the exchange of these items. Both within and outside of Wanigela, pots are also required as an accompaniment to the transfer of bride price given by the man's family to a woman's family when a couple decides to live together.

If a Wanigela man or woman wants a pot, they approach a potter who is a relative: in such a small place, those who want pots can find kinship connections to potters. The existence of this social relationship sets up the expectation that the approach can be made. The making of pots for someone who asks is a normative, and expected, response. Some recompense may be made to the potter for the time that the work takes her away from her household duties and this may take the form of food. Generally, although there are exceptions, money is not exchanged for the provision of the pots between people who are closely related. Thus, the making of pots and their commissioning is largely set within the context of kinship, that is, social connection. People from villages outside of the area might also be able to make such social connections to the potters that they approached or they may have to commission pots to be made.

---

[9] However, despite this, I did take the collection to the PNG National Museum and obtained a permit for the museum's records as a form of protection against future questions arising around the absence of such a document.

However, in parallel to the acquisition of pots within the resources of the extended family, pots can be, and are, sold for cash. This typically happens at the markets outside Wanigela in neighbouring villages. Here, a woman might demand cash for pots, or alternatively make her transaction in a traditional exchange. If seeking cash, then there was a standard rate according to the size of the pot. During the period 2001–2003, tourists did not come to Wanigela, but they did go to Tufi where a dive resort operated. The Tufi market therefore held the potential for sale to tourists, as did the resort shop.

But it was rare to see pots on sale at the market in Wanigela. On the first occasion that I saw one there, I bought it. This resulted in my being chided for buying a pot when I had only to ask for one. My purchase was clearly incomprehensible in Wanigelan eyes: pots were gifted to people within a known social context and sold to people who were not known. I should have sought to acquire pots from the women with whom I was interacting socially, and not sought them from outside of this group.

What, then, were the implications for me in making a collection of pots for the museum? How could I achieve the anthropological objectives I had in mind and collect in a manner acceptable to Wanigela?

A Methodology for Collecting

From a disciplinary perspective, I was interested in any changes in pot making and how these might reflect changes in social practices. I wanted to document a number of aspects to achieve this aim. These included: the distribution of pot making across Wanigela, manufacturing techniques (the museum held adequate data to assess this using the earlier collections which included photographic records from 1904 to 1910 and also from the 1960s collection) and the contemporary use of pots, either in the home or in trade; I was also interested in the designs on the pots and wanted to identify these and consider their relationship to similar designs that appeared on barkcloth held in the museum collection. Finally I wanted to make a collection which would represent Wanigela broadly, and not favour any particular village of clan. The latter was particularly important to me because I had envisaged buying the collection and felt that it was important to strive for a fair distribution of financial benefit across the community. Each of the above points is addressed separately below:

Documenting the Distribution of Pot Making Across Wanigela

To achieve the greatest coverage of pot making, I set out to meet all the potters living in the 12 villages in Wanigela. There were no specialist villages (the distribution and age of potters and the villages is published elsewhere Bonshek 2008).

Quickly comprehending that I wanted to learn about pot making, the women decided to organise demonstrations and to teach me to make pots. They orchestrated five demonstrations on the basis of village residence. Analysis of my review of marriage and residence patterns (Bonshek 2005) revealed a high level of inter-marriage between the different clans living in Wanigela, which supported the even, if low, distribution of pottery skills throughout all the villages, a phenomenon which reflects marriage patterns in which women leave their natal villages to live with their husbands.

Documenting Manufacturing Techniques

I participated in and recorded pot manufacture, which emerged as remarkably uniform in technique: there was no substantial variation between the village groups. The women talked about pottery making as a 'Wanigela' activity. The technique also remained consistent with that described by Tuckson and May in the 1960s and by Money at the turn of the nineteenth century. I also queried women about how they had learnt how to make pots and from whom.

Surveying Contemporary pot usage

I undertook a household survey in which I made an inventory of the number of pots in each household I visited and whether or not any of the women residing there (or visiting) was a potter and what uses the pots were put to (such as local exchange, for sale at market, domestic use, held as mementoes of a relative, gift or a commission).

Discussing designs

Using photographs of the pots held in the museum collection, I asked potters about the designs on the pots (and on other object types), some of which had been identified with specific clan names by Percy Money.

In summary, I felt that the fact of the wide distribution of pottery skills across the villages was an important detail that should be captured in the acquisition of the pots I collected for the museum, especially as village alliances existed (demonstrated in the women's need to stage 5 demonstrations). This kind of information about pots and their manufacture a description of the human-object relationship, was absent from the earlier collections and the literature. I was interested to know who was making pots, for how long, who had taught the potters their skills and where potters were living. I viewed the pots as the material outcome of the intangible heritage of the pot making that I wanted to document.

Emic Considerations in the Human-Object Relationship

While obtaining a pot from every potter in Wanigela would have been a way to secure the fullest representation of Wanigela pot making, such an attempt was complicated by my developing social relationships with a core group of women. Over time, as I increasingly interacted with women who were either directly looking after me or associated with those who did so, the idea of buying pots not only receded from my mind, but was viewed by this core group as not an appropriate way for me to acquire a collection. The women of Wanigela should, they said, give me the pots for the museum's collection. They also wanted me to tell them how many pots I wanted and what types of pots. In short, their sense of a collection was something that would accommodate what I wanted.

By this time, their sense of what a museum collection might be had received some consideration. Throughout my stay of 15 months, I had shown photographs of the museum collections and discussed with men and women what was there and who had placed the collections there. The collector Percy Money was of interest because he was a figure who continued to exist in collective memory of older people and regular churchgoers (the latter incorporated a large proportion of the village residents). The women remarked that many of the pot shapes (or forms) in the museum's collection were no longer used or made. The abundance of decorative elements on these historic pots was also noted largely for the skill that it demonstrated. The women had admired of the work of their grandmothers.

However, their offer to make what I wanted, as a kind of commission, compromised my sense of how Wanigela women might choose to represent themselves in the making of such a collection. So, I in turn was reluctant to dictate what I wanted in the collection—although I did want it to be 'representative' of Wanigela more broadly. By being 'representative', I understood the reflection of the creative energies of Wanigela potters, hopefully unaffected by my influence, drawing upon the work of potters residing across Wanigela: in short, at the time I felt geographic spread to be desirable. Also my interest in the distribution of a particular skill (pottery making) made the acquisition of 'artworks' unnecessary from my point of view. I was interested in 'material culture', not 'art'.

And indeed Wanigela women seldom voiced what we might refer to as an 'aesthetic' of pot making. Rather, they understood every woman had the potential to be a potter, and the degree of skill of any individual was rarely commented upon. However, women with greater experience could tell and identify the work of others even though pots do not carry a maker's mark. If an individual pot was evaluated, it was on the basis of the thinness of the pot wall and, inseparable from thinness, the weight of the pot. The thickness of the pot affects the efficiency of the pot in cooking. The curvature of the pot also received comment on occasion, but only when the maker was not known. More broadly, the act of critically appraising someone else's work, or the role of a single potter as a connoisseur, was not customary. Once a woman could make a pot (i.e. she was no longer learning the basic techniques), her work was as good as the next potter's. The decorative elements rated little mention in terms of a local aesthetics of design, although clan designs were significantly different, carrying information about the owner of the pot and certain prohibitions on use (see Bonshek 2008). However, such designs were noted for their existence, not the quality of their execution. The acquisition of the 'best' work in Wanigela would therefore not represent a meaningful category of information from a Wanigelan perspective. All Wanigela pots were equally authentic or valid, reflecting the qualities and skills of Wanigela women.

Thus, a number of difficulties surrounded my purchase of a pot collection. Collecting could not proceed on the basis of acquisitions from the 'best' potters; to achieve broadest geographical distribution required abandoning the desires of my closest advisors to restrict myself to women with whom I had interacted; but pursuing the broadest geographical distribution would ensure young and old potters were included, and the maximum number of clans and diverse expertise (even if the latter were not acknowledged locally). The longer I resided in Wanigela, the more problematic my proposed purchase became.

A Resolution

By the time I felt I knew how to proceed, I was aware of two things: first, that my interactions in regard to pot making were being mediated through potters who were also members of the Anglican Church group, the Mothers' Union and second, that the local clinic was very poorly stocked with medical equipment. Working on the knowledge that pots were by their nature, potentially exchangeable objects, I suggested to the potters in the Mother's Union that instead of approaching potters individually and acquiring pots directly from them for money, I invite all potters to 'donate' a pot to the proposed collection, and instead of paying them their asking price, I would pool the monies to buy a blood pressure machine, stethoscopes and thermometers for the clinic (all the items that the medical officer had told me he lacked and desperately needed). They agreed to this suggestion and were happy to make a contribution to the acquisition of medical equipment for the clinic. That the community of Wanigela as a whole should benefit, through the use of the equipment, was an outcome that was considered by them to be very satisfactory. In addition, while Mothers' Union membership the MU membership included women from throughout the villages of Wanigela, potters who were not members were invited to participate.

Conclusion

In the end, the women contributed a collection of 15 pots, mostly, but not exclusively, made by the potters who belonged to the Mothers' Union. The pots in the 'donation' came from a number of villages in Wanigela and largely drew upon the work of older women.

Most of the pots made for the museum were either cooking pots made for trade and exchange or flowerpots.[10] The latter are given as gifts to people on all sorts of occasions and are visibly prominent when people are leaving the villages (e.g. at the airstrip). This composition of pot forms mirrors the museum's 1960s collection made by Tuckson and May and is also reflected in the photographic collection made by Brian Egloff during the same period.

However, the collection also offered a non-verbal commentary by two women on clan association and affiliation. One, a young woman who had recently started making pots, put a clan design onto the pot that she donated: she explained that this was the first time she had created such a design on a pot; a second potter placed a design on her pot which depicted a landmark relating to an origin story that she had previously recounted to me (in the context of a dispute over access to land). Her inclusion of this story, via a pictograph on the pot, was a claim for acknowledgement of her clan. As such, it was a bold statement, which now places her story in an archive which will outlive her. And further, she has placed her clan in the museum, where it cannot be dislodged. A third potter recreated a *simom* (water pot), a form which is no longer made and seldom seen. She told me she wanted to make the old style of pot, and it was the first *simom* that she had attempted and that the Money collection had inspired her to make this form.

These three examples are particularly interesting because they materialise visual (and tactile) forms of an earlier tradition, seldom seen publically in Wanigela today. While there are pots carrying clan designs such as those in the Money collection in Wanigela homes, they are stored safely out of sight as family mementoes of earlier generations. So the collection represents not a revival perhaps, but a reaffirmation of the potential for pottery to act as visual and tactile media for the expression of clan association and affiliation.

But the 2003 collection also represents another form of social identity of great importance to people today. Mediated through the efforts of the Mothers' Union, and a member of a neo-Pentecostal group, it affirms the way in which women identify themselves today as Christians and Wanigelans. While Christianity is an 'introduction' to Wanigela, imported through the efforts of Abbott, Money and Chignell nearly a century ago, it is now the national religion of PNG and the channel for social activities (as well as infrastructure) across the nation. While viewed as an 'introduction' in historical (disciplinary) perspective, Christianity is now an integral (not additional) aspect of Wanigela life. While missionaries made the first collections from Wanigela at the turn of the twentieth century, in the twenty-first century, it is the actions of Christian Wanigelans that have mediated the most recent acquisition.

From a 'disciplinary' perspective, the 2003 collection also represents physical evidence of a continuing tradition and technical knowledge through practice. But together with the data gathered on who makes pots and the documentation of the intergenerational transmission of pottery-making knowledge, it appears that pottery production is greatly reduced and is being maintained largely (but not exclusively) amongst the older generations of women.

---

[10] Flower pots were also included in the earlier Tuckson collection of the 1960s.

Whether pottery making continues into the future will reflect Wanigelans attitudes to traditional aspects of their lives and the value they place upon such objects in terms not only of their expression of social identity and but also economic necessity. Regardless of whether younger Wanigela women adopt or abandon pottery making, the new acquisition and the data collected from all the potters allows a 'disciplinary' reflection upon cultural continuity, change and expressions of social identity in contemporary Wanigela and enables a commentary on the forces of change occurring locally.

Codes of ethics and guidelines governing a museum's acquisition of materials provide a conceptual framework which establishes the need for consideration of social values as well as legal requirements and increasingly, the economic resources available to support new acquisitions. However, how ethics are operationalised in 'ethical practice' is not always clear cut or self-evident: making sure that people are adequately (as a minimum) recompensed is a paramount consideration, but the role of monetary payment (often associated with the legal & ethical transfer of ownership for museums) may not be easy to define or establish in any particular place or time. However, the combination of a research agenda which acknowledges the local sensibilities concerning the production of both material and intangible knowledge, rather than the acquisition of an object(s) alone, provides a way in which ethics can be implemented effectively rather than paid lip service to. It also provides unexpected results.

I hope that my acquisition of the pots was carried out in a manner that accords with the traditional ways of giving and receiving pots. I have tried to present the method of my making this particular collection and to voice the concerns I met with and articulate these with the anthropological objectives of making a museum collection. But as Sayers reflects, ultimately it will be others who will judge the ethical nature of my acquisition of pots from Wanigela.

References

Alexander, E., & Alexander, M. (2008). *Museums in motion: An introduction to the history and functions of museums*. Lanham: AltaMira.

Allen, L., & Hamby, L. (2012). Pathways to knowledge: Research, agency and power relations in the context of collaborations between museums and source communities. In Byrne, S., Clarke, A., Harrison, R., & Torrence, R. (Eds.), *Unpacking the collection. Networks of material and social agency in the museum* (pp. 209–229). London: Springer.

Australian Museums. (1989). *Policies and principles of collection management*. Sydney: Australian Museum.

Australian Museums. (2008). *Ethnographic collection development strategy, 2008-2012*. Sydney: Australian Museum.

Australian Museum. (2014). Cultural Collections Acquisition Policy, 2014-2017. www.Australianmuseum.net.au/Our-policies . Accessed 2 September 2014.

Belk, R. (2006). Collectors and collecting. In C. Tilley, W. Keane, S. Küchler, & P. Spyer (Eds.), *Handbook of material culture* (pp. 534–546). London: Sage.

Bennett, T. (1995). *The birth of the museum: History, theory, politics*. London: Routledge.

Besterman, T. (2006). Museum ethics. In S. MacDonald (Ed.), *A companion to museum studies* (pp. 432–441). Chichester: Wiley-Blackwell.

Bonshek, E. (1989). *Money, pots and patterns: The Percy Money collection of bark cloth and pottery held at the Australian Museum.* Masters Qualifying thesis, University of Queensland.

Bonshek, E. (2005). *The struggle for Wanigela: Representing social space in a rural community in Collingwood Bay, Oro Province, Papua New Guinea.* Doctoral dissertation, Australian National University, Canberra.

Bonshek, E. (2008). When speaking is a risky business: Understanding silence and interpreting the power of the past in Wanigela, Oro Province, Papua New Guinea. *Journal of Material Culture, 13*(1), 85–105.

Bonshek, E. (2011). Collecting relations: Contemporary collecting in Papua New Guinea. *Journal of Museum Ethnography, 23*, 7–20.

Bonshek, E. (2012, August). *The complications of reflecting upon the past: Research and museum collections.* Paper presented in the session Shifting Traditional Museum Boundaries: Research, Agency and Power Relations, Australian Anthropological Society, Brisbane.

Busse, M. (2000). The National Cultural Property (Preservation) Act. In K. Wimp & M. Busse (Eds.), *Protection of Intellectual, biological and cultural property in Papua New Guinea* (pp. 81–95). Canberra: ANU Asia-Pacific Press.

Chapman, W. R. (1985). Arranging ethnology: A. H. L. F. Pitt Rivers and the typological tradition. In G. W. Stocking Jr. (Ed.), *Objects and others. Essays on museums and material culture* (pp. 15–48). Madison, WI: University of Wisconsin Press.

Commonwealth of Australia. (2009). *Collecting cultural material: Principles for best practice. A resource for Australia's collecting institutions.* Canberra: Department of the Environment, Water, Heritage and the Arts.

Conn, S. (2010). *Do museums still need objects?* Philadelphia, PA: University of Pennsylvania Press.

Council of Australian Museums Association. (1993). *Previous possessions, new obligations: Policies for museums in Australia and Aboriginal and Torres Strait Islander peoples.* Melbourne: The Council.

Craig, B. (1996). *"Samting bilong tumbuna": The collection, documentation and preservation of the material cultural heritage of Papua New Guinea.* Doctoral dissertation, Flinders University of South Australia, Adelaide.

Edson, G. (Ed.). (1997). *Museum ethics.* London: Routledge.

Egloff, B. (1979). *Recent prehistory in Southeast Papua.* Canberra: Australian National University.

Genoways, H. (Ed.). (2006). *Museum philosophy for the twenty-first century.* Oxford: AltaMira.

Hein, H. (2000). *The museum in transition: A philosophical perspective.* Washington, DC: Smithsonian Institution Press.

Humphrey, C., & Hugh-Jones, S. (1992). *Barter, exchange and value: An anthropological approach.* Cambridge: Cambridge University Press.

International Council of Museums. (2013). *ICOM code of ethics for museums.* Paris: ICOM.

King, M. E. (1982). The ethics of ethnographic collecting. *Council for Museum Anthropology Newsletter, 6*(4), 2–8.

King, J. (1997). Franks and ethnography. In M. Caygill & J. F. Cherry (Eds.), *A. W. Franks: Nineteenth-century collecting and the British Museum* (pp. 136–159). London: British Museum Press.

Knell, S. (Ed.). (2004). *Museums and the future of collecting.* Farnham: Ashgate.

Lidchi, H. (2012). Great expectations and modest transactions: Art, commodity and collecting. In G. Were & J. C. H. King (Eds.), *Extreme collecting: Challenging practices for 21st century museums* (pp. 131–156). New York: Berghahn.

MacDonald, S. (2006). *Collecting practices. A Companion to Museum Studies.* Chichester: Wiley-Blackwell.

McLeod, M. (1993). *Collecting for the British Museum.* Milan: Carlo Monzino.

Museums Australia. (2005). *Continuous cultures, ongoing responsibilities: Principles and guidelines for Australian Museums working with Aboriginal and Torres Strait Islander cultural heritage.* www.museumsaustralia.org.au

O'Hanlon, M. (1993). *Paradise: Portraying the New Guinea Highlands.* London: British Museum Press.

O'Keefe, P., & Prott, L. (Eds.). (2011). *Cultural heritage conventions and other instruments: A compendium with commentaries.* London: Institute of Art and Law.

Peers, L., & Brown, A. (2003). *Museums and source communities: A Routledge reader.* London: Routledge.

Perrot, P. (1997). Museum ethics and collecting principles. In G. Edson (Ed.), *Museum ethics.* London: Routledge.

Quinnell, M. (2000). "Before it has become too late": The making and repatriation of Sir William MacGregor's official collection from British New Guinea. In M. O'Hanlon & R. L. Welsch (Eds.), *Hunting the gatherers: Ethnographic collectors, agents and agency in Melanesia, 1870s-1930s* (pp. 81–102). Oxford: Berghahn.

Russell, R., & Winkworth, K. (2010). *Significance 2.0: A guide to assessing the significance of collections.* Canberra: Commonwealth of Australia.

Sandell, R., & Nightingale, E. (2012). *Museums, equality and social justice.* Abingdon: Routledge.

Sayers, R. (1991). Museum collecting in a postmodern world: A Korean example. *Museum Anthropology, 15*(3), 8–12.

Specht, J. (1979). Anthropology. In R. Strahan (Ed.), *Rare and curious specimens: An illustrated history of the Australian Museum 1827-1979* (pp. 141–150). Sydney: Australian Museum Trust.

Stanley, N. (Ed.). (2007). *The future of indigenous museums: Perspectives from the Southwest Pacific.* Oxford: Berghahn.

Stocking, G. (Ed.). (1985). *Objects and others: Essays on museums and material culture.* Madison, WI: University of Wisconsin Press.

Thomas, N. (1991). *Entangled objects: Exchange, material culture and colonialism in the Pacific.* London: Harvard University Press.

Tuckson, M., & Patricia, M. (2000). *The traditional pottery of Papua New Guinea.* Adelaide: Crawford House.

Vergo, P. (Ed.). (1989). *The new museology.* London: Reaktion.

Weil, S. (2002). *Making museums matter: A reflection on the nature of museums.* Washington, DC: Smithsonian Institution Press.

Wetherell, D. (1977). *Reluctant mission: The Anglican Church in Papua New Guinea 1891-1942.* St. Lucia: University of Queensland Press.

Williams, F. E. (1923). *The collection of curios and the preservation of native culture.* Port Moresby: Papua Government Printer.

Chapter 10
Tourism, World Heritage and Local Communities: An Ethical Framework in Practice at Angkor

Richard Mackay and Stuart Palmer

Introduction: Ethics and Cultural Heritage

Ethics is about answering the question 'what ought one do?' It is concerned with the pursuit of what's good and doing what's right. Or we might simply say that ethics is about making better decisions. Ethical decision-making processes seek to facilitate informed, reflective and deliberative choice of best action and outcomes which take account of decision maker and stakeholder values and principles whilst responding to contextual circumstance. However, in practice, conflicting perceptions or rankings of values as well as external pressures can obscure a clear view of 'what to do?' Conflicting values can arise in cultural heritage management both internally where heritage values are contested and externally where heritage values conflict with values of non-heritage professionals such as local communities (Scarre and Scarre 2006:3).

Nowhere is this challenge more apparent than at World Heritage sites with both mass tourism and living resident local communities. At the World Heritage site of Angkor, Cambodia, the combination of rapidly growing tourism and the intangible heritage of a massive lived-in sacred landscape provides an opportunity to explore the interaction between human rights, intellectual cultural property and heritage management and the role that an ethical decision-making framework can play in navigating that interaction. At Angkor, by contrast with other World Heritage sites with living indigenous communities and enduring cultural traditions (see Titchen 2002), traditional cultural practices were not recognised in the initial

R. Mackay (✉)
Godden Mackay Logan Pty Ltd Heritage Consultants,
78 George Street, Redfern NSW 2016, Australia
e-mail: richardm@gml.com.au

S. Palmer
St James Ethics Centre, Sydney, Australia
e-mail: stuart.palmer@ethics.org.au

© Springer Science+Business Media New York 2015
T. Ireland, J. Schofield (eds.), *The Ethics of Cultural Heritage*,
Ethical Archaeologies: The Politics of Social Justice 4,
DOI 10.1007/978-1-4939-1649-8_10

World Heritage List citation in 1992 (see Mackay and Sullivan 2008; UNESCO 2013) but are now understood to be fundamental to both the 'official' value of the place to organisations like UNESCO and, importantly, to Khmer people for whom Angkor is both 'home' and a symbol of nation. However, this 'culture' also has important 'economic' value to the ever-growing tourism sector. There is currently a significant disconnect between the beneficiaries of the economic value and traditional owners of the cultural value. The question which arises is how to make cultural heritage management decisions within an ethical framework?

This chapter commences with an outline of ethical decision making which is rooted in Western philosophical exploration of ethics. More proximately the material draws on tools, models and concepts used in practical engagement by applied ethicists in Australia with public, private and not-for-profit organisations across a wide range of sectors and industries. These tools, models and concepts are informed not only by Western ethical traditions but also by work and research in psychology, cognitive science and organisational studies (see Carroll and Shaw 2013 for a recent work on ethical decision making in individual lives, organisations and professions which draws insight from these and other sources). Our particular way of thinking about ethics and ethical decision making (with the roots and sources mentioned above) has the potential to limit the insight we are able to offer to those approaching ethics from other directions and traditions. However, we hope that the 'theoretical' ethical elements we advance are general enough to accommodate a wide variety of approaches to ethics. And indeed part of the purpose of this chapter is to explore similarities and differences between the theoretical ethical decision-making framework we describe and actual practice of decision making in cultural heritage management.

An Ethical Decision-Making Framework

To answer the question 'what ought one do?' it is helpful to consider four elements: values, stakeholder relationships, decision-making principles and pressures on decision making. These elements are common to both the decision-making framework described below and to values-based cultural heritage management (see UNITAR 2013; Demas 2000), recognising that individuals and organisations do not necessarily articulate their frameworks in a way which uses this terminology or observes strict distinctions between the different elements.

What Are Our Values?

Our values are the things we consider fundamentally valuable and important. In this context we're trying to identify core, higher level values, rather than instrumental values which we see as means to achieve some more fundamental goal. In relation to a particular domain of activity, there may be some values which are intrinsic to the ethical conduct of that activity: for example, fairness on the sporting field, justice in the practice of law and knowledge at a university. Other values may not have this intrinsic connection—for example, one might or might not value creativity in the ethical conduct of a career in finance. Cultural heritage values are usually defined as the attributes that make a place 'important' to a community and are usually assessed and defined according to 'aesthetic', 'historic', 'scientific' or 'social' or similar attributes (see e.g. Australia ICOMOS 1999).

What Are Our Stakeholder Relationships?

Good decision making requires the identification of stakeholders and taking account of their relevant interests. Stakeholders, whether colleagues, clients, partners or local communities (and beyond), will typically exert different types of claim on a decision maker, depending on the nature of their relationship. It is often important to distinguish between stakeholder interests and desires. When a diabetic comes to a doctor asking for medication to facilitate the consumption of more chocolate, the doctor will typically have regard to what they consider to be in the best long-term health interests of the client, rather than simply prescribing the medication best suited to the patient's request. Of course in many cases, the expressed desires of a stakeholder will indicate the stakeholder's interests. Related to this, and of particular relevance to communities local to culturally significant places, an ethical response should typically be made in a way which has careful regard to the way that local community members experience and perceive the issue, as well as to their social context and the imbalance of power that may exist between local people and authorities. Community participation needs to be meaningful and to include 'negotiation', rather than just adopting the values and practices of the expert (Waterton et al. 2006).

What Are Our Principles?

Principles are the rules or tests which are applied to help select the right and best way of advancing values in the interests of stakeholders. Such principles may not necessarily direct what should occur in a particular situation. Rather they require honest and thorough engagement with available choices. The best way to understand the nature and role of what are known as 'thin' principles of this type, following Bernard Williams' distinction between thin and thick ethical concepts (Williams 1985:129), is to consider some examples: the golden rule (i.e. treat others as you would have them treat you); put yourself in the shoes (position, perspective, background) of others affected by the decision. How will they feel about it? The sunlight test—imagine the decision you are proposing to make will be on the front page of the newspaper tomorrow; Which choice maximises benefits over harms? Which choice best advances your values? Which choice best develops the good character of those involved? Which choice best protects the rights and dignity of the individuals affected? (These examples of principles draw on a number of different approaches to ethical decision making, including virtue ethics, deontological ethics and consequentialism—see e.g. Frankena 1973.)

What Are the Other Influences and Pressures on our Decision Making?

The final element of the framework addresses actual practices of decision making and action. A decision-making structure that considers values, stakeholders and principles assumes that it is possible to populate and apply that framework in a rational way. Of course an assumption of decision-making rationality is often unrealistic, and it is important to take account of non-rational (or less rational) influences and pressures, for example, following unthinking custom and practice; over-discounting long-term impact or over-emphasis on short-term or easily measurable goals; tribalism or groupthink; undue attention paid to powerful, noisy or nearby stakeholders; cognitive bias and distortions (e.g. belief perseverance, confirmation bias, cognitive dissonance); unconscious bias based on gender, race, age or culture; and time pressure. It is important to recognise and think about ways to take account of the impact of such influences on decision making and counterbalance them where they pose a threat to the quality of decision making. For example, diversity of those involved in the decision-making process may mitigate the effect of confirmation bias (which can incline us to see evidence which supports our existing point of view but to discount contrary evidence).

Decision-Making Processes: Ethics and Heritage

The above elements of an ethical framework (values, stakeholder relationships, principles and pressures) need to be assessed (and reflected on periodically) to provide a foundation for ethical decision making. The challenge then becomes ensuring that these foundational elements are actually put to work in the practice of decision making, and organisations will often develop a decision-making process designed to help ensure this happens. An 'ethical decision-making process' should include the following components: identifying relevant facts (and unknowns), relevant values and their implications; identifying assumptions, perspectives and pressures; identifying relevant stakeholder relationships and interests and ensuring appropriate voices are heard; framing the issue or dilemma, for example, identifying competition between values, between stakeholder interests; brainstorming all the possible options; assessing the application of relevant policies, laws and norms; applying the principles to evaluate the different options; and planning implementation of the decision chosen. These elements of good decision making emerge from the practice and philosophy of ethics, but they align strongly with current models for heritage management (e.g. Australian Heritage Commission 2002; China ICOMOS et al. 2004; Kerr 2004; Australia ICOMOS 1999) which usually describe a methodology that involves steps such as gathering and analysing documentary, physical and oral evidence; assessing heritage values, usually according to statutory criteria; identifying relevant constraints and issues; consulting with associated people; framing the issue or dilemma, for example, identifying competition between values, between stakeholder interests; brainstorming all the possible options, applying relevant statutes and policies; preparing heritage management or conservation policies; preparing implementation strategies; and monitoring progress and reviewing and adjusting the plans.

In short, and perhaps unsurprisingly, the underlying process of values-based heritage management is an ethical framework, intended and predisposed to deliver optimal outcomes which take account of both decision maker and stakeholder values and principles. Effective heritage management documents are effective precisely because they are ethically founded and designed to be cognisant of and responsive to relevant values, stakeholder perspectives, principles and pressures. This is not to ignore the growing corpus of critique which highlights weaknesses in heritage practice, including the power imbalance between institutions, regulators, experts and communities, nor that many heritage documents and projects are ineffective (Smith and Waterton 2009:139; see also the summary provided in Poulios 2010). Whilst these criticisms have merit, they also draw attention to the extraordinarily challenging position of the ethical heritage manager who, in assessing the values, principles and stakeholder relationships which are to guide decision making, must often take account of very diverse—and sometimes very unfamiliar—perspectives on which values, principles and stakeholder relationships ought to play that guiding role. There is a power relationship implied by the fact that the heritage decision maker is the person making this assessment. But this flows from the fact that he or she carries the decision-making authority—and responsibility. An alternative would be for him or her to relinquish decision-making (or recommendation making) authority. The power imbalance might be removed but then the benefit of the heritage professional's expertise and experience (not to mention his or her ethical decision-making skills) is lost. In our assessment, values-based approaches to heritage management do strive to be inclusive, transparent and ethical.

Figure 10.1 includes a 'heritage management process' drawn from the *Burra Charter* (Australia ICOMOS 1999) which can be seen as combining both the process of identifying key elements of an ethical framework in the context of a particular site, along with a series of decision-making steps designed to put these elements to work. Alongside this heritage management process are listed the foundational elements of an ethical framework already described, together with components of a 'generic' ethical decision-making process (drawn from a model designed by St James Ethics Centre). The figure indicates connections between the heritage process and the general ethical framework and decision-making process.

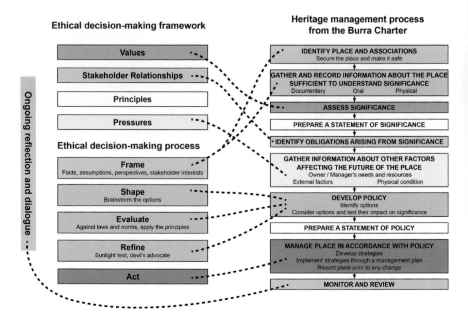

Fig. 10.1 Comparison of the Burra Charter's heritage management process with an ethical framework and ethical decision-making process

The Ethical Decision-Making Framework in Practice in Heritage Management?

How is the theoretical ethical decision-making framework described above actually applied in heritage management? The comparison below addresses similarities and differences according to the four elements of the theoretical framework described above in light of a current project at Angkor, which involves World Heritage values, local community stakeholders, a range of guidelines and principles and major tourism pressures. The consideration is drawn from personal experience of cultural heritage decision making in Australia and Asia; well-accepted practice guidelines such as *Ask First* (Australian Heritage Commission 2002), the *Burra Charter* (Australia ICOMOS 1999) and the China Principles (China ICOMOS et al. 2004); international treaties and declarations which address the rights of stakeholders and local people; and the Angkor Heritage Management Framework project (Godden Mackay Logan Pty Ltd 2013a). However, by way of context for ensuing observations, it is helpful to pause briefly and to contemplate the majestic place that is Angkor.

Angkor

Angkor is an iconic and internationally recognised heritage place which inspires and amazes through its monumental scale, scenic cultural landscape, deep and continuing history and superb artistic achievement. Stretching over some 400 km², the

Angkor World Heritage Park contains the magnificent remains of the different capitals of the Khmer Empire, from the ninth to the fifteenth century, including massive reservoirs, ancient roads, and famous temples like Angkor Wat, the Bayon, Banteay Srei and Ta Prohm. The site vividly expresses Khmer architecture, engineering and town planning and is laden with cultural, religious and symbolic values, as well as containing many individual sites of high architectural, archaeological and artistic significance (UNESCO 2013). Perhaps more than any other World Heritage site, Angkor is recognised as a symbol of culture and nation, featuring in every version of the Cambodian flag since independence. Over the last two decades, there has been a sustained national and international conservation effort at Angkor, which has seen the site removed from the List of World Heritage in Danger (Beschaouch 2010).

Values

Values play a central role in decision making for heritage places. Indeed the identification of values is fundamental to heritage identification processes, which requires regard to be had to the features of a site which embody natural and/or cultural attributes. For example, the inclusion of Angkor on the World Heritage List in 1992 was based on a judgement (UNESCO 2013) that the place satisfied World Heritage criteria (i), (ii), (iii) and (iv):

Criterion (i): The Angkor complex represents the entire range of Khmer art from the ninth to the fourteenth centuries and includes a number of indisputable artistic masterpieces (e.g. Angkor Wat, the Bayon, Banteay Srei).

Criterion (ii): The influence of Khmer art as developed at Angkor was a profound one over much of Southeast Asia and played a fundamental role in its distinctive evolution.

Criterion (iii): The Khmer Empire of the ninth to fourteenth centuries encompassed much of Southeast Asia and played a formative role in the political and cultural development of the region. All that remains of that civilization is its rich heritage of cult structures in brick and stone.

Criterion (iv): Khmer architecture evolved largely from that of the Indian subcontinent, from which it soon became clearly distinct as it developed its own special characteristics, some independently evolved and others acquired from neighbouring cultural traditions. The result was a new artistic horizon in oriental art and architecture.

The articulation of these features of the site provides a ready-made road map to the key site values which the heritage decision maker should seek to conserve. Importantly though, heritage management practice is not limited to the advancement of only these first-articulated heritage values. As understanding grows of the site and its context and communities (including recognition that the so-called 'past' civilisation lives on beyond the 'brick and stone' record), so does the heritage professional's understanding of the heritage values of the site—for example, a greater recognition of its contemporary intangible cultural values. In practice this growing understanding is realised as subsequent value assessments, culminating (in the case of Angkor) in preparation by Cambodia of a new' Statement of Outstanding Universal Value' for the consideration of the World Heritage Committee, which overtly recognises the importance of Angkor's intangible heritage (see Godden Mackay Logan et al. 2012 and Lloyd and Khuon in press). This development of understanding of heritage values derives of course not just from growth of site-specific knowledge. Greater recognition of intangible alongside material heritage values also reflects general developments in understanding of the nature of heritage values and the rights of living communities within (and beyond) the profession. The Convention for the Safeguarding of the Intangible Cultural Heritage is both a product of, and contributor to, this developing understanding, with the measures it outlines for safeguarding intangible heritage at a national and international level (UNESCO 2003). Increasingly this heritage is not only conceived as a social condition but also as a community right and asset:

> The heritage of indigenous peoples is comprised of all objects, sites and knowledge, the nature or use of which has been transmitted from generation to generation and which is regarded as pertaining to a particular people or territory. The heritage of an indigenous people also includes objects, knowledge and literary or artistic works which may be created in future based on its heritage (United Nations Commission on Human Rights, Economic and Social Council 1995, Definitions).

This focus on the interplay between intangible heritage, indigenous people and the rights that vest in the 'value' of this heritage continues. An International Expert Workshop on the World Heritage Convention and Indigenous Peoples which was organised by the International Work Group for Indigenous Affairs was held in Copenhagen as recently as September 2012, in association with the 40th Anniversary of the World Heritage Convention. Among other findings this workshop determined that:

> Indigenous peoples must be recognized as rights-holders and not merely stakeholders in any decisions affecting them, in accordance with their distinct status and rights under international law and in particular, their right of self-determination (International Work Group for Indigenous Affairs 2012).

Obviously a developing broader understanding of heritage values does not automatically translate into practice. In the context of Angkor, concerns have been expressed about the limited regard paid in some cases to intangible elements (and some tangible elements) of cultural heritage. Winter (2009:112) has noted the systemic disconnect between traditional architectural or monumental heritage and continuing history, observing that:

> In piecing together Angkor's history much less attention has been given to the Khmer inscriptions found among the temples or the evidence pertaining to the ongoing presence of animism. Indeed, within an account of architectural splendour and pristine glory, anthropological accounts that might reveal oral histories or the transmissions of cultural traditions across generations have been largely overlooked.

More recently Lloyd and Im (2013:228) lament that 'At many heritage places the management of intangible heritage is typically considered as an afterthought to the preservation and presentation of monumental remains or natural sites'. However, on a more positive note, the Authority for the Protection and Management of Angkor and the Region of Siem Reap (APSARA) is currently developing a specific policy to advance the protection of, and respect for, intangible cultural heritage in the Angkor region (Hor 2011).

Stakeholders and Stakeholder Rights and Interests

The identification of heritage stakeholders and understanding of their rights and interests is at the heart of many current issues and challenges in heritage management. Whilst a key motivation for heritage conservation is the interest that all people have in the world's heritage, it is also obviously crucial to recognise the way in which the heritage-related rights and interests of different people will differ. Once again this is an area where there has been development in the profession's thinking, in this case its understanding of the nature, relationship and priorities between rights and interests of different groups. Some important examples are the recognition of the special interests which local communities have in continuing and developing their own cultural traditions and practices and, more recently, in sharing in the economic benefits of the use of local natural and cultural heritage. A logical next step from recognising the cultural value of intangible heritage and community traditional practices is to recognise the economic value of cultural heritage as intellectual property. This is more easily said than done; for a long time there has been '…widespread unfair exploitation of the cultural heritage <…..> for commercial and business interests' (WIPO-UNESCO 1999. article 2).

Related to this issue is an increasing appreciation of the key role which appropriate management of items of heritage value can play in sustainability and development of local communities; and the central role which local communities ought be allowed to play in any decision making concerning their heritage as well as directly participating in heritage conservation, use and development. Articles 11.1, 12.1, 23 and 31.1 of the 2007 United Nations Declaration on the Rights of Indigenous Peoples (United Nations 2008) particularly acknowledge the rights to self-determine, practice manage and develop cultural heritage, traditional knowledge customs and cultural expressions. The cultural rights of local communities thereby fall within the overall discipline of human rights and, as such 'provide the right to maintain and develop a specific culture or cultural identity <and are> clearly pertinent to the protection of intangible heritage' (Lloyd 2009:56).

The Kyoto Vision published by participants gathered in Kyoto on the occasion of the Closing Event of the Celebrations of the 40th Anniversary of the World Heritage Convention in 2012 affirmed and extended this principle within the context of a broader agenda for sustainability:

> We are convinced that a people-centred conservation of the world's cultural and natural heritage is an opportunity to provide critical learning models for the pursuit of sustainable development and for ensuring a harmonious relationship between communities and their environment. The concept of heritage is fundamental to the logic of sustainable development as heritage results from the dynamic and continuous interaction between communities

and their environment. Heritage sustains and improves the quality of life of people…
benefits derived from well- protected cultural and natural heritage properties should be
equally distributed to communities to foster their sustainable development and there should
be closer cooperation with management bodies and experts (Kyoto Vision 2012).

These perspectives and observations highlight the need to pay particular heed to
the economic and educational circumstance of local people, who are seldom in an
equal power relationship with either site management authorities or decision
makers. There is a need on the one hand to break the pattern of tourism providing
the smallest relative benefit to the poor in least developed countries (UNCTAD and
WTO 2001) and on the other to recognise that heritage tourism offers a viable strategy to address poverty in these nations. Further stakeholder considerations attach to
the nature and circumstances of the people themselves. Consultation mechanisms
need to be appropriate and friendly, built on communication, engagement and trust.
This may require that resources be directed towards establishing trust and long-term
relationships, as well as nonthreatening techniques that empower people to express
opinions and desires, free of external influences or fears.

Principles

Thin decision-making principles are intended to facilitate informed and good faith
decision making, without being formulated in a way which direct a particular course
of action in a particular case. Often principles of this type are not written down in
formal articulation of the values, rights and interests which are to be taken into
account in decision making—for example, in the United Nations and UNESCO conventions and declarations already mentioned above. Although these documents often
refer to 'principles', these principles are in many cases *thicker* principles like a 'principle of intergenerational equity' which—at least in part—is intended to describe the
particular outcome which is to be pursued (in this case equity between generations).

This is not to say that principles like the sunlight test and golden rule are not
applied in practice by heritage professionals, but it is difficult to make general comment. However, some of these familiar ethical principles or tests may be framed in
a way which is more specific to the heritage advisor, for example:

- A *sunlight test* which requires the advisor to imagine that the proposed recommendation will be on the front page of the local newspapers of significant stakeholder groups
- An*other person's shoes* test which requires the advisor to follow a thorough
  consultation process regarding the relevant issues with representatives of affected
  groups
- A *golden rule* which asks the advisor to imagine that the natural or cultural heritage is heritage of the advisor's own cultural group and to imagine the local
  children are children of their own

All three of these tests are relevant to the circumstances of local communities
and tourism pressures at Angkor.

Other Influences and Pressures

Various factors may stand in the way of the effective protection and management of intangible cultural heritage:

- The specific cultural perspective of the heritage professional (or site manager or regulator) which may place greater value on tangible heritage (such as temples or carvings) rather than intangible heritage (such as traditional medicines or ceremonies)
- A tendency to emphasise or focus on areas for which there are established skill sets, experience and frameworks (such as well-established missions working at Angkor)
- The general ongoing influence of past practice

In this regard Viñals and Maryland (2012:46) observe:

> The impacts involving the intangible values and functions of heritage are very often more important than the physical ones, but have received less attention both from World Heritage site management bodies and from the academic world as they are sometimes difficult to detect, measure and value and even harder to deal with.

This observation too is true at Angkor where two decades of successful collaboration on monumental repair is now finally being joined by initiatives directed at local community support, as well as a policy framework which recognises the need to deliver benefits to local people so that they can continue to enjoy cultural traditions and practice, to live sustainably in the Angkor Park and to share in the resources generated from the industry that 'sells' their culture to visitors (Godden Mackay Logan Pty Ltd 2012, 2013a; Hor 2011; Lloyd and Khuon in press; Lloyd and Im 2013). Importantly, this change is leading towards a more sustainable place and a more sustainable community, recognising that '*a balance needs to be achieved between the use of heritage as an economic asset and heritage as a cultural resource, without compromising preservation or sustainable development*' (Negussie and Wondimu 2012:99).

Whilst there is, of course, a long way to go, at least one current 'pilot project' which is being implemented as part of the Angkor Tourism Management Plan offers an example of sustainable and culturally appropriate use of heritage as a local economic asset, as well as a vignette of the ethical framework for decision making in practice.

Managing Tourism at Angkor

Angkor's traditional cultural practices are integral to the social fabric of contemporary communities but are also now recognised as part of the heritage value of the Angkor World Heritage site and the Cambodian nation: 'local people have a legitimate and significant role within the Angkor Park and... their existence and activities contribute to the outstanding universal value of the site' (Lloyd and Khuon in press; see also Mackay and Sullivan 2008; Khuon 2006; Im 2003, 2007; Hor 2011) (Fig. 10.2).

Fig. 10.2 Buddhist ceremonies and practice are but one element of Angkor's rich intangible heritage (Photo: Georgina Lloyd 2010)

Angkor's intangible heritage is reflected in 'localised animistic and Brahmanic beliefs, the daily activities of people who live around the monuments of Angkor, continuing Buddhist practices and traditional livelihood activities' (Lloyd and Khuon in press). This 'intangible' heritage is increasingly threatened by growing tourism. International visitation to Cambodia has grown from c118,000 in 1993, the year after Angkor was inscribed on the World Heritage List, to c3.5 million 2012. The vast majority of international tourists visit Angkor, as do Cambodian nationals, whose presence is not recorded by ticket sales numbers, as they are entitled to free entry (Kong and Horth 2012). Tourism impacts are many: large visitor numbers alter the environment and ambience of sacred spaces, tourism development has environmental and social consequences, and community lifeways change in response to both tourist expectations and demographic shifts as younger generations especially seek employment away from villages in the tourism industry.

And yet, despite these social impacts, the effects of tourism do not provide widespread economic benefits to the more than 130,000 Khmer who actually live within the Angkor World Heritage Park, nor to the many hundreds of thousands more who live in the surrounding Siem Reap Province (Hall et al. 2014). The disconnect between the heritage value of the place, the economic powerhouse of burgeoning tourism and the rights of the local people as owners of the heritage which is being presented and sold to tourists gives rise to a challenging ethical issue for cultural heritage management. Siem Reap is already a poor province in a poor nation: Cambodia ranks 138 out of 186 countries on the UNDP Multidimensional Poverty Index, with more than 45 % of the national population living in multidimensional poverty—measured according to health education and living standards (United Nations Development Programme 2013). Given that tourists at Angkor are paying to visit a Khmer place and learn about Khmer culture, there would seem to be a strong case that tourism at Angkor should be delivering substantive economic benefits to local Khmer people.

There is also a strong case that tourism at Angkor should encompass the more recently recognised intangible traditional cultural values. But as Winter and others have noted, the 'living heritage' values of the site have been largely ignored, by policies focused on structural conservation and tourism (Winter 2007). However, this practice is changing. The collaborative development of a Tourism Management Plan offers an integrated approach to tourism and heritage management at Angkor (Godden Mackay Logan Pty Ltd, The APSARA National Authority and UNESCO 2012). The Tourism Management Plan (or 'TMP') is part of a broader 'Heritage Management Framework' (HMF) project being undertaken through collaboration between UNESCO, the Royal Government of Cambodia and the Australian Government (Godden Mackay Logan Pty Ltd 2013a).

Both HMF and the TMP use a 'values-based' methodology in which the values of the site are identified and agreed, issues affecting those values are considered and analysed, stakeholders are consulted and involved, and then policies and actions, which address the issues and retain the values, are developed (Australia ICOMOS 1999). In this regard, the TMP has in effect adopted a version of the above 'ethical framework' for decision making. In particular, whilst the TMP may reflect a light-framed decision-making model, the outcome has been directed by local community perspectives (the other person's shoes test), has been publically exhibited and transparently prepared and endorsed (the sunlight test) and seeks to deliver better outcomes for all participants (the golden rule test). The resulting TMP seeks to manage the fast-growing tourism at Angkor through six key policy initiatives:

- Providing positive visitor experiences by encouraging and promoting different opportunities, recognising that different visitors have different expectations and needs
- Reducing site impacts through visitor education, management of visitor flows and better information delivery
- Partnering with industry to provide incentives and new products for tourism operators
- Offering benefits for local people through greater participation of local communities, direct economic benefits and greater recognition, acceptance and celebration of local cultural beliefs, practices and traditions
- Improved governance which responds to the practical realities of the resources that are available to the Cambodian Government; and stakeholder engagement through consultative implementation and opportunities for the people and organisations involved in tourism to participate in the process

Whilst all six initiatives are integral to the cultural change that will be needed to implement the TMP successfully, the delivery of genuine, self-evident benefits to local people is particularly imperative, not only as an ethical obligation but as an outward and visible sign of the underlying paradigm shift (Hall et al. 2014). Therefore, another related element of the HMF is a series of 'pilot projects' which demonstrate how such changes might work in practice. One such project, which demonstrates diversification of the visitor experience and development of community-based tourism, as a tool to address rural poverty, is the 'Community

Tour for Baray Reach Dak'. This project demonstrates a new approach to tourism management and stakeholder involvement and addresses directly the often-highlighted, but seldom-solved, problems of inequity in benefit distribution from cultural property:

> An inequity gap exists in benefits distributed to many rural communities whose cultural heritages are being appropriated and exploited by multiple commercial entities for tourism purposes and personal gain. Little, if any, of the profits realized benefit the local community- the actual creators and owners of the local culture (George 2010: 376).

Community Tour for Baray Reach Dak

The Community Tour for Baray Reach Dak was originally conceived as an opportunity to foster the development of a community-based tourism 'product' within the Angkor World Heritage Park. Whilst the Angkor HMF project team has facilitated the 'pilot project', it has been conceived and is being operated by local people. The tour extends and expands the visitor experience at the Preah Khan temple, by adding a walking tour or 'natural circuit' in the nearby forest and an opportunity for a boat trip on the nearby 'North Baray' in a traditional Khmer wooden boat. Whilst there have been some previous community tourism initiatives at Angkor, including ox-cart tours, and local craft manufacture and sales (Khuon 2006), the focus on this initiative has been concurrent delivery of outcomes that reflect the interests of the local community, the APSARA National Authority and the tourism industry (Hall et al. 2014).

The North Baray is a large constructed Lake which has recently been repaired and refilled by the Department of Water Management. 'Baray Reach Dak' is the local community name for the lake. Refilling of the Baray allows a reinterpretation of both the Baray itself and the associated temples and surrounding environment, including the relationship between ancient hydrological management, the traditional use and association of the temples and the beliefs and customs of contemporary communities. For the visitor there is an emerging opportunity to understand that the place has values and meaning that transcends the stereotypical 'ruin in the jungle'. For the people of Leang Dai and Phlong, the two local villages, there are both cultural and economic opportunities—including particularly the prospect of employment adjacent to home (rather than in Siem Reap), direct income from tourism and skills acquisition for young people.

Members of the HMF Project team and APSARA staff from the HMF Technical Committee and Community Liaison Team have worked with the villagers using a participatory planning approach: the 'Stepping Stones for Tourism' (Stepwise Heritage and Tourism 2013). This method combines community needs and aspirations with local tourism product development, and heritage conservation (Hall et al. 2014). The outcome of this interactive and inclusive process is a unique offering to visitors: a guided walking tour through a beautiful forest, with engaging explanation of the medicinal and other properties of the forest plants, followed by a trip in a small wooden Khmer boat, across the Baray through submerged forests water lilies

Fig. 10.3 Participatory planning methods have involved local people in all aspects of the developing Community Tour for Baray Reach Dak (Photo: Nicholas Hall 2013)

and birds, to the Neak Pean temple (Godden Mackay Logan Pty Ltd 2013b). In the initial stages the HMF Project team and APSARA staff continue to provide 'hands-on' support, but the villagers take the tourist bookings, sell tickets, guide the tours and operate the boats. In time, other tours and food or craft sales can be added to the visitor offer. Initial feedback from tourists is enthusiastic and very positive (Journeys Within 2013) (Figs. 10.3 and 10.4).

The emerging business should soon provide income to more than thirty individuals, spread across the two villages, as well as funds for a common community fund. In time, the entire enterprise will be independently operated by the local communities. Of course, problems and challenges remain, including particularly striking a balance between directing and supporting those involved in the growing business and allowing them to self-determine and 'learn by doing'. The danger of the former is an entrenchment of the expert adviser's approach, as THE only way. By contrast, without some ongoing involvement of those with experience in community-based tourism, the new business and the individuals involved may struggle to prosper. By advising and mentoring, rather than directing and managing, the Angkor HMF team is hoping to encourage independence, even if the business moves in unexpected directions. What is significant is that the enterprise is concurrently fostering a continuation and celebration of Khmer culture by local Khmer people AND delivering genuine economic benefits to the owners of that culture. It is also a small step in fostering a wider understanding and enjoyment of Angkor's intangible heritage as a lived-in sacred landscape.

Fig. 10.4 Visitors enjoy the natural environment and quiet solitude during their boat journey on Baray Reach Dak. The new experience spreads the tourist load and provides income to local villages at Angkor (Photo: Richard Mackay 2012)

The project is timely, not only as an exemplar of how the TMP can work in practice, delivering concurrent and multiple policy outcomes for the place, its residents and visitors, but also as real-world implementation of APSARA's policy for 'Sustainably Safeguarding Intangible Cultural Heritage at Angkor', particularly to 'recognise the right of all villagers to their intangible heritage and their obligation to respect, protect and receive benefits from their heritage' (Hor 2011, policy 9 (ii)). From an ethical perspective the project stands on a strong values-based foundation that seeks to conserve and interpret the multiple values of the place; the process has engaged with, and indeed been driven by, the perspectives of the key stakeholders; the response addresses the pressures of increasing tourism and importantly the total project complies with established principles for the rights of local people to enjoy and benefit from their own culture and heritage.

Conclusion

There are strong parallels between ethical decision-making frameworks and values-based cultural heritage management. Both approaches require a clear understanding of (and ongoing reflection on) values, stakeholder viewpoints and interests and external issues or pressures. This understanding, together with the application of decision-making principles, helps build clarity of overall purpose and objectives.

Neither approach provides an 'easy answer' but rather they offer a transparent method for ensuring that relevant factors are uncovered and appropriately considered and weighted in decision making, fostering the exploration of innovative solutions to ethical and heritage challenges and ultimately grounding robust decisions and strategies. For places with multiple values and competing pressures, application of an ethical framework sits comfortably with heritage management practice and can facilitate outcomes which are particularly cognisant of stakeholder perspectives, desires and rights. Managing Angkor's intangible heritage is assisted by an ethical approach which not only recognises multiple heritage values but also the fundamental rights and legitimate economic entitlements of local communities who share their rich and enduring heritage with ever-increasing hordes of enthusiastic visitors.

Acknowledgements This paper presents a framework that is derived from the work and experience of the St James Ethics Centre, an Australian centre for applied ethics, working with public, private and not for profit organisations and professional associations. The case study draws heavily upon the Angkor Heritage Management Framework project being undertaken by Godden Mackay Logan Pty Ltd for UNESCO, the Royal Government of Cambodia and the Australian Government, whose support is gratefully acknowledged. We also particularly thank Dr Georgina Lloyd, Nicholas Hall and Prof Sharon Sullivan for their generous assistance and our Khmer colleagues for the privilege of working on and at Angkor and amid their culture and their traditions.

References

Australia ICOMOS. (1999). *The Burra Charter: The Australia ICOMOS Charter for Places of Cultural Significance*. Available via DIALOG: http://australia.icomos.org/publications/charters/ Accessed April 2, 2013.

Australian Heritage Commission. (2002). *Ask first: A guide to respecting indigenous heritage places and values*. Canberra: Australian Heritage Commission.

Beschaouch, A. (2010). Angkor saved, prosperity on the way. In *Angkor: Fifteen years of international cooperation for conservation and sustainable development* (pp 18–26). Phnom Penh: UNESCO ICC (International Coordinating Committee for the Safeguarding and Sustainable Development of the Historic Site of Angkor [and] Phnom Penh),

Carroll, M., & Shaw, E. (2013). *Ethical maturity in the helping professions: Making difficult life and work decisions*. London: Jessica Kingsley.

China ICOMOS, in association with the Getty Conservation Institute. (2004). *China principles: Conservation and management principles for cultural heritage sites in China*. http://www.getty.edu/conservation/our_projects/field_projects/china/china_publications.html. Accessed May 2, 2013.

Demas, M. (2000, May 19–22). Planning for conservation and management of archaeological sites: A values-based approach. In J. M. Teutonico & G. Palumbo (Eds.), *Management planning for archaeological sites: An international workshop organized by the Getty Conservation Institute and Loyola Marymount University* (pp. 22–50). Los Angeles: Getty Conservation Institute.

Frankena, W. (1973). *Ethics*. Englewood Cliffs, NJ: Prentice-Hall.

George, W. (2010). Intangible cultural heritage, ownership, copyrights, and tourism. *International Journal of Culture, Tourism and Hospitality Research, 4*(4), 376–388.

Godden Mackay Logan Pty Ltd. (2013a). *Angkor Heritage Management Framework*. http://www.gml.com.au/resources/angkor-hmf/. Accessed April 30, 2013.

Godden Mackay Logan Pty Ltd. (2013b). *Natural Circuit at North Baray Angkor Park*. http://www.gml.com.au/resources/angkor-hmf/naturalcircuit/. Accessed May 1, 2013.

Godden Mackay Logan Pty Ltd, the APSARA National Authority and UNESCO. (2012). *Angkor World Heritage Area Tourism Management Plan*. International Committee for the Safeguarding and Development of Angkor and Surrounding Areas. Available via DIALOG. http://www.gml.com.au/resources/angkor-hmf/. Accessed April 30, 2013.

Hall, N., Richard, M., & Sullivan, S. (2014). Taming tourism at Angkor. In B. Baillie (Ed), *Angkor: Heritage Tourism and Development. Multidisciplinary perspectives in archaeological heritage management*. New York: Springer.

Hor, R. (2011). APSARA Authority: ICH safeguarding in the Angkor living site, Siem Reap. *Intangible Cultural Heritage Courier for Asia and the Pacific, 8*, 13.

Im, S. (2003). Angkor: A living heritage site. *Report for living heritage sites programme, first strategy meeting*, Bangkok: SPAFA Headquarters.

Im, S. (2007). Social values and community content. In *Living with Heritage: Report of the living with Heritage Technical Committee*. Phnom Penh: APSARA Authority.

International Work Group for Indigenous Affairs. (2012). World heritage and indigenous peoples: A call to action. *Resolutions of an international expert workshop on the world heritage convention and indigenous peoples*. Copenhagen. http://whc.unesco.org/uploads/events/documents/event-906-1.pdf. Accessed May 4, 2013.

Journeys Within. (2013). A fresh approach to Angkor Park. *Blog Post*. http://www.journeyswithin-travelblog.com/2013/04/09/a-fresh-approach/. Accessed May 1, 2013.

Kerr, J. S. (2004). *The conservation plan: A guide to the preparation of conservation plans for places of European Cultural Significance* (6th ed.). Sydney: National Trust of Australia.

Khuon, K-N. (2006). *Angkor: Site management and local communities*. Unpublished paper delivered to the Angkor—Landscape, City and Temple conference, University of Sydney.

Kong, S, & Horth, V. (2012). *Tourism Statistics Annual Report 2012*. Cambodian Ministry of Tourism, http://www.tourismcambodia.org/images/mot/statistic_reports/tourism_statistics_annual_report_2012.pdf. Accessed May 1, 2013.

Kyoto Vision. (2012, November 8). *Published by participants gathered in Kyoto on the occasion of the closing event of the celebrations of the 40th anniversary of the world heritage convention*, http://whc.unesco.org/en/news/953/. Accessed May 4, 2013.

Lloyd, G. (2009). *The safeguarding of intangible cultural heritage: Law and policy. A case study of Angkor*. Doctoral Dissertation, University of Sydney.

Lloyd, G., & Im, S. (2013). Cambodian experiences of the manifestation and management of intangible heritage and tourism at a World Heritage site. In R. Staiff, R. Bushell, & S. Watson (Eds.), *Heritage and tourism: Place, encounter, engagement* (pp. 228–250). London: Routledge.

Lloyd, G, & Khuon, K-N. (in press). Safeguarding Angkor's intangible heritage. In B. Baillie (Ed.), *Angkor: Heritage Tourism and Development*. New York: Springer.

Mackay, R., & Sullivan, S. (2008). *Angkor: Heritage values and issues*. Sydney: University of Sydney.

Negussie, E., & Wondimu, G. S. (2012). Managing world heritage sites as a tool for development in Ethiopia: The need for sustainable tourism in Lalibela. In M.-T. Albert, M. Richon, M. J. Viñals, & A. Witcomb (Eds.), *Community development through world heritage* (pp. 93–99). Paris: UNESCO.

Poulios, I. (2010). Moving beyond a values-based approach to heritage conservation. *Conservation and Management of Archaeological Sites, 12*(2), 170–185.

Scarre, C., & Scarre, G. (2006). Introduction. In C. Scarre & G. Scarre (Eds.), *The ethics of archaeology: Philosophical perspectives on archaeological practice* (pp. 1–12). Cambridge: Cambridge University Press.

Smith, L., & Waterton, E. (2009). *Heritage, archaeology and communities*. London: Duckworth.

Stepwise Heritage and Tourism. (2013). *Stepping stones for tourism*. Available via DIALOG, www.steppingstonesfortourism.net. Accessed April 16, 2013.

Titchen, S. (2002, May 15). Cultural heritage and sacred sites: World Heritage from an Indigenous perspective. *Presentation to the world heritage from an indigenous perspective conference*. New York, www.dialoguebetweennations.com/N2N/PFII/English/SarahTitchen.htm, Accessed April 27, 2013.

UNCTAD and WTO. (2001). The least developed countries and international tourism. Tourism in the least developed countries. *Published for the third UN conference on the least developed countries*, Madrid: World Tourism Organisation.

UNESCO. (2003). *Convention for the Safeguarding of the Intangible Cultural Heritage*. http://portal.unesco.org/en/ev.php-url_id=17716&url_do=do_topic&url_section=201.html. Accessed May 4, 2013.

UNESCO. (2013). *Angkor. World Heritage List.* http://whc.unesco.org/en/criteria/. Accessed May 4, 2013.

UNITAR (United Nations Institute for Training and Research). (2013). *The Management and Conservation of World Heritage Sites 2013 Workshop.* http://www.unitar.org/hiroshima/management-and-conservation-of-world-heritage-sites. Accessed May 12, 2013.

United Nations. (2008). *United Nations Declaration on the Rights of Indigenous Peoples 2007.* http://www.un.org/esa/socdev/unpfii/documents/DRIPS_en.pdf. Accessed May 4, 2013.

United Nations Commission on Human Rights, Economic and Social Council. (1995). *Principles & guidelines for the protection of the heritage of indigenous people.* E/CN.4/Sub.2/1995/26, GE. 95-12808 (E). Elaborated by the Special Rapporteur, Mrs. Erica-Irene Daes, in conformity with resolution 1993/44 and decision 1994/105 of the Sub-Commission on Prevention of Discrimination and Protection of Minorities. http://ankn.uaf.edu/iks/protect.html. Accessed May 4, 2013.

United Nations Development Programme. *Human Development Index.* http://hdrstats.undp.org/en/countries/profiles/KHM.html. Accessed April 27, 2013.

Viñals, M. J., & Maryland, M. (2012). Heritage, tourism and local community interactions within the framework of site management. In M.-T. Albert, M. Richon, M. J. Viñals, & A. Witcomb (Eds.), *Community development through world heritage* (pp. 40–47). Paris: UNESCO.

Waterton, E., Smith, L., & Campbell, G. (2006). The utility of discourse analysis to heritage studies: The Burra Charter and social inclusion. *International Journal of Heritage Studies, 12*(4), 339–355.

Williams, B. (1985). *Ethics and the limits of philosophy.* Cambridge: Harvard University Press.

Winter, T. (2007). *Post-conflict heritage, postcolonial tourism, culture, politics and development at Angkor.* London: Routledge.

Winter, T. (2009). The modernities of heritage and tourism: Interpretations of an Asian future. *Journal of Heritage Tourism, 4*(2), 105–115.

WIPO-UNESCO. (1999). *Regional Consultation on the Protection of Expressions of Folklore for Countries of Asia and the Pacific.* http://www.wipo.int/meetings/en/details.jsp?meeting_id=3726. Accessed April 30, 2013.

Chapter 11
A Matter of Trust: The Organisational Design of the Museo de la Libertad y la Democracia, Panama

Ana Luisa Sánchez Laws

Introduction

The shadows of the military dictatorship that ruled Panama between 1968 and 1989, and of the invasion that brought it to an end, still lurk in the consciousness of many of that generation. As civilian testimonies reveal:

> On September 22, 1988, they (the Panamanian Defence Forces) searched my office and took me into custody… They told me "we are going to kill you, you know, you are next"… I had nowhere to lie down, no food, and nowhere to go to the toilet… They showered me and put me in front of a large air conditioning duct until I started to tremble, they let me get dry there, while they were interrogating me. Four times this happened… One of those times, a pond of water formed around my feet, and a guard took an electric cable and put it in the pond, laughing… they took me to Tocumen Airport with handcuffs and a hood over my head… they forced me into the plane at gunpoint, threw my passport at me and told me 'you will never come back'. I was in exile for a year, until December 30, 1989 (after the invasion). Even though I fight it, I still can't handle certain stories. Some nights, I have recurrent nightmares… this is what this type of torture does to you (Alberto Conte, member of the Civilian Crusade, interviewed for a special supplement of *La Prensa*, 1992, n.p.).
>
> It was a Thursday, Thursday the 20th. I was studying; I had an exam at university the next day. I thought nothing was going to happen. Nothing like that had happened before in Panama, that was something from the movies. Friends of our family called and told us to get out of our house, U.S. soldiers were surrounding El Chorrillo. We moved to the second floor of my brother's house to hide. The house caught fire, and when we were going to run away, the stairway fell down. We ended up in the balcony. There were some U.S. tanks coming, we asked them for help. They just told us to jump. My mom did not want to jump, she was afraid, so I jumped first. I hit myself in the spine but I thought I was fine. We ran to safety. A year later, I started to lose movement in my arms and legs, and I lost my sight. My life was truncated, my dreams, my ambitions (Yolanda, resident of El Chorrillo, interviewed by Clea Eppelin, 2005).

A.L. Sánchez Laws (✉)
Media Arts and Production, Faculty of Arts and Design, University of Canberra,
Bruce, ACT 2601, Australia
e-mail: Ana.SanchezLaws@canberra.edu.au

© Springer Science+Business Media New York 2015   185
T. Ireland, J. Schofield (eds.), *The Ethics of Cultural Heritage*,
Ethical Archaeologies: The Politics of Social Justice 4,
DOI 10.1007/978-1-4939-1649-8_11

This is a history where there are no clear winners. More than anything, it is a history of betrayal. Consider the US military invasion that ended the dictatorship. On the one hand, the community that supported the invasion had many reasons to feel betrayed. It never imagined the magnitude of the human costs of calling in a foreign power. During the 2 weeks of sustained military activity, whole neighbourhoods were burnt to ashes. More than 4,000 Panamanians were caught in the line of fire, and a lack of consensus remains over how many died; many were buried in a hurry in communal graves (Hockstader 1990; Human Rights Watch 1991; Freed 1991). The community that supported the dictatorship, on the other hand, felt betrayed by a leader (General Manuel Antonio Noriega) who fled to the safety of the Vatican embassy while a battle was fought on the streets on his behalf (Larmer 1989). The result of this history is a shared distrust in the political system, in the media and, above all, amongst members within and between communities.

What happens with museums in countries with a history of political violence such as Panama, where decades of corruption and abuse have resulted in low trust in institutions and low trust in cooperative behaviour in general? And why would it be important for a museum to collaborate in building trust between and within communities? This chapter deals with the role of museums in a historically violent society. Specifically it asks how a social history museum can help rebuild trust within a community and to what effect. More broadly it examines the role of a community organisation in rebuilding trust in a democracy and its institutions in a country with a history of conflict.

The issue is timely. A new museum is currently in the making in Panama, the Museo de la Libertad y la Democracia. This is a project in Panama City for a museum about the representation of the country's human rights violations, with emphasis on the period between 1968 and 1989. It is a private community initiative aiming to redress the exclusion of the military regime and invasion that dominates governmental museum narratives, as two decades after the invasion and end of the dictatorship, established Panamanian museums still either remain silent or address these events only temporarily.[1]

Hardin (2002) has argued that in situations of distrust, where strong leaders and state institutions have been the problem (e.g. in the Soviet Union), the best alternative to rebuild trust is to create weak institutions and leaders, so as to remove the source of the problem.

My interest in museums comes from a similar perception. Museums can influence public opinion, but they do not have the legal power to limit it. They are weaker kinds of organisations, yet they can be very pervasive forces in identity building. Museums have the potential to promote positive relations in a community yet may not be able to replace the essential source of trust that a primary unit such as the family represents.[2]

---

[1] This topic is dealt with in more depth in Laws and Luisa (2011).

[2] For a discussion of intermediate institutions as sources of trust and a critique of Robert Putnam's ideas of civic engagement, see Job (2007).

In essence, museums are weak yet influential enough to be interesting organisations for situations in which trust in government and trust in community cooperation have been shattered. Yet although the idea of the museum as an institution of trust is not new, the role of the museum in shoring up trust in the context of conflict is still not well understood.

Approach

After mapping the concept of trust and how it relates to the work of museums, the chapter goes on to consider the specific case of the Museo de la Libertad y la Democracia through the lens of the *value of trust* and *its sources* and in the issue of defining *the object entrusted*.

In what concerns *value*, trust will be explained as an important heuristic for individual and collective decision-making and also as underpinning cooperative behaviour in society. For the *sources* of trust, my main interests will reside in the museum as a place to facilitate the emergence of sources of trust (e.g. via enabling open discussions amongst communities in a relatively safe environment) and in the issues surrounding the museum as a source of trust itself. In relation to defining *objects entrusted*, I will examine current provisions for forms of heritage relevant to the memories of the dictatorship and invasion. Some shortcomings in current definitions about what ought to be preserved in national heritage legislation are raised. These shortcomings point to a lack of recognition of the symbolic importance of this heritage. This is further discussed in a comparison between the Panamanian situation and solutions to similar problems in other countries in the Latin American region. While the focus is on the Museo de la Libertad y la Democracia, I bring in solutions from other Latin American experiences because the lessons that can be learned from them are important for putting the Panamanian case in context for the purpose of evaluating its efforts so far.

The chapter concludes by way of a proposed organisational design. I argue that in the context of a politically violent history, the new museum initiative's success hinges on several forms of trust building. For the Museo de la Libertad y la Democracia to succeed in its mission, it is necessary for it to nurture transparent relations among stakeholders, to harness existing legal frameworks and to construct open channels of communication with the community. Frameworks from international institutions may help in addressing gaps in concepts of heritage and in garnering support for the memory work concerning the periods of conflict. With this approach to trust building, the museum may avoid being drawn into polarised discussions about "how" the military regime and invasion should be represented. Its mission will be well defined within the push to collect and make available evidence about this period to future generations of Panamanians.

Before discussing trust and museums in situations of conflict, I start with a more general delineation of trust as it relates to museums.

Trust in Museums

Trust is understood as a social contract between two or more parties. While contractual conceptualisations of trust suggest a zero-sum game (i.e. A trusts B to take care of C), trust is a much more complex matter. As Baier (1986), Jones (1999) and Gambetta (1988) suggest that trust can be affected by power asymmetries in the relationship, by context and by the "agenda" of each party and the parties involved.

The tripartite definition proposed by Baier (1986) is well known: A trusts B to take care of C, and this means that A gives some discretionary power to B over C. C has to be very important for A (Baier 1986). It has to be valuable enough for the trustor (A) to experience the trustee's (B) power as a risk (Gambetta 1988), and it also involves vulnerability (Rousseau et al. 1998).

Nooteboom (2008:259) sees trust as a "four-place predicative: a trustor (1) trusts a trustee (2) in some respects (3), under some conditions (4)". Nooteboom (2008) also argues that some risk is involved. In particular, the trustee has to have opportunities to take advantage of the trustor. There are, however, many nuances to the above. These include kinds of trust, dynamics of trust, power asymmetries in trust, the value of trust, sources of trust, contexts of trust and the parties involved. I will focus on just three of these, namely, the value of trust, the sources of trust and the object entrusted.

Value of trust	Extrinsic: relationships are less costly when trust is involved, as investment in supervision is reduced. Intrinsic: a relationship based on trust is valuable in itself (Nooteboom 2008). Trust has value as a necessary component of enabling collective hope (Braithwaite 1998)
Sources of trust	Social expectations and norms ("thin trust") and personalised and specific sources ("thick trust") (Nooteboom 2008, after Williams 1988). Trust as coming from the family and modified in interaction with the government (Job 2007)
Object entrusted	The object entrusted is valuable and unique (Baier 1986). The object helps establish whether it is trust or mere reliance

The above table provides an overview of some known theoretical discussions upon these aspects. A more detailed explanation is presented below.

The Value of Trust

Nooteboom (2008) refers to the extrinsic benefits of trust for achieving social and economic goals (the cost of trust). If there is trust in the relationship, it will be more effective, as fewer resources will be invested in surveillance. In terms of its intrinsic value, a relationship based on trust can be valued for itself. Deutsch (1973) also notes that relations without trust fall into the most consuming type of power, which is coercive and conditional. Luhmann (1979) points out that trust can be used to reduce complexity, and it is an important heuristic in our decision-making. Trust, in sum, can make our relationships with the world and with each other smoother and easier.

Baier (1986) has addressed how to establish the value of a trust relationship through an expressibility test, which demands for partners to be explicit about what they are relying upon for trust to exist. Depending on the answer, this expressibility may destabilise the trust relationship (e.g. if one part is relying in the other's weakness or misplaced beliefs as the basis of trust), or it may strengthen it (when the party expresses its reliance in the other's competence and goodwill).

For museums, trust is invaluable. Without trust, the public would not even go to exhibitions, for how could they accept the knowledge presented? Without trust, the task of collecting would be incredibly hard, for how could anyone endow the museum with objects? Trust is implicit in all relations surrounding the museum, even if it is not explicitly stated.

Sources of Trust

The sources of trust are complex and varied and range from personal attributes to institutional settings. Nooteboom (2008), for example, lists several heuristics from social psychology that can be useful to understand the sources of trust. He notes the "availability heuristic", where trust can emerge from comparisons to near events or situations in memory; the "representativeness heuristic", where trust comes from comparisons with similar events or situations in memory (stereotypes); and "anchoring and adjustment", where a comparison is made to a base value (first impression) with subsequent incremental adjustments of that value then taking place.

Another way to look at the sources of trust is to follow Williams (1988) and Nooteboom (2008) in their descriptions of "thin" and "thick" sources of trust. Thin trust comes from institutions that enforce it (contracts, reputation, values, norms, kinship, morality). For example, Fukuyama argues that trust implies the expectation of members of a community or group for cooperative behaviour (Fukuyama 1995), yet the social-norm-based trust he describes could be considered as only part of those types of trust coming from thin sources. Thick trust is based on specific relations and is personalised (via hierarchy, dependence, empathy, routinisation, identification, affect or friendship). This would include processes of identification, oneness and connectedness (Braithwaite 1998). When derived from recognising similar traits, trust can be easily enlarged and also misplaced (Nissenbaum 2004).

Undoubtedly, an important source of thin trust in the museum is its perceived competence, and this of course includes that of its staff. Museums depend on the professionalism of curators, conservators and exhibition designers, which is in turn "certified" by universities. The museum's trustworthiness also grows in strength through membership in organisations such as the International Council of Museums (ICOM). Even when they are not staff, the reputation of other individuals participating in the museum adds to its trustworthiness. For example, a high-profile human rights activist on the museum board can bring credibility to the organisation. Yet this also depends on the position of these stakeholders within the organisation.

We can also refer to Nooteboom's (2008) distinction between trust in competence and trust in intentions. An additional source of trust in the museum comes from its still largely untainted image of neutrality and lack of (evident) political alignment. By and large, the public trusts that the museum's intentions are honest and for the benefit of society, as it is a not-for-profit organisation.

Museums also have experience with thick trust, via identifying themselves with the values of the community. This is done in several ways. The community is invited to participate in the making of exhibitions and collections through the provision of artefacts (a source of identification once these are on display). Another way is to involve the community more structurally as cocurators. In both cases, the "them" becomes "us".

In what concerns the museum as a source of trust in itself, the impact of intermediate organisations as sources of trust should not be taken for granted. Job (2007) problematises some assumptions in Putnam (1993, 1995) about intermediate organisations (such as clubs or associations) as sources of trust and points to Erikson's (1950s) ideas of the family as the cornerstone of trust building (1959). It is from our primary socialisation in the family that trust "ripples" into the rest of society (Job 2007). However, Job also points to how this trust is modified by the interaction between individual and government.

The role of museums as places for social change has been a matter of debate for practitioners and theoreticians for some time (New Museology being a clear reference; see, e.g. Vergo 1989, and, in Latin America, DeCarli 2003), yet there is still lack of consensus and insufficient empirical data to establish the actual power of these organisations. Job's (2007) empirical data from Australia shows a limited effect from middle-range organisations (and museums could be located in this category). Job speculates that policy-creating institutions and families are stronger sources of societal trust than community organisations.

More empirical research is needed to clarify whether museums that are involved in creating or executing policy have indeed a significative impact in building societal trust and whether museums that stay away from participating in policy making end up having no effect in nurturing trust and have thus very low impact in their communities.

I argue that in the particular case of Panama, museums can be said to sit between the primary socialisation (as educational institutions) and government spheres of life. Panamanian museums have traditionally been explicit governmental means of enforcing cultural policy, and their role as educational institutions was established in law early on with the first projects for museums in the early 1900s (Sánchez Laws 2011).

It may be more appropriate to view sources of trust in museums under the loupe of *trust norms* (Braithwaite 1998). These are norms that emerge when an agreement has been made upon some common goals, and the question becomes how to achieve those goals and gain support from the community. Braithwaite refers to exchange and communal trust norms. Exchange trust norms have to do with rational decisions about trust. Transparency and information about an organisation cater to those types of norms and so do reputation and adherence to respected bodies. Communal trust norms have to do with harmony and with feelings of connectedness. For organisations, when they are perceived to share the values of the community and to *care* for the well-being of community members, they are appealing to types of communal trust that are found in the family. Communal trust norms are close to social connectedness and shared identities (Braithwaite 1998).

For Braithwaite, once a decision to cooperate (which implies a decision to trust) is made, both types of norms come into play and need to be balanced in order to reach the common goal. This is a theoretical move based on empirical data that shows it is necessary to bridge the divide in the trust literature between those who conceive trust as a calculated relationship and those who stress ideas of care.

The Object Entrusted

As has been pointed out above, C, or the object entrusted, has to be something vulnerable, valuable and unique. It can be something material, but it can also be something intangible (feelings, emotions, memories, secrets).

The obvious objects entrusted to museums are artefacts. These are items of archaeological importance; they constitute material historical evidence. In the ethical frameworks available for museums, provisions for such kinds of artefacts are extensively developed (from issues of conservation to issues of repatriation and so on). Recent changes in the materials that support evidence (in the form of audiovisual recordings or digital documents) mean that currently the concept of heritage and its safeguarding are in revision. In Latin America, the concept of documentary heritage is being used to justify the value of heritage related to histories of conflict and thereby being used to promote its preservation.

As noted above, the idea of documentary heritage comes from recent concerns in the heritage sector about the preservation of new forms of material culture, such as audiovisual and digital materials. Audiovisual and digital materials have become predominant forms of evidence of the heritage of our contemporary world, yet international bodies such as UNESCO and ICOM have only recently addressed the issue of preserving this type of material. This is understandable: the technology is just over a hundred years old, and electronic technology is even younger. The pace of change from storing crucial information about our world in durable artefacts to storing it in the more ephemeral digital formats has been intense and extremely fast paced. The call is then to begin to consider a future form of museum artefacts that departs substantially from the types of material artefacts that have so far characterised collections.

As with other types of artefacts, there are a number of criteria that need to be met for audiovisual and digital materials to be considered trustworthy and important enough to be preserved. For example, for documentary heritage to be accepted into UNESCO's Memory of the World Programme, applicants have to comply with the following criteria:

- *Integrity*, which means proving that the artefact has not been manipulated or damaged
- *Authenticity*, which can be certified by an external body that attests to the source
- *Uniqueness*, for example, that it is a document of restricted access
- *Value*, which is dependent upon its relevance for the local community and the world

The framework of documentary heritage, on the one hand, helps back up the need for museums to preserve everything from papyrus to floppy discs. It opens up the concept of heritage to go beyond archaeological objects to include contemporary forms of memory. The Memory of the World Programme, on the other hand, has prompted the development of human rights archives such as Paraguay's "Archives of Terror", Argentina's "Human Rights Documentary Heritage 1976–1983—Archives for Truth, Justice and Memory in the struggle against State Terrorism" and the "Human Rights Archive of Chile". In the case of documents about conflict in Latin America, this type of material is seen as empowering the community to prevent similar situations through knowledge and awareness.

Against this backdrop of trust and how it relates to museums, I now turn to a discussion of the case of museums in post-conflict situations.

Trust at the Museo de la Libertad y la Democracia

The above discussion provides the basis for a rich analysis of trust in the case of the Museo de la Libertad y la Democracia. As above, I will concentrate on *the object entrusted* as both the documentary heritage and in symbolic form the sensitive memories of conflict; the *sources of trust in the museum,* which can help it establish an enduring relationship with the broader community; and *the value of trust* as a form of collective therapy that the museum can use to foster positive cooperative behaviour in the community.

The Object Entrusted: Documentary Heritage

Documentary heritage is interesting in the Panamanian context because it remains absent from any type of national heritage legislation. Law 14 of the 5th of May 1982 about "Custody, conservation and administration of Historic Patrimony of the Nation" regulates the heritage sector in Panama. The traditional area of interest in Panamanian state policies and legislation has been the preservation of pre-Columbian and Colonial artefacts. These are the two archaeological periods that have provided the bulk of artefacts in government museum collections. There is a gap in protection for documentary heritage, and this gap is problematic because it condones evading the coverage of recent history of conflict, since many materials will be audiovisual.

Documentary heritage has to first be recognised via legislation, through the work of museum staff or through the efforts from the community to become an object worthy of being entrusted. While the community may already recognise the importance of preserving the memories of conflict, there needs to be an appropriate institutional framework that enables transfer of such materials to the museum, which is an important step in safeguarding them.

Sources of Trust: Representativeness by Inclusion of Diverse Stakeholders and Organisational Transparency

Exchange trust norms/thin sources of trust are present in the new museum project in several forms. Initially, the Museo de la Libertad y la Democracia will rely mostly upon the reputation of individuals on the board to build trust in the organisation. At the origin of the project is the common reputation of the members of the board as part of the anti-dictatorship movement. While this type of reputation is proof of a commitment to democracy, it may also come across as politically biased. In a situation where consensus is sought over the reality of human rights violations and the need to prevent those from happening again, it is important to make room for sectors of the Panamanian society that while agreeing with the regime in some regards (in particular with the view of the USA as "the enemy") would not condone these violations. It is important also to understand the sense of defeat and divisiveness that surrounds the community response to this period, as this testimony shows:

> (This whole period) was like a family where some had abused others, where, in a moment of crisis, some responded by hiding under the bed, others by accusing each other... many different responses. The country needed a magnanimous, generous, compassionate response to the crisis, but this did not happen. So it is very difficult for us to recognize that we did not respond united, that we did not respond as a country, but as individuals... (Consuelo Thomas, poet and cultural activist, interviewed by Ernesto Jara, 2005).

From conversations with the executive director of the project, it is clear that the museum board is struggling to prevent the project from becoming the object of political manipulations or from being as biased. This would drive the focus away from human rights to the unfruitful discussion about political parties. Broadening the diversity of stakeholders is vital in this regard.

One of the alternatives chosen to broaden the palette of "stakeholder reputation" has been to outsource the exhibition design to curators from Chile who worked in the project of the Museo de la Memoria and also to use the services of a Brazilian architect for the design of the building. These external figures may more easily come across as politically unbiased. More recently, however, the board has also started to contact prominent historians and other museum professionals in Panama to collaborate in the project. Thus, there are current moves to expand the diversity of reputation of stakeholders by including merit-based reputation.

Another exchange trust norm/thin source of trust may be the museum's compliance with a legislation geared at enhancing democratic practices in Panama. One example is the legislation related to transparency in public and private organisations. In Panama, the matter is regulated by Law 6 of the 22nd of January 2002 about transparency in public management. Article 2 states that "Private enterprises that provide public services of exclusive character are required by law to provide any information required by the users of this service, in relation to it". Article 9 states that "In attention to the principle of publicity, State institutions are required by law to make available in printed form and in their websites to publish periodically up to date information about their themes, documents and policies", including the internal regulations, strategic plan, handbooks of internal procedures, description of the organisational structure, localisation of documents and person in charge of them and forms and procedures to obtain more information.

An organisation such as the Museo de la Libertad y la Democracia has an opportunity to set an example in this matter. Hybrid private-public museums in Panama have not made this kind of documentation accessible in the past. The National Institute of Culture, INAC, the body administrating all state museums, complies with the publication of such documents in the transparency section of its website but only at the global level of the institution, not at the level of individual museums. Adherence to the law of transparency for its access to documents can be a way for the Museo de la Libertad y la Democracia to heighten trustworthiness.

Communal trust norms/thick sources of trust are intrinsic to the genesis of the Museo de la Libertad y la Democracia: it is the product of like-minded individuals that shared a repudiation of the military regime's abuses, in addition to coming from a similar socio-economic stratum of the Panamanian society. The problem then becomes the inclusion of a wider range of stakeholders. Driving identification beyond that of class or political affiliation is an important challenge ahead for this museum.

The Value of Trust

An evident value of the work that the Museo de la Libertad y la Democracia can perform is that of helping build a collection of trustworthy evidence. This evidence in turn can be used to combat impunity as well as to restore the dignity of the victims by recognising the damage inflicted. Principle 3 on "The Duty to Preserve Memory" of the UN Set of Principles for the Protection and Promotion of Human Rights Through Action to Combat Impunity (1997) asserts the need for memory work after conflict:

> A people's knowledge of the history of its oppression is part of its heritage and, as such, must be ensured by appropriate measures in fulfillment of the State's duty to preserve archives and other evidence concerning violations of human rights and humanitarian law and to facilitate knowledge of those violations. Such measures shall be aimed at preserving the collective memory from extinction and, in particular, at guarding against the development of revisionist and negationist arguments (U.N. E/CN.4/Sub.2/1997/20/Rev.1, 2 October 1997).

In addition, the introduction to a report about the situation of violence in Colombia and the work of memory institutions provides the following reflections:

> The safeguarding of memory is supported in the belief that the victim's defeat is not definitive, that injustice is reversible, and the past can be redeemed. The strategy with the broadest acceptance in countries with a recent history of State terrorism is "forgive and forget". (Yet) forgetting is but another aggression towards victims. It cannot be read in any way other than as acceptance of the crimes that destroyed their integrity. With what moral coherence could the rights of future victims be defended? (Giraldo 2000, para. 41, translation by the author).

Two cases of efforts to preserve documentary heritage about the history of conflict in Latin America can shed further light upon the importance of this memory work. They are Paraguay's "Archives of Terror" and Chile's "Human Rights Archives".

The Archives of Terror are documents of the abuses of the 55 years of Alfredo Stroessner's dictatorship. In the application for the inclusion of the Archives of

Terror as part of the Memory of the World Programme, the symbolic value of these archives is stated. The archives represent the solidarity of a people in working to uncover the truth about the regime, and they also symbolise information as a means of empowerment against injustice. They are proof against repressors and help victims and their families understand what happened and the damage to society caused by this authoritarian regime. They have been fundamental resources in the work of the Truth and Justice Commission of Paraguay.

Chile's Human Rights Archives attest to the abuses of the Pinochet regime. For inclusion in the Memory of the World Programme, the applicants pointed to the archives' usefulness in prompting debate and to question the presence or absence of memories of human rights violations in the country. The archives help remind the public of how dictatorships function and thus can help them to better identify warning signs. They also provide empirical evidence of disappearances and repression and have been used in trials against General Pinochet in Europe.

In Conclusion

The above has been an attempt to establish grounds in which to justify the value and moral obligation of the heritage sector in Panama to engage in the preservation of evidence of its history of conflict and of the abuses perpetrated. One way of establishing this value is by discussing trust, its importance for society and democracy and the way in which museums can participate in nurturing it. It is argued that in a situation of post-conflict, the establishment of a trust relationship between museum and community on this matter is of symbolic value (it is a token of the joint compromise to combat impunity) and of practical value (as this heritage can in fact become evidence in legal prosecution, and trust in general is needed for the kind of social cooperation that democracy demands).

It has also been argued that a museum initiative's success hinges on an array of trust-building activities. For the Museo de la Libertad y la Democracia to succeed in its mission to address the dictatorship and invasion in the context of human rights, it is necessary for it to nourish transparent relations among stakeholders at personal and community levels (Braithwaite's communal trust norms—Williams' thick trust). In addition, the museum can harness existing legal frameworks in Panama and concepts and instruments from international institutions that address current gaps such as the safeguarding of documentary heritage (exchange trust norms—thin trust). By grounding its activities in this way, the museum may avoid being drawn into polarised discussions about "how" the military regime and invasion should be represented. Its mission would be defined by the vital need to collect and make available evidence about this period to future generations of Panamanians.

With the knowledge that we have at the moment, it is not possible to state that a museum will help solve widespread distrust generated by government corruption or past misdeeds. Hopefully, interest will continue to grow in expanding our understanding of the role of museums as reminders of how cycles of violence may unfold and thus may be prevented.

References

Baier, A. (1986). Trust and antitrust. *Ethics, 96*(2), 231–260.

Braithwaite, V. (1998). Communal and exchange trust norms: Their value base and relevance to institutional trust. In M. Levi & V. Braithwaite (Eds.), *Trust in governance* (pp. 46–75). New York: Russell Sage.

Chile Human Rights Archive. Available at http://www.unesco.org/new/fileadmin/MULTIMEDIA/HQ/CI/CI/pdf/mow/nomination_forms/chile_human_rights.pdf

Conte, A. (1992). Special Edition. La Prensa Newspaper, n.p. Panama City: Panama.

DeCarli, G. (2003, July–December). Visión de la nueva museología en América Latina: Conceptos y modelos. *Revista ABRA*:1–22.

Deutsch, M. (1973). *The resolution of conflict: Constructive and destructive processes*. New Haven, CT: Yale University Press.

Eppelin, C. (2005). "20/89" (Documentary). San Jose: La Pecera Producciones.

Erikson, E. H. (1959). *Identity and the life cycle: selected papers*. New York: International Universities Press.

Freed, K. (1991, October 27) Panama tries to bury rumors of mass graves. *The Los Angeles Times*.

Fukuyama, F. (1995). *Trust: The social virtues and the creation of prosperity*. New York: Free Press.

Gambetta, D. (Ed.). (1988). *Trust: Making and breaking social relations*. Oxford: Basil Blackwell.

Giraldo, J. (2000). Memoria Histórica y Construcción de Futuro. Introducción a la primera entrega del informe COLOMBIA NUNCA MÁS. Website.

Hardin, R. (2002). *Trust and trustworthiness*. New York: Russell Sage.

Hockstader, L. (1990, October 6). In Panama, civilian deaths remain an issue. *The Washington Post*.

Human Rights Watch. (1991). *Human rights in post-invasion Panama: Justice delayed is justice denied*. Human Rights Watch Website. Available at http://www.hrw.org/reports/1991/panama/

Jara Vargas, E. (2005). "20/89" (Documentary). San Jose: La Pecera Producciones.

Job, J. A. (2007). *Ripples of trust: Reconciling rational and relational accounts of the source of trust*. Doctoral Dissertation, Australian National University, Canberra.

Jones, K. (1999). Second-hand moral knowledge. *Journal of Philosophy, 96*(2), 55–78.

Larmer, B. (1989, December 27). Panama's 'Dignity Batallions' betrayed by Noriega. *The Christian Science Monitor*.

Sánchez Laws, A. L. (2011). *Panamanian museums and historical memory*. Oxford: Berghahn.

Luhmann, N. (1979). *Trust and power*. Toronto, ON: Wiley.

Memory of the World Committee, UNESCO. http://www.unesco.org/new/en/communication-and-information/flagship-project-activities/memory-of-the-world/homepage/

Nissenbaum, H. (2004). Will security enhance trust online? In R. Kramer & K. S. Cook (Eds.), *Trust and distrust in organizations: Dilemmas and approaches* (pp. 155–188). New York: Russell Sage.

Nooteboom, B. (2008). Forms, sources and processes of trust. In R. Bachmann & A. Zaheer (Eds.), *Handbook of trust research* (pp. 247–263). Cheltenham: Edward Elgar.

Putnam, R. (1993). *Making democracy work: Civic traditions in modern Italy*. Princeton, NJ: Princeton University Press.

Putnam, R. (1995). Bowling alone: America's declining social capital. *Journal of Democracy, 6*, 65–78.

Rousseau, D., Sitkin, S., Burt, R., & Camerer, C. (1998). Not so different after all: A cross-discipline view of trust. *Academy of Management Review, 23*, 393–404.

Vergo, P. (1989). *The new museology*. London: Reaktion.

Williams, B. (1988). Formal structures and social reality. In D. Gambetta (Ed.), *Trust. Making and breaking cooperative relations* (pp. 3–13). Oxford: Basil Blackwell.

Chapter 12
Forget About 'Heritage': Place, Ethics and the Faro Convention

John Schofield

> *Everyone has the right freely to participate in the cultural life of the community, to enjoy the arts and to share in scientific advancement and its benefits.*
>
> Faro Convention: Article 27 [extract]

Introduction

The degree to which heritage practice conforms to the articles of the UDHR, and other comparable documents (see Bonnici 2009:54), and the extent to which it can therefore be considered 'ethical' in these terms are increasingly relevant considerations not only for those working within the heritage sector (e.g. Langfield et al. 2010; Silverman and Ruggles 2007) but for everyone who participates in heritage activities, for every member of every 'heritage community' (after Faro, see Council of Europe 2009). As people increasingly want to engage with their personal and cultural pasts, it is necessary that heritage practitioners and professionals find ways for this to be achieved, ways that are meaningful (e.g. in the sense of being culturally and socially relevant) and ethical. These two considerations are not necessarily compatible. For example, what people do in terms of engagement should not compromise the ability of others to do the same; any engagement must be respectful of other values attached to the heritage being studied; and engagement must be inclusive in terms of opportunity. Here I take a very specific line in exploring these issues, one

J. Schofield (✉)
Department of Archaeology, University of York, King's Manor, York YO1 7EP, UK
e-mail: john.schofield@york.ac.uk

© Springer Science+Business Media New York 2015   197
T. Ireland, J. Schofield (eds.), *The Ethics of Cultural Heritage*,
Ethical Archaeologies: The Politics of Social Justice 4,
DOI 10.1007/978-1-4939-1649-8_12

that draws closely on the spirit and content of the 2005 European Framework Convention on the Value of Cultural Heritage for Society (also known as the Faro Convention, or simply 'Faro'). With an eye to the UDHR and notably Article 27 (above), this chapter uses examples to illustrate how some of the ethical implications of Faro can be accommodated within heritage practice. In short, the implementation of Faro can facilitate people's 'free participation' in the cultural life of the community and protect the cultural rights which are 'indispensable for dignity and the free development of personality' (Article 22). The chapter will also demonstrate how the implementation of Faro is realistic, provided heritage leaders ('experts') realign their priorities and curb their desire (or sense of obligation) to 'lead'. Zimmerman et al. (2010), in their study of homelessness in the United States, describe this approach as 'translational', recognising that as heritage practitioners or archaeologists, we sometimes need to surrender power and authority to achieve real success.

The chapter will briefly examine the Faro Convention within a wider heritage policy context, before presenting some examples that combine to demonstrate ethical practice and procedures which are closely aligned with the terms and the spirit of Faro.

Faro: A Framework for Ethical Practice

For many, heritage encompasses the iconic places of deeper history, places associated with notable events and individuals who did more than most to create the contemporary world. We are all familiar with castles and great houses, the ruins of past civilizations and examples of monumentality. These exist the world over, their universality recognised through myriad approaches to heritage protection including UNESCO World Heritage status and, in the UK, scheduled monuments which are of 'national importance' and listed buildings of 'historic interest', for example. But to limit our definition of heritage to only these things is to misunderstand the nature of heritage as something which is created by contemporary thought and social action; heritage, simply, does not exist as a set of things (after Smith 2006) but rather as a multitude of approaches and perspectives that refer to how we think about and choose to manage those things. Heritage, in other words, can be whatever we want it to be. The Heritage Lottery Fund (HLF) is an organisation within the UK which exists to promote heritage, including its social and community benefits, and while they retain the word 'heritage' (as they must), they usefully present it in such a way as to make it more accessible: 'We do not define heritage, instead we encourage people to identify their own heritage and explain why it is valued by themselves and others' (HLF 2012:10).

People have long taken interest in their surroundings, their local places. Places are central to defining human experience, just as routeways are significant in connecting those places, supporting narratives of a journey made or generating connectivity across landscape. People feel attached to places, and everyone feels this attachment to some degree (Read 1996). The landscape therefore is full of stories, and stories make memories. It is those memories that shape our conceptions of heritage and which make it inevitable that we attach a complex range of values to the places that matter to us (also negative values to those which don't). It is the inevitability and universality of valued places filling our world that give heritage strong social relevance and purpose. For all these social reasons (not to mention those which are economically and politically driven), heritage has become central to our experience of the world.

More often than not, it is places created or used within recent memory that comprise people's everyday landscapes. Through studies like *Edgelands* (Farley and Symmons Roberts 2011), people are becoming increasingly aware that ordinary, everyday places are significant, not only for personal reasons but for society. There is thus a further problem of definition. Take, as an extreme example, those countries where legislation restricts the definition of heritage to buildings or places over 50 years old. Not only does this reflect misunderstanding of the concept of heritage (as above, that it is more perceived than real), it also denies the existence of modern heritage, of the heritage we ourselves have created. It therefore serves to disenfranchise whole communities who value this modern heritage over more ancient remains. In an opinion poll in 2000 (English Heritage 2000), results highlighted the popularity of modern heritage in the UK (75 % of the people questioned agreed that some post Second World War heritage should be preserved, a figure rising to 95 % of the 16–24 age group). Recent heritage therefore matters, especially to young people. It is problematic therefore that, for some, modern heritage remains a contradiction in terms.

Many people have no interest in Stonehenge, or other monuments on the World Heritage List, or (in the UK) the Schedule of Ancient Monuments, yet they will value the place they were born, or a garden, or a street corner, for some memory associated with it. Slowly, steadily, this view of the wider landscape and its diversity is being articulated, in the media and in everyday thought. As development continues to change our familiar landscape, people increasingly feel the impact of change and the speed and significance of it. People are also now (with widespread access to the Internet and social networking/media) more aware of how to engage the process, how to object or to voice opinions.

The 2005 Faro Convention (after UDHR) is very clear that everyone in society has the right to participate in the heritage of their choice and that this right accords with their basic human rights. While some member states appear reluctant to endorse this European convention, its principles can nonetheless form the basis for a new approach to heritage and to public engagement with the historic environment, in much the same way as the principles of the Australian Burra Charter (Marquis-Kyle and Walker 2004) were adopted and used beyond its country of origin. And, significantly, Faro is not alone. The 2000 European Landscape Convention[1] (see Anon 2008) defines landscape in terms of perception and recognises that landscape has a 'public interest role in the cultural, ecological, environmental and social fields' and is a 'key

---

[1] http://www.coe.int/t/dg4/cultureheritage/heritage/Landscape/default_en.asp (accessed 10 May 2013).

element of individual and social well-being and that its protection, management and planning entail rights and responsibilities for everyone'. In 2008 English Heritage issued its *Conservation Principles*, noting that the 'historic environment is a shared resource' which people value, and which

> ...each generation should therefore shape and sustain ... in ways that allow people to use, enjoy and benefit from it, without compromising the ability of future generations to do the same. Heritage values represent a public interest in places, regardless of ownership (English Heritage 2008:19).

A further conservation principle is that

> ...everyone should be able to participate in sustaining the historic environment, by having the opportunity to contribute his or her knowledge of the value of places, and to participate in decisions about their future, by means that are accessible, inclusive and informed (English Heritage 2008:20).

This inclusivity is represented also in heritage values. *Conservation Principles*, for instance, defines 'communal value' as 'deriving from the meanings of a place for the people who relate to it, or for whom it figures in their collective experience or memory' (English Heritage 2008:31). Social value is further defined as being associated with

> ...places that people perceive as a source of identity, distinctiveness, social interaction and coherence. Some may be comparatively modest, acquiring communal significance through the passage of time as a result of a collective memory of stories linked to them. They tend to gain value through the resonance of past events in the present, providing reference points for a community's identity or sense of itself (English Heritage 2008:32).

But nowhere is this idea of 'everybody's heritage' better or more strongly expressed than in Faro, which recognises:

- The need to put people and human values at the centre of an enlarged and cross-disciplinary concept of cultural heritage
- That every person has a right to engage with the cultural heritage of their choice, while respecting the rights and freedoms of others, as an aspect of the right freely to participate in cultural life enshrined in the Universal Declaration of Human Rights (1948)
- The need to involve everyone in society in the ongoing process of defining and managing cultural heritage[2] (see Council of Europe 2009)

In a world in which everyone has their own heritage, to which they attach particular values, values that are often hard or even impossible to articulate beyond recounting a story, an intimate experience, how might heritage practice encompass and encourage such diversity, such breadth? How can everyone get involved in ways that are meaningful, that enhance well-being and that ensure an effective (affective) participation in social practice? Some examples follow which illustrate in *extremis* how

---

[2] http://conventions.coe.int/Treaty/en/Treaties/Html/199.htm (accessed 10 May 2013).

local communities can participate in ways that are socially constructive. In all of the examples, socially disenfranchised groups are the focus of heritage-based research, although significantly 'heritage' is a word barely used. Landscape is a term most people understand, one way or another, and place is also a word that can resonate (helpfully) in a multitude of ways. The argument is presented here that using alternate words to heritage may be a prerequisite to achieving ethical heritage practice.

Case Studies

The case studies that follow briefly describe three situations (all urban) where members of local 'heritage communities' have been encouraged to define and participate in the heritage of their choice. All three projects were created or implemented within a framework which accords closely with the terms of Faro and the UDHR. Each project defined a community and its neighbourhood and sought to create opportunities for people to think about and articulate views on this neighbourhood: what they like and dislike about it, the notable or significant places with which they identify and the reasons behind these judgements, and thoughts often also on the future—what should happen to the area or specific places within it. The projects all create opportunities for expression, dialogue and representation. How those 'minority' views are then incorporated into official, authorised heritage is another stage. We have already seen how minority and local views are often underrepresented in defining heritage, but what about active participation in its management? Some aspects of heritage management are open to public participation (making representations to planning committee meetings or suggesting buildings for statutory designation or for inclusion on local lists, responding to opinion polls or questionnaires). The problem of course is that these processes might themselves be excluding and thus discriminatory. People who are illiterate cannot make written representations; people with mental health issues may not feel able to attend what would seem intimidating planning committee meetings, or even talk with a planning officer. Either we accept that or we explore new ways to achieve public engagement, ways that allow everyone to participate—with the growth of social media, this should not be hard to accommodate. There are two issues therefore which resonate throughout these case studies: definition of heritage (place) values and the articulation of views and opinions.

Valletta: Joe's Place

From circa 1700 until the 1970s, the Mediterranean island of Malta was a British colony, with a large naval presence. Typically Malta was a base or staging post for thousands of British (and later American) ships and their crews as they patrolled the central Mediterranean. Malta's capital city, Valletta, is a heavily fortified sixteenth-century city, and it was here that sailors came for their regular 'runs ashore'. And the street they made for was Strait Street, a long narrow street that ran from one end of Valletta to the other. This was a street of bars, music halls, fast-food outlets, hotels and lodging houses in some of which there was prostitution. Sailors drank to excess, fought and brawled and fraternised with the local women and with the barmaids and prostitutes in particular. Strait Street (part of which was known as 'The Gut') was a lively place. The author Thomas Pynchon was stationed in Malta in the 1950s, and it is most likely his experiences that later appeared in the narrative of his novel *V*. For example, in one passage, he describes one of his leading characters approaching the street thus:

> Strada Stretta; Strait Street. A passage meant, one felt, to be choked with mobs. Such was nearly the case: early evening had brought to it sailors ashore from HMS Egmont and smaller men-o-war; seamen from Greek, Italian, and North African merchantmen; and a supporting cast of shoeshine boys, pimps, hawkers of trinkets, confections, dirty pictures. Such were the topological deformities of this street that one seemed to walk through a succession of music-hall stages, each demarcated by a curve or slope, each with a different set and acting company but all for the same low entertainment. (Pynchon 2000:468)

A recent project has documented the stories of Strait Street and the places associated with them (Schofield and Morrissey 2013). In addition to a photographic survey of the buildings and a study of the street's social history, the project also involved a series of interviews with residents, of which there are now very few, at least in the more notorious section of the street, in The Gut. Malta is predominantly Roman Catholic, rendering many of the activities associated with Strait Street unacceptable to polite Maltese society. So when Malta declared independence in 1964, the navies withdrew and the bars and musical halls sustained by the naval presence closed down, nothing replaced them. Such was the stigma attached to Strait Street and The Gut that the street remained unused and—to many—unloved. Yet for those who do remain, resident above the former bars of Strait Street, its former dancers, barmen and (potentially) prostitutes, this is a significant place, a treasured place and a place heavily laden with memories, good and bad. These people live at the margins of Maltese society. They feel excluded and their voices go unheard. People rarely walk into Strait Street, and the Strait Street community rarely venture out. The divisions within this small, compact European capital city are stark and uncompromising.

In undertaking this project, a significant objective was to redefine Maltese heritage. Previously this heritage was confined to palaces and fortifications, the pomp and ceremony and the galleries and museums, the things—in other words—that led to Valletta gaining World Heritage status. This is where the tour guides take cruise ship passengers. The only tourists in Strait Street are former sailors, returning with wives and families to relive old times. Amongst publications of Malta's Midsea Press is a heritage series comprising books on the Neolithic temples, the Knights of St John and the Phoenicians. Now, additional to that is the book on Strait Street (Schofield and Morrissey 2013). As the book concludes, why not place former bars like the Egyptian Queen alongside the palaces and the barmaids and policemen everyone remembers alongside those who founded Valletta? They are all part of the story, and arguably the more recent they are, the more relevant they are to contemporary society. Take Joe. Joe lives above the former Cairo Bar where he was the star attraction. His views about Strait Street and what should happen to it are every bit as valid as anyone else's, or they should be. Yet it is unlikely anyone will ask his opinion. He has been ordered with an eviction notice, as his flat is no longer considered fit for habitation. But he does not want to leave. 'Why should I?' he said. 'All of my memories are here'.

Bristol: Jane's Place

A similar situation exists in Bristol's Stokes Croft, an area of the city which has long had a reputation for petty criminality and alternative lifestyle. It was once beyond the city limits, and people were excluded from Bristol onto Stokes Croft. Now it is an area occupied by students and artists amongst others and forms a focal point for the city's homeless community (Kiddey and Schofield 2010).

Bristol is a major British city and a city constantly changing, often through major developments determined through a planning process that is democratic (the Council members are publicly elected) and which encourages public participation (anyone can make a representation and express their views). Many of Bristol's buildings are listed, and there are specially designated 'Conservation Areas', whose character should be 'preserved or enhanced'. But who gets to choose? Who decides which buildings and which places matter, and who decides what should happen to them? Whose heritage is this? Whose place is it?

The Heritage & Homelessness Project sought to widen participation and to give a voice to those arguably closer than anyone to these places: the people constantly on the street and for whom these places are an everyday experience. Which places in Bristol do homeless people value most, and what sorts of places are the most significant? How are these decisions made, and what scope is there for representing their views? A separate but related project concerns the homeless community in York, a very different British city. In both cases the approach is entirely collaborative. There are no 'leaders', although there is facilitation. This is heritage from the ground up—from the street. In both cases there were no formal workshops or questionnaires with specific and tightly defined questions. This project involved meeting, walking and talking. Conversation not conservation. In one such conversation and during a walk around Bristol, Jane took Rachael Kiddey to her special place. The following account is taken from Kiddey (2013):

Jane was laughing as she led fellow colleagues and me up Park Street towards Berkeley Square and said in a mock posh accent, 'I always insist on the best address!' Jane sped up as we reached some stone cellar steps and walked down them. To our left was the back entrance to a pizza restaurant kitchen and to our right were three recessed arches. 'When I used this place (in 2003 and 2006)' Jane began,

> I wouldn't show no-one. You can't, right, because soon as someone knows where you skip [sleep], it's ruined. They'll want to come too and you'll get moved on because there's too many of you or they'll bring people back with them or you'll get back one night and find it full.

She pointed to the back step of the kitchen.

In them days, the staff who worked here would sometimes leave me out a bowl of Spaghetti Bolognese or a bit of pizza on a plate, with cling film over it. It was kind actually. Sometimes there would even be a whole cigarette for me too. But if there wasn't, I used to pick up the ones they'd only half smoked because they didn't have time to finish it. This was a good place.

Standing in front of three dimly lit arches crammed with bins and catering crates, I asked Jane to tell me exactly where she slept. She pointed to the last arch (now grilled off).

I slept in this one because the hot air vent blows right into the archway and it keeps you warm. Honestly, I could take my clothes off … and sleep just in my sleeping bag and PJs! With that vent blowing hot air and Patch [Jane's dog] curled up with me, I was warm.

Jane demonstrated how she would take off her two coats, wet trousers and a jumper and lay them over the hot vent, resting her trainers over the top. 'In winter, I wear my PJs under my clothes. Extra layer of warmth,' she explained. 'The best thing about this place is that I could put dry clothes on the next day.'

Structurally, it was easy to understand why the 'hot skipper' appealed to Jane. Several basic human needs were addressed. The site was out of the wind, relatively warm; it offered a degree of privacy and there was often food and sometimes a whole cigarette, the symbolism of which made Jane feel welcome. The site was about a mile up-hill from the city centre which Jane said made it a 'safe place'. She explained,

when I skipped out every night, I'd sometimes bed down with other people, safety in numbers that way. But if I couldn't find them or when I was getting into domestic violence situations, I had no choice, I had to sleep on my own. The type of people who are going to attack a home- less person tend to be drunks, you know, stupid kinds of people who think it's funny to kick you or set your sleeping bag on fire with you inside. Not so many of them walk up this way because most of the clubs and that are down the other end of town so I was safer up here.

So concludes Jane's field guide to a place that holds significance for her. It is a place that contributed to her survival, and which is rich with positive and significant references to adaptation under duress, and to comfort, generosity and homeliness. Even hidden places, tucked away behind restaurants hold value.

Liverpool: Pyro's Place

In Liverpool the objective was a counter-narrative to authorised views of heritage that existed on two levels: one, the World Heritage status of the portside area of the city and its iconic architecture and grand designs. This is the face of Liverpool's heritage that most people recognise and identify with (if they live there) or encoun- ter (if they visit). A second level is the city's authorised popular music heritage—the legacy of its most famous export and global phenomenon, The Beatles (Roberts and Cohen 2013). This heritage comprises houses in which the band members were born or grew up, the places where they performed (and notably The Cavern Club) and locations immortalised in songs, such as Strawberry Fields and Penny Lane. Interestingly, for some, this is still a heritage that challenges the acceptable, authorised view. But just as The Beatles' music is no longer considered a challenge to authority (or 'the old ways'), so it is for their heritage, at least for the majority. The Beatles' legacy is now part of the establishment (not so, The Sex Pistols—Graves-Brown and Schofield 2011).

A recent project sought to 'decentre' the 'master-map' of Liverpool's authorised musical heritage, focusing on those areas where Mersey Beat barely reached and where its influence is certainly no longer felt. This counter-mapping of the city's musical heritage focuses on hip-hop, a genre not closely associated with Liverpool and whose musicians commonly articulate through speech and song their marginalisation within the city. Pyro, for example, a local hip-hop singer, created a literal counter-map for his neighbourhood of Wavertree. In Pyro's map (Lashua et al. 2010:140), Liverpool's rich (authorised) musical heritage is entirely absent. This map identifies 'cribs' or the houses of friends, the local places where he makes his music on home computers and the places where they hang out. The map also highlights the direction of Toxteth, another area of Liverpool and a different postcode from his own 'turf'. In the UK hip-hop and grime scenes, these postcodes matter; gang wars are fought over these boundaries. As Pyro says, Wavertree is a 'bubble', 'encompassing his everyday social worlds. The city centre is a world apart, as is college' (Lashua et al. 2010: 139). Pyro goes on to describe his bubble thus:

> Down here, there is not, there is not a lot of light. So when people are down, like, if you fall off track from when you are young, you're pretty much, ain't no help, that you're pretty much done. Do you know what I'm saying? That's probably universal to a lot of slums and to a lot of places, but it's just, for me, growing up in Liverpool, it's just, it's just fucked. (Lashua et al. 2010:140)

Thus Pyro portrays his life and music in terms of a bubble of social and cultural marginalisation. And it seems from all three examples that 'bubbles' are ubiquitous. They are certainly evident in Valletta and in Bristol, and again here. One of these cities is a World Heritage Site (and Liverpool contains one), two are major international port cities and cultural centres and one a recent Capital of Culture. Yet within these 'bubbles' are places of significance, valued places, and places valued by people heritage engagement initiatives rarely reach. In the case of Pyro, his map highlights the places that characterise his neighbourhood, his life. He would never refer to this as 'heritage', but it is his 'hood', and it matters for being so.

Discussion

Themes recur in these case studies. One concerns methodology and how far the heritage sector can (should it wish to) accommodate these minority and often alternative views, sometimes the views of people who position themselves outside of society. But it also begs the question, how far should one extend the search for heritage communities? Another theme concerns terminology and in particular the degree to which 'heritage' is, by definition, a divisive term. Are there not better alternatives? And finally, how can the sector prepare itself for a more socially engaged heritage practice? This theme touches on the important question of skill sets. To widen participation to this extent requires heritage practitioners who not only understand places and the range of values and conservation measures relevant to their upkeep but who also have the social skills to ensure they ask the right questions of the right people and gain access to those people in the first place. I have often wondered, why are there so few anthropologists employed in the heritage sector? I shall return to this question below.

On methodology, experience has shown that traditional heritage methodologies work well for certain sectors of society and notably the professional and educated middle classes. We can ask questions and send out questionnaires. We can encourage participation in community projects leading to parish maps, for example (Clifford 2011), with the confidence that results will be informed, illuminating, meaningful and often outstandingly creative. Apply the same methods to another (in this case underprivileged or socially deprived) community, and it simply doesn't work. Yet the sector appears reluctant to adjust its working practices to the needs of more marginal interest groups, even though this may only require slight adjustment to established practices. The memory mapping of Common Ground's Parish Maps (Crouch and Matless 1996), for example, could not work for a group of poorly educated young musicians in one of the most socially deprived areas of Liverpool. Yet by adapting this methodology and adjusting the language used to present it, maps were generated that *are* comparable. Another example is the distinction between the questionnaire (a staple methodology for gathering heritage information) and the conversation. A questionnaire has the distinct advantage of being structured, presenting a series of questions or comments (the same for everyone) that typically generate simple factual answers that can then be analysed and presented in a summary form. But for people who are suspicious of authority or who have criminal records or even people who feel they are disadvantaged by a poor education, this will not work. Such a process is discriminatory (by excluding a specific group of people) and is thus unethical. In these cases, a conversation may work better, with simple notes in a notebook to record the relevant observations and comments. In Malta, this approach, 'bimbling' (after Anderson 2004) through a landscape to generate a web of interrelated stories and experiences, produced a series of narratives about the meaning and significance of what, for many, is a forgotten place, with a degree of eloquence that other forms of survey could never achieve.

Terminology also has the capacity to divide and disenfranchise. The very word 'heritage' drips with authority, with its implications of importance and the iconic. Heritage is for 'us', not for 'you'. A recent collection of essays (Schofield 2013) highlights the relevance of Faro in these terms and for a diversity of communities: it contains chapters dealing with the homeless community, a prostitutes' graveyard in London, places that are significant through entirely fictional events and the LGBT community, amongst others. In many of these chapters, as in the case studies briefly described above, 'heritage' is a word rarely used. It is of course heritage that we are speaking of, but the same concept can helpfully be presented in other ways.

The word 'place' is an obvious alternative and one most people claim to understand. 'Which places around here would you most wish to see survive into the future?' is a question most people are more likely to understand compared to 'What are the area's most significant heritage assets?' The vocabulary also largely determines what people think the questioner wants to know. A question on 'heritage' is likely to be interpreted as meaning buildings or monuments that are special and iconic in the local landscape or where some significant event unfolded. However, most respondents would interpret a question about 'places' as referring to a combination of the iconic *and* the everyday (arguably with an emphasis on the latter). It is a matter of perception, therefore, but also a matter of presentation. Persisting with the word heritage in public engagement exercises will exacerbate the exclusion some groups already feel and skew the responses away from the everyday. As it is the everyday that matters most to the majority of people, this is a question that needs resolution.

Finally, the sector is lacking one of the key skill sets for ensuring better and wider social engagement: the very people who specialise in human engagement with each other and with place, social scientists and anthropologists. Thinking specifically of the UK and large parts of Europe, how many social scientists and anthropologists are employed within the heritage sector? Answer: very few. And how many heritage jobs (museums, agencies, etc.) specify as essential (or even desirable) social scientific skills or training, in qualitative methods, for example? Answer: again, very few. There are two questions which could helpfully therefore be addressed with immediate effect: why do organisations not seem to prioritise (even want) these skills, and why are they content to then expect staff without the relevant training to undertake such work? This is not the place for that discussion, but it is a genuine concern and one of the reasons heritage practice cannot currently align closely with Faro. Heritage should be as much (if not more) about people as about place, yet heritage practice emphasises place over people. This raises the fundamental question of how ethical heritage practice actually is.

Conclusion

In his thought-provoking essay, Thomas (2008:144) reassessed the role of authority in archaeological heritage management in the twenty-first century. The essay refers to the same market research described earlier, conducted in the UK in 2000 into people's attitudes to heritage, which demonstrated widespread support for it, but noting that heritage was also a personal matter, that the relevance of heritage to individuals is a key issue and that heritage is significant in contributing to meaning in people's lives. People have their own views of heritage and will no longer simply accept the official view. Thomas goes on to argue, in ways that align closely with Smith's (e.g. 2006) 'Authorized Heritage Discourse', that the role of heritage officials ('experts') in future should be as guides and facilitators. That

> Experts should use their knowledge and skills to encourage and enable others to learn about, value and care for the historic environment. They play a crucial role in discerning, communicating and sustaining the established values of places, and in helping people to refine and articulate the values they attach to places (English Heritage 2008:20).

But this may not go far enough. Heritage is one of those things on which everyone has a view and everyone has expertise. One is reminded of the comment made in support of NIMBYs ('Not in My Back Yard') a few years back: that they are 'experts at living where they do'. People with strong ties to a place are experts. They know what matters and why, and they know (in their own terms, obviously) the impact of change and development on the local area. We should find better ways of listening to what they have to say and accommodating those views in heritage practice and policy formulation where appropriate (recognising the reverse argument that promoting access can also empower groups resistant to change, sometimes for exclusionary [even racist] reasons). This doesn't mean an end to the old ways but merely the introduction of new ways. As Robert Palmer (2009): 8) has so eloquently stated,

> Heritage involves continual creation and transformation. We can make heritage by adding new ideas to old ideas. Heritage is never merely something to be conserved or protected, but rather to be modified or enhanced. Heritage atrophies in the absence of public involvement and public support. This is why heritage processes must move beyond the preoccupations of the experts in government ministries and the managers of public institutions, and include the different publics who inhabit our cities, towns and villages. Such a process is social and creative, and is underpinned by the values of individuals, institutions and societies.

Heritage matters. Places define our lives, and in these places stories are generated that become embedded in the landscape as memories. These memories are literally everywhere, fresh and raw where they remain exposed, yet worn and only partly remembered as they gradually succumb to the passage of time and eventually become buried and forgotten. Where these stories have a material trace, archaeologists may uncover the trace and create narrative around it. All of this is heritage, and as heritage it belongs to everyone. The trouble is many people feel their stories do not matter; they are somehow less important, irrelevant even within a broader (e.g. national) narrative. That's the trouble with heritage. It resonates with the grand narrative, the big stories of the past, leaving all of the other stories in its wake. But talk about 'place' and 'landscape' and perception changes. Landscape is everywhere. We all have a stake in it. And place too is a universal—everyone has access to places of one kind or another. If we are serious about heritage being 'for everyone' and aligning precisely and without question to the UDHR, then the entire sector needs to draw inspiration from Faro. If we are to avoid the risk of heritage being branded elitist, we need to reassess what it means and redefine heritage practice.

References

Anderson, J. (2004). Talking whilst walking: A geographical archaeology of knowledge. *Area*, *36*(3), 254–261.

Anon. (2008). European landscape convention: An extract. In G. Fairclough, R. Harrison, J. H. Jameson, & J. Schofield (Eds.), *The heritage reader* (pp 405–407). London: Routledge.

Bonnici, U. M. (2009). The human right to the cultural heritage: The Faro convention's contribution to the recognition and safeguarding of this human right. In Council of Europe (Ed.), *Heritage and Beyond* (pp. 53–58). Strasbourg: Council of Europe.

Clifford, S. (2011). Local distinctiveness: Everyday places and how to find them. In J. Schofield & R. Szymanski (Eds.), *Local heritage, global context: Cultural perspectives on sense of place* (pp. 13–32). Farnham: Ashgate.

Council of Europe. (2009). *Heritage and beyond*. Strasbourg: Council of Europe.

Crouch, D., & Matless, D. (1996). Refiguring geography: Parish maps of common ground. *Transactions of the Institute of British Geographers New Series, 21*(1), 236–255.

English Heritage. (2000). *Power of place: The future of the historic environment*. London: English Heritage.

English Heritage. (2008). *Conservation principles: Policies and guidance for the sustainable management of the historic environment*. Swindon: English Heritage.

Farley, P., & Roberts, M. S. (2011). *Edgelands: Journeys into England's true wilderness*. London: Jonathan Cape.

Graves-Brown, P., & Schofield, J. (2011). The filth and the fury: 6 Denmark Street (London) and the sex pistols. *Antiquity, 85*(329), 1385–1401.

Heritage Lottery Fund. (2012). *Heritage lottery fund strategic framework 2013-18. A lasting difference for heritage and people*. London: Heritage Lottery Fund.

Kiddey, R. (2013). Punks and drunks: Counter-mapping homelessness in Bristol and York. In J. Schofield (Ed.), *Who needs experts? Counter-mapping cultural heritage* (pp. 165–179). Farnham: Ashgate.

Kiddey, R., & Schofield, J. (2010). Embrace the margins: Adventures in archaeology and homelessness. *Public Archaeology, 10*(1), 4–22.

Langfield, M., Logan, W., & Craith, M. N. (Eds.). (2010). *Cultural diversity, heritage and human rights: Intersections in theory and practice*. London: Routledge.

Lashua, B., Cohen, S., & Schofield, J. (2010). Popular music, mapping and the characterization of Liverpool. *Popular Music History, 4*(2), 126–144.

Marquis-Kyle, P., & Walker, M. (2004). *The illustrated Burra charter: Good practice for heritage places*. Burwood: Australia ICOMOS.

Palmer, R. (2009). Preface. In Council of Europe, *Heritage and beyond* (pp. 7–8). Strasbourg: Council of Europe.

Pynchon, T. (2000). *V*. London: Random House. [1961].

Read, P. (1996). *Returning to nothing: The meaning of lost places*. Cambridge: Cambridge University Press.

Roberts, L., & Cohen, S. (2013). Unauthorising popular music heritage: Outline of a critical framework. *International Journal of Heritage Studies, 19*(1), 1–21.

Schofield, J. (Ed.). (2013). *Who needs experts? Counter-mapping cultural heritage*. Farnham: Ashgate.

Schofield, J., & Morrissey, E. (2013). *Strait Street: Malta's 'red light district' revealed*. Malta: Midsea Books.

Silverman, H., & Ruggles, F. (Eds.). (2007). *Cultural heritage and human rights*. New York: Springer.

Smith, L. (2006). *The uses of heritage*. London: Routledge.

Thomas, R. M. (2008). Archaeology and authority in the twenty-first century. In G. Fairclough, R. Harrison, J. H. Jameson, & J. Schofield (Eds.), *The heritage reader* (pp. 139–148). London: Routledge.

Zimmerman, L. J., Singleton, C., & Welch, J. (2010). Activism and creating a translational archaeology of homelessness. *World Archaeology, 42*(3), 443–454.

Index

Printed by Printforce, the Netherlands